riot grrrl

revolution girl style now!

black dog
publishing

Dedicated to
Andy Roberts, Mathew Fletcher,
and all the grrrls who were
and are part of the riot

Yeah, well, that's why I was so disappointed when I heard that Polly Harvey was definitely *not* a feminist!

No one wants to be called a 'feminist'. Why not? 'interested in women', or 'girl-positive' - t definition i've heard - is that a bad thing?

It's that whole thing, you know, yourself a feminist, then you're man-hating dyke. It's like talking to that girl, telling book *Angry Women*, and J "What, you mean they ca and stuff like that. Peop i mean, i can unders doesn't think of hers either. I'm just n a shock, when y when you thought

change

c. I
in our
t to the
donna".
about at
gative. It's
seem like
t taken seriously.

ir appearance, or morals,
ead of their ideas! We

TABLE
OF CONTENTS

Eve. Courtney Love. Yoko Ono

Can you tape a prostitu...

Does a prick tease deserve to be raped?

and therefore guilty victims?

Ripper case said, as the police official on the Yorkshire

Are there 'innocent victims'

Why is it a girls clothes are relevant to her rape?

In the skinbag world boys don't desire girls, girls tempt boys.

'Prick Tease' is a powerful insult.

It can make a girl feel guilty

for not sleeping with a boy.

Make her feel obligated.

Or perverted,

because a 'prick tease' is anything but innocent.

For her, sex is a game.

you know she's asking for it

her power over men and She know

torments them with it. Slut.

She doesn't take men's dicks quite as seriously as she should

performer. The men had come to see the women. They hadn't anticipated having their pants pulled around their ankles and their cocks revealed to other men. But it was Zarina's intention to round on the men, not turn them on—to humiliate and frighten them. This was part of the act.

WORD

I'm waiting — I'm waiting — waiting

alternate gyno at strength

PRICK TEAZE

NOTE FROM THE EDITOR
NADINE MONEM

Riot grrrl culture spread like wildfire. It might have officially started in Olympia, Washington during the early 1990s, but it had hundreds of beginnings in bedrooms, classrooms, bars and clubs all over North America and Europe. Riot grrrl was reinvented through every young woman who took it up and made it her own, and through every band, zine and agit-prop art attack those women undertook. Riot grrrl was a movement without leaders or a centralised ideology, but rather made leaders out of anyone who chose to pick up the task of carving out a cultural place for herself where there wasn't one before. This was empowerment writ large: inspiring, alarming and forever changing the face of feminist resistance.

Here is the story of riot grrrl told in (at least) four voices, turning the pages of this book is like entering into a heated conversation where experiences, opinions, reservations and celebrations are falling on top of one another to create a sense of the joyful chaos that typified this movement. This is not a eulogy, or an attempt to relegate riot grrrl to its rightful place in history, rather this is a first attempt at looking at what happened, why it happened and what's happening now. Many of us no longer call ourselves riot grrrls, but relish in our shared history and the memories of how we became politicised and empowered to make those politics our own through cultural experimentation.

All of the authors in this book have built their accounts around their own experiences of the movement, and their research into the oral histories of those who were around at the time. We wanted this volume to stand in opposition to the media representations that poisoned riot grrrl in so many ways all those years ago, to offer an alternate account of the motivations and aspirations of the third wave, one that might be closer to the hearts and minds of those involved. So, DIY historical analysis at its best, we've scrabbled together our stories, snapshots, zines, flyers and books to provide a sense of the political and visual world the movement came out of, and the cultural production it continues to inspire. This is riot grrrl, this is revolution girl style now, and this is your invitation to see it for yourself.

"Prick Teaze" Flyer outlining some of the concerns and themes taken up by the riot grrrl movement, produced by Huggy Bear.

FOREWORD
BETH DITTO

I am sitting here. In my bed. It is 10:30 am. I woke up to write a piece about what riot grrrl means to me. This is the fourth piece I have worked on this morning alone, all of them different. Lately there have been a lot requests for my opinion, for which I am grateful. As with music, it has become a serious career built on radical ideas laid out for me by the sister that came before me. I am here, in a band, living (no matter how measley or well) from my art, speaking and looking and feeling just the way I wish. When I look around I see Erase Errata, Mika Miko, The New Bloods, Rock 'n' Roll Camp for Girls, I am reminded that we are all direct descendants of a movement, love it or hate it, called riot grrrl. A movement formed by a handful of girls who felt empowered, who were angry, hilarious, and extreme through and for each other. Built on the floors of strangers' living rooms, tops of Xerox machines, snail mail, word of mouth and mixtapes, riot grrrl reinvented punk. It, as with any legit movement, has a strong aesthetic that the 1990's would be nothing without. Therefore the bands, art and movements to come would be nothing without. Clip art had never been so dangerous, a psychic death-defying Patty Duke to be taken seriously. For the first time in history valley girls were feared. Riot grrrl made it, and still makes it, possible for me to get up in the morning and say to myself, "I can do any fucking thing I want!" Riot grrrl was by far one of the most undeniably effective feminist movements, turning academia into an accessible down-to-earth language, making feminism a trend for the first time in history. Before the riot grrrls, feminism was only available to kids lucky enough to go to college, but riot grrrl gave a name, a face, a sound to feminist frustration. Nirvana and Sonic Youth spread the message via white boy privilege, which they owned. Those of us lucky enough to really get it dug deeper, kept our ears to the dirt waiting for any rumble of the underground. Riot grrrl is alive. The essence is still out there in groups like Guerilla Girls and Tracy and the Plastics, and it's all very necessary. Every time a music magazine devises a category for the sexiest woman, every time another picture of Bob Dylan makes it on the cover of *Rolling Stone*, or there is a three-page spread on the same regurgitated boy band after boy band, our efforts are being ignored. Every time I am backstage and I hear the snicker of some dude rock band like a high school hangover laugh at me, I remember dorky=cool. I remember the Bikini Kill lyrics "that girl she holds her head up so high". I recall stories about Team Dresch getting beat up by 'punk' dudes at shows and I remember, it isn't what it was, and as long as I am alive it never will be again. I hear some people try to undermine the movement, as with any real threat of change, but it is no doubt what shaped my life. Until I found riot grrrl, or riot grrrl found me I was just another Gloria Steinem NOW feminist trying to take a stand in shop class. Now I am a musician, a writer, a whole person.

The best answer to the question "Stones or Beatles?" was muttered this winter by a genius named Guy Picciotto while laying down demos for a record he was producing. When the question was asked for about the thousandth time, as usual, always in studio conversation: "Stones or Beatles?" Guy said simply: " The Smiths". Ever since then when asked Ramones or Sex Pistols? "I will always say: "The Slits" or better yet turn around and ask: "Heavens to Betsy or Bratmobile?".

Front cover of Ladyfest, London, 2002. Programme
featuring Beth Ditto.
Image courtesy of Cazz Blase

LADY FEST LONDON 2002

FESTIVAL PROGRAMME

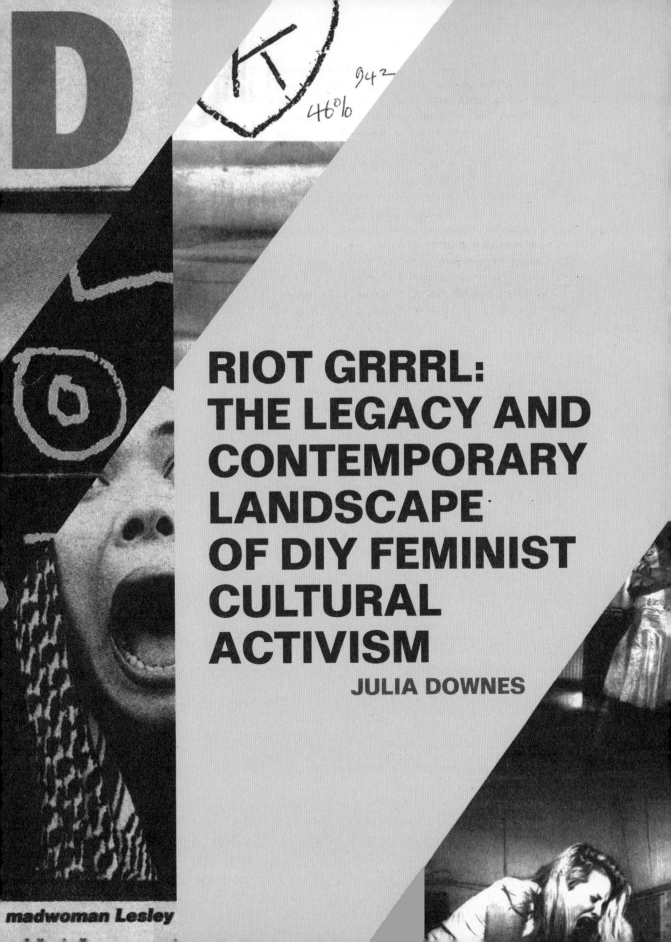

RIOT GRRRL:
THE LEGACY AND
CONTEMPORARY
LANDSCAPE
OF DIY FEMINIST
CULTURAL
ACTIVISM

JULIA DOWNES

madwoman Lesley

I know what we wanted to start, and I know we started something, but I don't really know what happened. And I don't think anyone can really tell you.[1]

A spectre of mystery haunts those interested in documenting and writing about riot grrrl. It feels like an unwarranted invasion into the safe spaces of female youth, like reading that hidden diary, decoding a secret myth, or eavesdropping on a slumber party. Writing about riot grrrl is risky. Girls keep secrets for a reason. Writing can destroy and distort meanings, intentions and experiences by twisting them into an uncomfortable order: confinement in language and linearity. Accounts of riot grrrl produced by dominant culture have easily fallen into these traps. Riot grrrl has been understood as a fashion, a phase, as punk, as dead, as violent, as man-hate, and ultimately, as a failure. The effect of which produces a set of meanings that reaffirm cultural power in masculine hands. Riot grrrls have had their messages and slogans co-opted, diluted and sold back in the form of girl-powered commodities and all-girl pop groups. Those involved in is creation have been excluded from profiting from this mainstreaming of the movement, left unable or unwilling to churn out another grrrl story or manifesto, and refusing to align themselves or conceptualise their youth within terms that have become alien from their own experiences. The opportunity to write a history of riot grrrl is like walking a tight rope, blindfolded, over hot coals with a bad sense of balance. But this might be a symptom of how much the movement means to me. How much these women and their ideas have personally inspired me and keep encouraging new generations of girls and women to explore their own creativity, political identity and expression. Nonetheless, I felt a need to keep as close as I possibly could to riot grrrl words, stories and meanings. Therefore, in writing this history I resisted relying upon mainstream media representations, to instead favour the voices of riot grrrl in their own words, as expressed in oral histories and panel discussions I've recently been involved with, as well as those conducted by the Experience Music Project (EMP) in Seattle, Washington. Instead of reproducing a music, American or fashion-centred history, I wanted to re-situate riot grrrl as a radical political movement, philosophy and cultural catalyst which continues to provide girls and women with vital inspiration and encouragement worldwide. By resisting the traditional depictions of girlhood, feminism and consumer culture, riot grrrl enabled the proliferation of new generations of cultural creators and activists. Women and girls found their own voices and power in music, art, literary and political discourses. Riot grrrls began to rewrite and figure out for themselves what it means to be a girl, a feminist, an activist, a musician or an artist. It opened up the possibility to share our experiences, tell our own stories and create our own language. A riot grrrl history is an insight into a provocative moment in modern day feminism, youth resistance and popular culture. Like girl germs, it's infectious.

PRECURSORS: DIY AND THE LEGACY OF CULTURAL SUBVERSION

> People who talk about revolution and class struggle without referring explicitly to everyday life, without understanding what is subversive about love and positive about the refusal of constraints, have corpses in their mouths.[2]

The 'Do it Yourself' (DIY) ethic of counter-cultural production was initially developed by the Situationist International (SI) who formed in 1957. The SI was a collective of avant garde artists who operated throughout Europe, the most well known of whom was Guy Debord who was based in France. Dissatisfied with the conditions of modern society the SI revolted against the dominant discourses, images and ideas of capitalist consumer culture, known as the *Spectacle*, and sought to incite a revolution by employing cultural tactics that exposed contradiction and openly critiqued society. Employing the tactic of *détournement*, the SI took quotes, symbols and representations from mainstream society and produced counter-cultural artefacts (journals, graffiti slogans, posters, cartoon strips) to subvert intended meanings. This opened up a space in which the viewer could resist dominant cultural representations and gain access to a consciousness critical of the mainstream. Crucially, the SI also encouraged others to express their frustrations through doing their own forms of cultural subversion in their everyday lives, "a revolutionary organisation must always remember that its objective is not getting people to listen to speeches by expert leaders, but getting them to speak for themselves".[3]

These disruptive tactics of everyday DIY cultural subversion were taken up within various 1960s and 70s political and radical social movements inspired by the New Left, civil rights and anti-war movements. Particularly relevant precursors for riot grrrl were social movements and subcultures that used youth-orientated, theatrical, artistic and stylistic tactics of resistance such as the Mods, Punks, Fluxus, Hippies, Yippies and The Diggers. For instance, The Diggers, a group based in San Francisco, combined spontaneous street theatre and anarchistic action with political art happenings, providing free music events, food, medical care, transport and temporary housing. Feminist, women's liberation and lesbian gay bisexual transgendered and queer (LGBTQ) movements also drew upon this legacy of DIY cultural subversions to resist and establish control over the negative representations of women, feminism and LGBTQ individuals and concerns in popular culture. Since the 'second wave' of feminism in the 1970s there has been a strong legacy of producing and distributing independent media. Publications such as *Ms* in America and *Spare Rib* and *Shocking Pink* in Britain thrived in this new environment and feminist bookstores, such as the Amazon Book Store Cooperative, provided crucial cultural spaces for the feminist community.

Feminist and lesbian collectives created their own separatist music community, known as womyn's music, which encompassed all women-run record labels, distribution networks, and women's music festivals. The sound that came out of this culture was amongst the first musical narratives of lesbian experience created by lesbians themselves. In the 1980s and 90s social movements like the AIDS Coalition to Unleash Power (ACTUP), Guerrilla Girls, Queer Nation and Lesbian Avengers disrupted and drew attention to the contradictions and inequalities that still endured in a so-called free and democratic society.

For instance, as a response to homophobia, violence and lack of queer visibility, Queer Nation began a series of visibility actions including holding 'Queer Nights Out' in straight-identified bars and areas to protest against the restriction of queer affection and socialising to gay bars. This legacy of reclaiming cultural space can be seen in contemporary queer dance actions such as Dykes Can Dance in New York City. The Guerrilla Girls are a long-running collective of anonymous women set up in 1985 who use the pseudonyms of dead artists, gorilla masks and humour to produce posters, actions, billboards, plays, performances and projects which expose and protest against sexism, racism and social injustice in art, culture and politics. Riot grrrl sought to build upon this rich legacy of politicised DIY cultural subversion to expose and resist the contradictory and marginalised experiences of modern-day girlhood.

OLYMPIA AND WASHINGTON, DC: GIRL TOWN AND BOY CITY

I've always felt Olympia is a female town. Olympia is a 'she' and DC is a 'he'.[4]

From the moment I set foot in Olympia in 1981, it was clear to me that girls ruled this town.[5]

We really looked to the scene in Olympia as inspiration and for networking, and just to connect with other girls, because it seemed like Olympia had a history of strong women doing cool things and being creative.[6]

The story of riot grrrl kicks off in the small, picturesque American town of Olympia in Washington State. On the edges lies the liberal Evergreen College, known for its artistic, alternative and radical freethinking individuals. Historically, Olympia has benefited from an enduring gender-balanced music scene, support for independent means of producing

Front cover of *Riot Grrrl*, no 15, featuring the K Records logo, International Pop Underground convention and DIY advertisements for Heavens to Betsy and Bratmobile. Image courtesy of Susan Corrigan.

Opposite: Queer Nation Demonstrations drew attention to the inequalities faced by LGBTQ groups in North America and Europe,

art and music as well as a strong feminist artistic and cultural legacy. For instance, in the early 1980s Olympia was the home of a collectively owned store called Girl City in which artists such as Stella Marrs, Dana Squires and Julie Fay created art and performances. Stella Marrs also later founded Satellite Kitchens, a visual arts studio open to the local community. Lois Maffeo hosted an influential women-centred rock radio show on KAOS, Olympia's community radio station whose policy dictated that 80 per cent of music broadcast had to be independent. The Olympia-based independent K Records label was set up in 1982 by Calvin Johnson, who also hosted the 'Boy Meets Girl' KAOS radio show and later formed Beat Happening with Heather Lewis, Laura Carter, and Bret Lunsford. Candice Peterson, who interned at K Records in 1986 as part of her Evergreen programme, became the co-owner of the label in 1987.

K Records initially focussed on documenting bands based in Olympia, releasing cassettes before moving onto a series of 7" vinyl releases in 1987, known as the International Pop Underground. This was in contrast to nearby Seattle with its focus on bar venues and drug culture, which therefore restricted the experience of live music to those who were 21 and over. A special atmosphere, spirit and attitude was created within the Olympian music scene, fostering upbeat all-ages community shows.

> The Olympia music scene, anytime anybody tried to do a bar show it would always be a flop. Like the only thing that would fly here was all-ages shows... people still danced at shows in Olympia, and everybody knew each other.... The energy here is really different.... I can think of very few bands from Olympia who don't really look at punk rock from the DIY angle. Like punk rock isn't a sound, punk rock isn't a look, punk rock is about what your intent is for making your music... punk rock is all about believing that you can do it yourself. You don't need a big record label, you don't need a manager, you don't need worldwide appreciation or acceptance. You're just doing it because it's the right thing to do, or it's an important thing to do.... Olympia's really a stronghold for that... we kind of exist in a different world.[7]

Beat Happening, inspired by bohemian ideals, created lo-fi twee-pop music and revelled in a celebration of amateurship, cuteness and innocence, a set of ideas that was later mockingly termed 'love rock'. One key element of Johnson's aesthetic was the return to youth, childhood and adolescence and accompanied celebrations of the pastimes of a bygone era. As Bruce Pavitt explained, "it's small town, baking pies, slumber parties, fetishising this romantic, old world, small-town 1950s culture."[8] Beat Happening encouraged its audiences to build supportive non-competitive communities, creating an atmosphere and message that opened up creative opportunities and possibilities for many women and girls who were later involved in riot grrrl.

I got into a band called Beat Happening. And that was in 1987. Not only did I see women could play music, but I could see that just... you can do it yourself—DIY—that's the first time I liked a punk band, and just saw that anybody could play an instrument. And you didn't have to be perfect. I could never be Andy Taylor. I could never be a guitar player in Duran-Duran. And I realised that was okay. I could still be good. And Heather Lewis was a woman playing guitar in that band, playing drums. They all switched instruments. To me, hearing that just opened up my mind. Opened all kind of doors for me.[9]

[Allison Wolfe] was from Olympia and she liked Beat Happening tapes and things like that, and I was like, I had just never heard anything like it. And it was just so like... liberating in this way, because it was so straightforward and it was so good, and it was still 'poppy' but it was... it was just so unique I was kind of like instantly like captivated by it. And also, you know, just kind of like meeting her and knowing there was all this other stuff happening. I just kind of realised that there weren't as many barriers to doing... making music or whatever as I had thought there were.[10]

Calvin Johnson, K Records and Beat Happening proved that anyone could make punk rock happen in their town, even in a small town like Olympia. In contrast, the independent punk scene in Washington, DC, was invested in a more aggressive fast-paced aesthetic, which championed technical ability: DC hardcore. Subsequently DC was dominated by a plethora of all-male hardcore punk outfits like Bad Brains, Scream and Minor Threat.

The independent record label Dischord—founded by Ian MacKaye and Jeff Nelson of Minor Threat alongside Nathan Strejcek in 1980—became the key outlet for music by local hardcore punk bands. Many involved in DC's hardcore punk scene advocated a straightedge ideology, which encouraged punks to abstain from the societal vices of drink, drugs and promiscuous sex. This often culminated in boys-only spaces, as the 'no girls allowed' signs visible in the Dischord house in the punk documentary *Another State of Mind* suggest. The culture of slam dancing at shows solidified a growing feeling and experience that in DC women remained on the sidelines as photographers, girlfriends or zine writers.

Despite the crucial involvement of women in the punk community and presence of all-female punk bands Chalk Circle and Fire Party, few women managed to occupy and command DC's elite punk platforms. A prescriptive hardcore sound evolved in DC which emphasised instrumental virtuosity and speed which, unlike independent punk culture in Olympia, troubled the meanings and values of punk and DIY and produced more gendered experiences of the punk scene. Experiences of gender discrimination, like being told that her guitar playing was 'good

BEAT HAPPENING

Front cover of self-titled Beat Happening Album.
Image courtesy of Cazz Blase.
Opposite: Riot grrrls at the Supreme Court in April
1992. © Pat Graham Photography
www.patgraham.org.

for a girl', led Sharon Cheslow to philosophise about the underlying meanings of punk circulating in the DC punk scene;

> I thought, no, no, no, that's not right. I should be good because I like what I'm doing. And it doesn't even matter if I'm good, because that's not what punk's about! It's about the ideas behind it and the passion behind it and the energy behind it.[11]

In response to the growing media representations of the punk scene as irrational and violent, the development of Positive Force DC enabled Washington, DC, to evolve into a highly politicised youth punk Mecca.

This long-standing activist organisation, founded in 'Revolution Summer' of 1985 by members of the punk community, is still active today and aims to empower youth and fight for social change by collectively organising benefits, protests and skill-sharing within their local community. It was from within this politicised punk community that women began to voice their contradictory experiences of feeling disenfranchised from their own alternative communities. Sharon Cheslow, member of Chalk Circle and DC punk photographer, explained;

> One of the reasons that riot grrrl developed is because a lot of the women and girls involved in the punk scene started to notice all these different ways that the punk scene was paralleling mainstream society. So we had all these ideas of how we were going to change society, and yet they were showing up right at our backdoor. And we all, in this community... we all felt that the personal was political. And so in order to really change things you had to look at what was going on right at your backdoor, and to address it.[12]

In 1988, Sharon Cheslow, Cynthia Connelly, Amy Pickering and Lydia Ely organised some group discussions that focussed on gender difference and sexism within the DC punk community for the June issue of the political punk fanzine *Maximum Rock 'n' Roll*. This experience laid the groundwork for the issues that became the agenda of riot grrrl.

That was a really important experience. And it really opened up the men for the first time to these issues of sexism and gender difference. They thought "Oh no! We're not sexist!" And they had to take a look, because so many of us women were saying there's something wrong here, we're noticing these differences. We are not getting the encouragement and support that we need. And how can we change things on this bigger level if we can't change things right here in our community.[13]

Despite women's involvement in the inception of punk and its potential in allowing women to challenge norms and ideas of the feminine while producing music, art and culture on their own terms, this potential never came to fruition in the everyday situations of women in punk underground scenes. Women involved in these alternative communities in Olympia and Washington, DC, began to put their feelings, frustrations and anger into words, creating a fanzine culture of what would later be dubbed 'angry grrrl zines'. These fanzines (or zines: self-published photocopied magazines) became a key site for women and girls to discuss, examine and resist the cultural devaluation of women with each other in a safe space.

A really important thing about riot grrrl is that we were all really inspired by punk rock and the idea that punk rock was all about like getting the access to the means of production and doing things your own way and doing it yourself.... But it seemed like even though people were doing all these creative things, there weren't enough women doing bands and fanzines and getting into positions of power, even in that scene.... There were a lot of shows that were all these guy-bands.... I felt really alienated from that, and that's why I think we were gravitating towards each other.[15]

In Olympia, Tobi Vail's punk feminist zine *Jigsaw* and Donna Dresch's queer-girl zine *Chainsaw* began in 1988 alongside Laura McDougell's *Sister Nobody*. The intentions behind starting a zine were simple for Tobi. "To try and meet other girls [and] express some kind of feminism. To try and put it out there. I felt like there was a void of females expressing themselves about music."[16] Fanzines soon became regular dreaming spaces and love letters exchanged between girls and women who yearned for an underground punk revolution they could call their own.

Right now, maybe CHAINSAW is about frustration. Frustration in music. Frustration in living, in being a girl, in being a homo, in being a misfit of any sort. In being a dork, you know, the last kid to get picked for the stupid kickball team in grade school. Which is where this whole punk rock thing came from in the first place. NOT from the Sex Pistols or LA But from the GEEKS who decided or realised (or something) to 'turn the tables' so to speak, and take control of their (our) lives and form a real underground. Which is

Minor Threat live on stage in the early 1990s. Image courtesy of John W Stuart.
Opposite: Allison Wolfe performing live with Bratmobile, one of the most important riot grrrl bands to come out of America. Image courtesy of John W Stuart.

ALSO where the whole heart of CHAINSAW comes from.[17]

I feel completely out of the realm of everything that is so important to me. And I know this is partly because punk rock is for and by boys mostly and partly because punk rock of this generation is coming of age in a time of mindless career goals.[18]

In a world before the internet, the main means of communicating and networking across America was through exchanging zines and writing letters. Erin Smith who wrote the kitsch-teen-pop-culture *Teenage Gang Debs* zine reflected on the unique character of this emerging network.

It is cool to find like-minded people, but [there] was something special about having this pen-pal and then kind of calling on the phone, and then hearing about this other person, and then reading their zine, and then mailing your zine out to people and just hoping somebody's going to understand it. There's something special and it's really sweet about the whole way it started up.[19]

This intimacy allowed for special connections, ideas and friendships to develop amongst girls and women, which would later prove crucial in the inception of riot grrrl. Through *Jigsaw,* Tobi Vail attracted the attention of Kathi Wilcox and Kathleen Hanna who would be her future band mates in Bikini Kill.

I used to read her fanzine *Jigsaw* and was really impressed with her approach—she was the first person I met who unapologetically focused her attention on girls in bands, specifically. And made it an issue. Like in interviews she would ask girls how it felt to be a girl in a band etcetera. It struck me as really unique because everyone in my college seminars was like, "You know, people are people, it's all the same. It doesn't matter if you're a boy or a girl." And she was acknowledging that there was a difference, especially if you are the girl in question.[20]
I hooked up with Tobi Vail, our drummer, because she did a fanzine called *Jigsaw*, which contained some of the most important writing I've ever encountered.... She takes huge risks in what she says, because she's actually living in a scene—she's not living miles away from everybody. She's writing about what happens directly around her in terms of going to a show, and what it feels like to be a woman at a show.[21]

Previous page: Bikini Kill, performing live at the Rock for Choice concert at the Sanctuary Theatre, Washington, DC, 14 April 1992. © Erica Echenberg/ Redferns www.musicpictures.com.
Left: Ian Svenonius and the NOU, playing live at The Embassy, Washington, DC, Fall 1992. © Pat Graham photography www.patgraham.org.

Alongside Beat Happening another band opened up the potential of youth, music and style to rework cultural space and instigate social change. The Nation of Ulysses (NOU) was a band based in Washington DC whose members James Canty, Ian Svenonius, Tim Green, Steve Gamboa and Steve Kroner played together between 1988 and 1992. NOU advocated an aesthetic that focussed upon revolution of the adult-centred world and the creation of a radical youth-centred community through style, language and music. Churning out manifestos, provocative shows and punk music, NOU asserted their intent to radicalise the world by destroying the past 'parent-culture' in favour of the revolutionary teenage 'zero generation'.

Ulysses explains: "The idea was to have a completely rotten attitude towards the whole adult world, meaning, in the long run, the whole established status structure, the whole system of people organising their lives around a job, fitting into the social structure, embracing the whole community. The idea in NOU (ROTTEN) was to drop out of conventional status competition into the smaller netherworld of ROTTEN teenagers and start one's own league." In the NOU, the core values of the straight world—sobriety, conformity, dullness, etc—are replaced by their opposites: hedonism, defiance of authority, and the quest for 'kicks'. These values we reflect in our language, our dress, noise—our entire new aesthetic.[22]

Tobi Vail first encountered information about NOU in Sharon Cheslow's fanzine *Interrobang?! #1* in 1989 and was instantly enamoured by their self-styled aesthetic and pseudo-political agendas and was inspired to create a band and youth movement which combined feminist politics, punk and style to resist the stale male-dominated punk underground culture of which she had become famously critical. The band was Bikini Kill, the movement was riot grrrl and the ideology was for Revolution Girl Style Now!

BEGINNINGS: REVOLUTION GIRL STYLE NOW!

Bikini Kill and Bratmobile (and our friends) had this idea we called the Revolution Girl Style Now! It was: "let's get all these girls to learn how to play instruments and change everything" and riot grrrl came out of that.[23]

Bikini Kill is more than just a band or a zine or an idea, it's part of the revolution. The revolution is about going to the playground with your best girlfriends. You are hanging upside down on the bars and all the blood is rushing to your head. It's a euphoric feeling. The boys can see our underwear and we don't really care. I'm so sure that lots of girls are also into revolution and we want to find them.[24]

Riot grrrl can be traced back to Tobi Vail, Allison Wolfe, Molly Neuman and Kathleen Hanna's joint conspiracy and vision for a 'Revolution Girl Style Now!' Acting as the philosophical bedrock for the bands Bikini Kill and Bratmobile, which became a reality around Olympia in 1990, these girls created a radical philosophy centred around encouraging girls and women across the country to subvert the stagnant male-dominated underground by creating their own music, art, writing and scenes.

We had been reading other people's fanzines and we knew that Bikini Kill had just started, and there was Calamity Jane and some other girl bands. And we were inspired by what they were doing and started networking with people in Olympia... we really just wanted to kind of start creating our own scene... we weren't really satisfied with what we were being handed as far as bands, the scene whatever... we were bored. So just trying to create our own fun, create our own scene. And it was pretty much girl-based.[25]

Originally based in Portland, Oregon, Kathleen Hanna moved to Olympia to attend Evergreen College, Kathleen's previous experience of music-making in bands like Amy Carter and Viva Knieval grew out of her involvement in setting up benefit shows whilst co-running the collective women's art gallery Reko Muse. Although initially interested in anti-racism activism, Kathleen spent a couple of years busy figuring out and working through issues around sexual abuse, teenage pregnancy and stigmatisation from her personal experiences, as well as from the women she counselled when volunteering at the domestic violence shelter Safe Space.

Heavily inspired by spoken word artist Kathy Acker and performance artist Karen Finlay, Kathleen sought out Tobi Vail to start the band Bikini Kill alongside Billy Karren and Kathi Wilcox, creating songs about "how to undo centuries of white-skin privilege, songs about the connections between class and gender, songs about being sexual that didn't cast me as a babe in a tight ZZ Top dress".[26] Meanwhile in nearby Eugene during the fall of 1989, Allison Wolfe and Molly Neuman discovered that they were next-door neighbours at the University of Oregon and became fast friends. Inspired and encouraged by the angry grrrl zine scene and bands like Beat Happening they began their own punk feminist fanzine, *Girl Germs*, and plotted to start a band.

Starting out as irreverent and spontaneous *a capella* intrusions at parties and shows around Eugene, Molly and Allison made outrageous random appearances in order to make their own entertainment. As Allison explains;

Eugene was the type of place where there's not much of a scene. You really have to create your own fun. So that's what we did. We really created our own scene. We started kind of singing songs—mostly other people's songs. Beat Happening songs, Lois songs, Go Team, whatever. And we would go around to different parties, usually hippie, beer-drinking parties. And when the band would take a beer break we would jump up to the mic and sing these silly songs... we would bring a tape usually of Salt 'n' Pepa stick it into the stereo and try to turn the hippie party into a dance party.[27]

The duo got a little more organised during one of their regular jaunts to Allison's home-town of Olympia; when Calvin Johnson asked them to play a Valentine's Day gig at the Surf Club. With the help of a friend who provided the pair with practice space and advice on song writing (which they subsequently rejected), Molly and Allison managed to play their first gig as Bratmobile with Bikini Kill and Some Velvet Sidewalk on 14 February 1991. Having been made aware of Washington DC-based guitarist Erin Smith, DC scene and NOU in late 1990, Molly and Allison decided to spend Spring break in Molly's DC home. The duo stayed at the home of NOU, a group house known as the Embassy, and met many women involved in the DC punk scene. Another line-up of Bratmobile, known as Bratmobile DC emerged in The Embassy involving Molly and Erin on guitar, Christina Billotte on drums, and Allison and Jen Smith singing. Expectations ran high as it turned out that the instigators of Revolution Girl Style Now, members of Bikini Kill and Bratmobile as well as the writers of the angry grrrl zine scene were to converge on DC in the summer of 1991.

Front cover of *Bikini Kill* no 1, "A Colour and Activity Book". Image courtesy of Julia Downes

Riot grrrl is...
BECAUSE us girls crave records and books and fanzines that speak to US, that WE feel included in and can understand in our own ways
BECAUSE viewing our work as being connected to our girlfriends-politics-real lives is essential if we are gonna figure out how what we are doing impacts, reflects, perpetuates, or DISRUPTS the status quo
BECAUSE we don't want to assimilate to someone else's (Boy) standards of what is or isn't 'good' music or punk rock or 'good' writing AND THUS need to create forums where we can recreate, destroy and define our own visions
BECAUSE we know that life is much more than physical survival and are patently aware that the punk rock "you can do anything" idea is crucial to the coming angry grrrl rock revolution which seeks to save the psychic and cultural lives of girls and women everywhere, according to their own terms, not ours
BECAUSE doing/reading/seeing/hearing cool things that validate and challenge us can help us gain the strength and sense of community that we need in order to figure out how bullshit like racism, able-bodism, ageism, speciesism, classism, thinism, sexism, anti-Semitism and heterosexism figures in our own lives
BECAUSE we are angry at a society that tells us Girl = Dumb, Girl = Bad, Girl = Weak
BECAUSE I believe with my holeheartmindbody that girls constitute a revolutionary soul force that can, and will, change the world for real.[28]

There was this definite feeling of movement forward, and we all had the same ideas and there was this confluence of energy. And it was this feeling of being compelled and a sense of urgency... there was this feeling that you could do things on a community level to change what was going on in society.[29]

It was in May 1991 that race riots erupted in Mount Pleasant. An African-American policewoman had shot a Latino man, however contradictory stories circulated about whether the man had lunged at her with a knife or whether he was actually shot whilst handcuffed. This incident sparked three days of intense civil unrest as hundreds of youth fought police in the streets and looted the neighbourhood requiring massive police mobilisation and the use of tear gas to defuse the situation. That same month the Supreme Court upheld the Bush administration's gag rule, which prevented federally-funded clinics from offering abortion counselling, threatening the Roe v Wade landmark decision that had made abortion legal in America. This turn of events created a social situation of urgency and frustration amongst the politicised punk underground in DC, it was within this emerging energy that led DC-based Jen Smith to write a letter to Allison.

We had this friend of ours, Jen Smith, who had written Allison a letter like in the Spring... there had been riots in Mt Pleasant where everybody lived at the time. So she wrote Allison a letter that said.... "We're going to have a girl riot this summer"... kind of like a call to arms... it was just a little like cute phrase that she had said in her letter... as you would write to someone and be lyrical or whatever...we like thought that was cool.[30]

The terms 'girl riot' and 'grrrl' re-emerged in Molly's dad's office as Molly and Allison were trying to come up with a catchy name for a new weekly zine they had made one evening. This is where the term riot grrrl was born:

It was just... me and Allison one night were like "let's make a zine tonight" And we were just going to have it be one page folded. And so we were at my dad's office and we were like... what are we going to call it? What are we going to call it? We just made like one square each. And we were like, let's just do one of these every week for the summer... let's just call it *Riot Grrrl*. I mean, I'm pretty sure that's how it started. We just wanted to call this zine something that was like catchy... we handed it out at shows because it was so cheap to make and so easy. And for some reason it was just like so perfect. Those two words were just like really good together at that time.... Tobi coined the phrase "grrrl" like as a kind of joke in her fanzine. Like she had called the newest issue of *Jigsaw* an angry grrrl zine and spelled it with three r's so we were like, oh that's cool too. So it's kind of like, you know, rip everybody off and put this thing together.... I think at that time we were interested in being inclusive and reaching out to people and connecting and sharing information... we didn't feel like access and inspiration and encouragement were available to other girls.[31]

The weekly zine ritual in Molly's dads office began attracting the involvement of their friends who were around DC that summer, including Erin Smith, Tobi Vail, Jen Smith, Erika Reinstein and Kathleen Hanna. The need and desire to reach out to more women and get together in the same space became more and more urgent, and the call for a riot grrrl (women-only) meeting was voiced in *Riot Grrrl* #3. The girls handed out *Riot Grrrl* zines, made announcements at gigs around DC and compiled lists of interested girls' phone numbers and addresses and many women involved in the DC punk scene responded. The first riot grrrl meeting, of what would become Riot Grrrl DC, was held at Jenny Toomey's house and weekly meetings continued to be held at various locations around the area including the Positive Force house. The meetings became crucial safe spaces, similar to

1970s feminist consciousness-raising groups, within which girls discussed and politicised their own individual experiences. Girls connected with, encouraged and supported each other, paving the way for collective action and a new feminist sub-cultural movement.

> We had the first meeting and about 20 women showed up. A lot of them had never been in a room with only women before, and were blown away by what it felt like: everybody had so much to say. That felt like an overwhelming response.[32]

> As we began thinking individually about how we experienced oppression on the basis of gender, we also started making connections with each other. We critiqued both popular culture and the underground culture in which we had participated.... Girls began drawing parallels between different experiences: shame at being fat and bitterness at caring so much about our looks; secret competitiveness with other girls, coupled with self-dislike for being jealous; the unsettling feeling that we could not communicate with a boy without flirting; the sudden, engulfing shock of remembering being molested by a father or stepfather when we were too small to form words for such a thing. Straight and bi girls talked about having to give anatomy lessons every time we had sex with a boy. Queer and questioning girls talked about isolation and about mothers bursting into tears when they learned their daughters were gay. Girls who wanted to play music talked about not knowing how to play a guitar because they had never gotten one for Christmas like the boys did. Girls who played music complained that they were treated like idiots by condescending male employees when they went to buy guitar strings or drum parts. We began to see the world around us with a new vision, a revelation that was both painful and filled with possibility.[33]

An early flyer for Riot Grrrl Press. Image courtesy of Julia Downes.

Riot grrrl rewrote feminism and activism into a punk rock rebellion and youth-centred voice that was felt to be missing from forms of feminism available in the 1990s. Feminism was seen to be addressing the concerns of older, middle-class, heterosexual and educated women and riot grrrl was seen to be a re-working of feminism to work through the needs, desires and issues in the situations specific to young girls and women in 1990s America;

> [Riot grrrl] focused on what the issues were to be a creative woman, to be young and to be creative. Whereas I think previous feminisms dealt with more economic issues: what was it like to be out in the workplace and not earning as much or what was it like to have children and not have daycare. Well none of us had children and even though we all had jobs and had maybe dealt with sexism on the job, our main focus was being writers and musicians and filmmakers and artists, and how that impacted our lives. And for us I

think that's how it was different, it was reclaiming feminism for our lives.[34]

The whole point of riot grrrl is that we were able to rewrite feminism for the twenty-first century... for teenagers there wasn't any real access to feminism. It was written in a language that was very academic, that was inaccessible to young women. And we took those ideas and rewrote them in our own vernacular.[35]

For me what riot grrrl meant was a way of making punk rock more feminist, because really (alternative music) was like this boys club for the most part. But also a way of making academic feminism more punk rock or more DIY... a lot of it with riot grrrl too was a reclamation of taboo imagery or things that were considered not feminist, but trying to reclaim those and say well actually girly can be feminist, lipstick and make-up people can be feminist, we can wear skirts and still be feminists. We can be cutesy and girly and whatever we want but we still should have rights and we still should be taken seriously.[36]

Riot grrrl also proposed a different way of conceptualising feminist activism, to move away from traditional state-focused protests like marches, rallies and petitions, towards an idea of cultural activism which incorporated everyday cultural subversions like creating art, film, zines, music and communities as a part of feminist activism.

I consider myself a cultural activist, rather than a political activist because I don't organise politics. I think that having women in positions of cultural power is really important for young girls and I can see that we inspire young girls and I can see that we inspire young women at our shows.[37]

We had all these images of protesting and we were able to do the double meanings in our own lives of the kind of violence that we live with in our own domestic lives that mirrored these kind of acts of aggression that the United States would perpetuate on people. I think that's one of the things that was great about people involved because they were so good at creating those images and those ideas that would catch on with people. It was a cultural activism... the kind of lyrics that people would write in songs. It was a really great rewriting of feminism, I think, by taking kind of ideas that were really in academic institutions and putting them into really simple song lyrics.[38]

This ethos of re-writing and re-working politicised ideas also applied to riot grrrl itself which was intended to remain a loose philosophy, made in such a way so people could take it on for their own identity and kind of change it by fleshing it out with their own ideas. Riot grrrl manifestos were added to, rewritten and re-worked to encompass a range of different issues and identities.

Riot grrrl gave people the tools and the language to maybe create community and talk with each other about what really is important. How do we create the networks that allow us to follow our bliss?[40]

That point... that it means different things, that the term riot grrrl has been able to be applied to so many different women's experiences or girls' experiences [that's] the most overwhelming and fantastic aspect of it... the fact that there are so many women who have done like really important things kind of inspired by or just simply like given the ideas or ratified their ideas by being supported by other women.[41]

Many women involved in the inception of riot grrrl chose not to be involved in these meetings: Erin Smith didn't go to any meetings and Tobi Vail, Christina Billotte and Jenny

KAOS
89.3 FM
OLYMPIA'S COMMUNITY RADIO STATION

BROADCASTING REPORTS ON THE INTERNATIONAL POP UNDERGROUND CONVENTION AT 9:20 AM, 1:00 PM AND 7:00 PM

TUES.-SAT.

KAOS FM programme for the K Records Pop
Underground Convention, 1991.

Toomey didn't return after the initial meetings. Kathleen Hanna became the only member of Bikini Kill to attend and a younger cohort of girls became involved in Riot Grrrl DC, including Erika Reinstein, May Summer, Mary Fondriest, Sarah Stolfa, Jasmine Kerns, Laura Soltaire, Tiffany Fabian, Amanda LaVita, and Claudia Von Vacano.

INTERNATIONAL POP UNDERGROUND: GIRLS NITE

The intensity of riot grrrl's Revolution Summer was solidified back in Olympia with K Records International Pop Underground (IPU) Convention held between 20 and 25 August 1991. The IPU opened with 'girl's nite', emphasising women performers and bands including Bikini Kill, Mecca Normal, Bratmobile, Heavens to Betsy, Lois Maffeo and 7 Year Bitch. The IPU is remembered as a watershed moment, producing intense emotional recollections from those involved as performers and audience members.

> Girl's nite will always be precious to me because, believe it or not, it was the first time I saw women stand on a stage as though they truly belonged there. The first time I had ever heard the voice of a sister proudly singing the rage so shamefully locked in my own heart. Until girl's nite, I never knew that punk rock was anything but a phallic extension of the white middle class male's frustrations.[42]

> It was just this kind of feeling of discovery and a sort of spark of this new kind of idealism and talent that was coming out that everyone was really taken by.[43]

> The International Pop Underground Convention in August of 1991, that was a huge deal because of the Girl Day. That was just nothing like.... I had never seen anything like that happen. And I just had the chills the whole day.[44]

> It felt... to be part of an all-girl bill... it felt really monumental and really special.[45]

Riot Grrrl Olympia was established from the energy of the IPU and meetings were held around Olympia including Allison Wolfe, Julie Lary, Nomi Lamm, Madigan Shive and Corin Tucker. 1991 was a critical year for those involved in riot grrrl as Allison Wolfe explained, "it felt like everything was changing... girls were taking over the whole punk rock scene of Olympia".[46] Riot grrrl bands, zines and chapters proliferated in Los Angeles, New York, Olympia and DC. Within Riot Grrrl DC the first convention was organised in summer 1992, benefit shows for Rape Crisis were organised, and Riot Grrrl Press was set up to help zine writers distribute their work.

Riot grrrl seemed to be defying limits, inspiring girls and rewriting feminism in a youth vernacular. As the Revolution (Summer) Girl Style Now wound down, expectations ran high of what riot grrrl could become next.

> Riot grrrl is so much. It will end up being so much more I am sure. Right now it isn't anything concrete, it's not a fanzine or a group or anything specific, although it is also all of those things. As of now, it has been a mini fanzine, and there have been some girls who met once a week calling themselves riot grrrls, talking about issues in and outside of punk rock that are important to us. But I know, and I'm sure some of you know that it is gonna be something BIG.... There's no copyright on the name so if you are sitting there reading this and you feel like you might be a riot grrrl then you probably are, so call yourself one.[47]

RIOT GRRRL DRAMA

> Girls traditionally, like girls who are socialised as girls, as feminine girls, I think have this really private thing about themselves like diaries, your room, that sort of thing, that is really isolated and you don't share it with anybody else. It was like all of a sudden all of the girls were in the same room, but somebody was trying to like take the room away from us.[48]

In July 1992 the first mainstream coverage of riot grrrl was printed in *LA Weekly*. This initial spark led to a media frenzy, forcing the radical underground community into the public eye, sparking multiple controversies. Publications including *Sassy, Off Our Backs, Newsweek, New York Times, Washington Post, Rolling Stone, Spin, LA Times,* and even *Playboy* covered riot grrrl, as the dominant culture became curious about this new girl-orientated movement. This media coverage was initially crucial as riot grrrl found a wider audience of girls and women and inspired the creation of riot grrrl chapters across America. However, the coverage also removed and/or ridiculed the radical and political aspects of riot grrrl, sensationalising it as an aggressive anti-men subculture or commodifying the movement into a genre of (bad) music or (anti-)fashion style.

> A scrawny boy stands by, watching the group and the bouncing sea of mohawked female fans in Pucci-print minis. They sport hairy legs, army boots and tattoos. Finally he yells: "Punk rock is just an excuse for ugly girls to get on stage!" In seconds, he's surrounded by an angry mob of girls, hopping and slam-dancing in a frenzy. He bolts to safety, chased by their jeers.[49]

> Five assumptions about riot grrrls
> 1. They can't play
> 2. They hate men
> 3. They're fakers
> 4. They're elitist
> 5. They aren't really a movement[50]

Connections to lesbian and queer sub-cultural producers such as Outpunk, Chainsaw and Candyass records were ignored as (male) readers were reassured of the heterosexual character of riot grrrl, "most riot grrrls still find boys for the usual teenaged thing" asserted *Newsweek*.[51] Attention was drawn to the sexualised bodies of riot grrrl, Tobi Vail was reported to be, "wearing only jeans and a bra" whilst audience members were, "taking off their clothes" and "rushing the stage".[52] A sense of astonishment is felt in *Newsweek*'s commentary that focuses on how, "grrrls marked their bodies with blunt five-inch high letters reading RAPE or SLUT" and struggled to comprehend how wearing "vintage little-girl dresses that barely make it past her hips" were "all the better to sing songs about rape

Front Cover of *LA Weekly* from 10–12 July, 1992, one of the first mainstream media attempts at covering the riot grrrl movement.

and exploitation".[53] Feminist philosophy was trivialised within statements such as, "riot grrrl is feminism with a loud happy face dotting the i"[54] and "better watch out, boys. From hundreds of once pink frilly bedrooms comes the young feminist revolution. And it's not pretty. But it doesn't want to be. So there![55] Riot grrrl was condemned as an individualistic apolitical outlet for a privileged elite of girls, as participants of the 1992 DC Riot Grrrl convention were described as, "mostly white, mostly middle-class, well-educated girls" and "serious and sombre and self absorbed".[56] In a move antithetical to the non-hierarchical model of riot grrrl, the media constructed its leaders of the movement, focusing on Kathleen Hanna, Bikini Kill and Bratmobile, as well as women musicians who were unrelated to and often openly critical of riot grrrl: Courtney Love of Hole and Kat Bjelland of Babes in Toyland. The coverage strove to portray Kathleen Hanna as pathological by constantly highlighting her 'history' of abuse and occupation as a stripper, going as far as printing false incest claims. For example *Newsweek* reported, "a former stripper who sings and writes about being a victim of rape and child abuse, Hanna represents the extreme edge of the grrrls' rage".[57] In order to curtail the misrepresentation of riot grrrl and reclaim power, a media blackout was called in 1992, those associated with riot grrrl were encouraged not to cooperate with the press. Nonetheless journalists continued to write about riot grrrl and those involved in the movement had conflicting opinions and experiences about the media attention.

> You have to look at what the media is doing, because they have a lot of power. And because we had all been talking about how power is manifested in society, well if we want to change that, then how can we take some of that power back? So one of the ways that we decided to take power back, and I think it was Kathleen's idea. Was to put a ban on the media. So by the time 1992 came around and all this media attention was happening, we were all prepared. We knew it was going to happen.... It wasn't that big of a surprise.[58]

> I was resented by certain people because I was getting attention that they weren't getting and even though I didn't ask for it and I never talked to the press, it was still happening... at the time it was really hard because the kind of attention I was getting was really negative... it was like feminist visibility in one way but it was really insulting like constantly calling me an abuse survivor and making out like I'd had all these crazy fucked up things happen to me and that's why I was a feminist.[59]

> None of us had any experience of the media, none of us ever expected that it would be something that would get, I mean we noticed that it was getting a lot of attention, but we thought of it in terms of people we knew and just group excitement... you didn't really think of it in terms of the media and how you'd be represented and having your image thrown back at you... it was overwhelming to see your friends all of a sudden in magazines and to see the whole world looking basically at the northwest... people coming in and trying to characterise everything and they ended up making caricatures out of everyone.[60]

Most of those involved in riot grrrl were shocked by the media attention in terms of its negativity, misinformation and journalistic attempts to discredit the ideas and actions of the people involved. As Corin Tucker argued, "there was never a serious article written about riot grrrl. I felt like it was outrageous the way that they just completely trivialised the entire movement as being a fashion statement and they never got the serious issue that young women have a lot to deal with in society and that we were serious feminists... it was deliberate that we were made to look like we were just ridiculous girls parading around in our underwear."[61] The positive effects of the blackout were highlighted, to encourage girls to find out about riot grrrl on their own terms, "it was kind of a good thing in this way, because it sort of let riot grrrl become whatever each girl who heard about it wanted it to be for them. And finding whatever power message they could find in it, that then they could use without it really being a media like 'this is what riot grrrl is about and you should buy it. It's for sale right now."[62] However, unequal financial gains were created as journalists profited from the documentation of riot grrrl producers, leaving them penniless, "they were making money off of our image. None of us had a single thing to show for it. None of us were making any money; I could barely pay rent. It was the industry of it all, the journalists were getting paid, the photographers were getting paid, we never were."[63] It became increasingly clear that those in bands had more to gain from media attention, as Allison Wolfe notes "it did help to sell more records and to have more people come to our shows. I mean Bratmobile and Heavens to Betsy toured in the summer of 1992 across the country... and people came to our shows and it went just fine, we didn't lose money. Which was probably due to the riot grrrl media attention."[64] A minority had no qualms with accruing media attention, "I was cool with it. I was into people covering our band. I was into people talking about me, about what I was doing, because I thought it was really validating.... It made my parents understand what I was doing."[65]

The turbulent relationship between the media and riot grrrl caused fragmentation within the movement, as Corin Tucker explained, "it was a really hard thing to go through because I think it really tore apart a kind of community feeling that riot grrrl had".[66] Internal inconsistencies and issues of privilege were brought to a national level, highlighting tensions already arising from within riot grrrl, "it was a really amazing thing and [the media] took it and like all the things about it that were maybe not quite right, or that were just goals trying to figure shit out, got really highlighted".[67] Inadequately-voiced issues of racial and class privilege, which permeated the riot grrrl community as well as the DIY punk communities from which it emerged, created internal conflict and feelings of frustration and anger at the common realisation that girl power was the exclusive realm for white middle class girls as Dasha, writer of *Gunk* zine, experienced.[68]

> I started iggling like a year into it, like started feeling funny about it just in terms of my whole position with punk rock and riot grrrl, because you know it was an odd position to be in... too many times be the only person of colour there, and feeling like no one gave a shit. This was an empowering movement for them which was only relative to a white middle class punk girl... it just became depressing and really hurtful to see that it would only go so far and that there was a total crazy powerful feeling about the whole environment and it was exciting. But it was also really sad in a way that like this is only what it is and its only for certain people and it was extremely frustrating to start realising that and start being like these aren't my people.[69]

The power implicit in the media's role in defining riot grrrl is that the media version has become the dominant history, which stands in contradiction to the experiences of those involved. Allison Wolfe examines this position, "it's sad because you'll look and [the media] is [taken as] fact, but it wasn't really what happened, but it's written this way, it's history".[70] Although the media allowed riot grrrl ideas to reach audiences globally, a sense of disillusionment was felt about what these audiences could take away from the media distortions of the movement, "it's really confusing, because I'm not sure what they really learned. What they really saw riot grrrl as".[71] Those involved felt the need to distance themselves and their activities from a term the meaning of which was no longer under the control of their communities, becoming more and more international.

TRANSATLANTIC SHIFTS

Young women and girls from across the world were also hungry to create girl-centred communities from which to revolutionise their music scenes, everyday lives and engage with feminist ideas in art, music, writing and culture. Riot grrrl migrated across the Atlantic as girls willed it into existence in the underground music scenes in Britain, Europe and Australia.

Britain has a strong legacy of punk, protest and youth politicisation, providing a fertile ground for DIY feminist cultural subversions. The production of radical feminist magazines like *Shocking Pink* and *Spare Rib*, allowed for the emergence of a discourse, aesthetic and means of production, from which to conceptualise issues around gender and sexuality.[72] Women's involvement in punk during the late 1970s, in bands such as The Slits, Siouxsie and the Banshees, the Adverts and X Ray Spex, saw women benefit from new opportunities available in punk DIY amateur aesthetics.

However, issues of gender and sexuality were suppressed during this period and punk was experienced as an asexual space.[73] This situation offered women cooperation as 'one of the boys' or as 'sexless', which subsequently prevented a confrontational exploration of resistant femininities and sexualities within punk. The 1970s also brought the publication of influential British feminist texts such as Germaine Greer's *Female Eunuch* and feminist consciousness-raising groups radicalised women around the country. Moving into the 1980s post-punk era, the effects of British feminism had trickled down to inform bands like the Au Pairs, The Raincoats, Marine Girls, Delta 5 and Ludus.

However, the mainstream became dominated by the sound of new pop with synth-driven bands such as Duran Duran, The Human League, Altered Images and Strawberry Switchblade gaining in popularity and DIY post-punk fell out of the media's favour. Out of the spotlight, the DIY aesthetic and independent means of production proliferated in the newly burgeoning indie-pop scene, as Nicky Wire described, "people were doing everything themselves; making their own records, doing the artwork, gluing the sleeves together, releasing them, sending them out, writing fanzines because the music press lost interest really quickly".[74] Fanzine culture proliferated with zines like *Hungry Beat* by Kevin Pearce, *Juniper Beri-Beri* by Aggi and Stephen of the Pastels, *The Legend!* by Everett True, *Are You Scared to Get Happy* by Matt Haynes and *Kvatch* by Clare Wadd. A collective of fanzine writers of the era also collaborated producing a series of zines with flexi-discs of many seminal indie-pop bands under the name Sha-la-la. Labels such as Creation, Postcard Records and The Subway Organisation released music by many notable bands of this era like The Pastels, Orange Juice, Jesus and Mary Chain, The Mighty Lemon Drops, The Shop Assistants, The Flatmates, The Soup Dragons, The Chesterfields and Razorcuts. In 1987, Clare Wadd and Matt Haynes set up the socialist and feminist inspired Sarah Records in Bristol, producing fanzines and releasing music by bands such as Tallulah Gosh and Heavenly. Although opinions surrounding the political intent and female involvement of the indie-pop music scene vary, Gregory Webster of Razorcuts argues that:

> It was political in the same way that punk was. It was rejecting the prevailing music scene at the time and going back to basics. In the environment (with bands like Simple Minds dominating the charts) playing three minute pop songs like the Ramones or the Ronettes seemed like a very political statement of intent.[75]

However shifts in the meaning of 'indie' in Britain began to emerge as bands like The Smiths broke through to the mainstream. As opposed to signifying a DIY mode of production, indie was reworked to refer to an increasingly popular sound, genre and style characterised as counter-cultural. British indie music cultures became dominated by music and culture produced by white men. Whereas punk, post-punk, and indie-pop allowed for the marginal involvement of women, this shift in the meaning of 'indie' as a popular commodity and genre led to a rigid reconstitution of a normative gender order in the indie public.[76] Teetering on the brink of the emerging Britpop scene and dissatisfied with the available indie scenes, British girls found themselves on the sidelines wanting more.

IN–GRRRL–LAND, SCATTERLAND & WAILS.

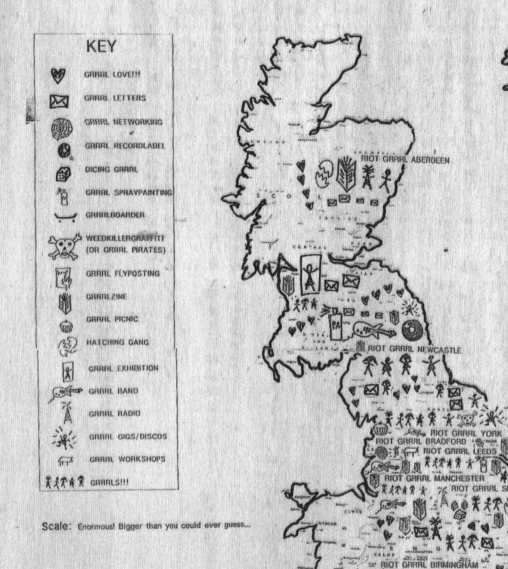

KEY

♥ GRRRL LOVE!!!

✉ GRRRL LETTERS

🕸 GRRRL NETWORKING

◉ GRRRL RECORDLABEL

🎲 DICING GRRRL

🧴 GRRRL SPRAYPAINTING

🛹 GRRRLBOARDER

☠ WEEDKILLERGRAFFITI (OR GRRRL PIRATES)

GRRRL FLYPOSTING

GRRRLZINE

🧁 GRRRL PICNIC

HATCHING GANG

GRRRL EXHIBITION

🎸 GRRRL BAND

📡 GRRRL RADIO

GRRRL GIGS/DISCOS

GRRRL WORKSHOPS

🕺🕺🕺 GRRRLS!!!

Scale: Enormous! Bigger than you could ever guess...

SEE?

"...as a woman I
have no country.
As a woman I want
no country. As a
woman my country
is the whole
world."
Virginia Woolf,
Three Guineas.

RIOT GRRRL ABERDEEN

RIOT GRRRL NEWCASTLE

RIOT GRRRL YORK
RIOT GRRRL BRADFORD
RIOT GRRRL LEEDS
RIOT GRRRL MANCHESTER
RIOT GRRRL SHEFFIELD

RIOT GRRRL BIRMINGHAM

RIOT GRRRL LONDON

RIOT GRRRL PORTSMOUTH

This map includes only those grrrls I know of from my
work with the Riot Grrrls of Leeds and Bradford – hence
the Northern bias. There are so many more grrrls I can't
know about, so it's up to you to fill in the gaps...

PUT YERSELF ON THE MAP!!

I [had] mostly been going out to indie pop type things and they were quite small. A lot of it was quite twee and there weren't many girls on stage for starters and there weren't any girls doing fanzines or anything like that and girls were people's girlfriends that were going along. It was always noticeable to me.[77]

RIOT GRRRL RUMOURS

News of this new American phenomenon called riot grrrl began to be transmitted across the Atlantic through K Records newsletters, mainstream press articles, underground press like *Maximum Rock 'n' Roll*, American bands on tour like NOU, letter-writing and paraphernalia brought back by Everett True who was busy covering the upcoming grunge scene in America for the *Melody Maker*. His house-mates Jon Slade and Jo Johnson were inspired by the music and fanzines that Everett would bring back. Amelia Fletcher, who was over in America during 1991 (as her band Heavenly were signed to K Records) learned about riot grrrl first hand and recognised the need for a similar scene in the United Kingdom.

I first heard about [riot grrrl] from the originators of it, Molly Neuman and Allison Wolfe... they'd invented the term: they started this fanzine and they just called it *Riot Grrrl*... that year everyone was kind of talking about this thing riot grrrl... I think we had lost a little bit of impetus and inspiration doing what we were doing [in the United Kingdom] and I think we'd become a bit tired so really [riot grrrl] invigorated us and got us all excited again.[78]

The character that British riot grrrl would take, however, was to be dictated and shaped by dominant cultural industries whose mainstream concept of indie, pub-centred music venue circuit and nationalised music media restricted, distracted and hindered an underground independent riot grrrl community to be developed and expressed in the same ways as was possible in across the Atlantic. Unlike America, with its DIY legacy of K Records, SST and Dischord enabling independent punk production, Britain lacked a coherent DIY punk infrastructure. British riot grrrl had to start from scratch, with a whole girl-orientated network and infrastructure to build.

Our situation was different to the one the American riot grrrls were responding to. The underground in London had deteriorated totally, there wasn't much of an alternative... 'indie' just became an abstract term for a style of music, not ideas or values, 'cause they were all selling out to major labels. The notion of selling out wasn't important. Punk rock wasn't important. Fanzines were seen as a sad joke, so we had to explain stuff that might have been obvious to American kids but was alien to young British kids. The reasons for being independent were snorted at.[79]

The way America is structured [into] urban and suburban environments [so] if you grew up in like a small town or suburb somewhere, you're more likely to be exposed to things like punk and hardcore which is where riot grrrl stemmed from... whereas in England, that doesn't really exist, there isn't that kind of suburban, like white boy angst rock in a DIY sense. We didn't have Black Flag and Fugazi building [it] up... there already existed a fanzine culture and a band culture for girls to kind of slot into, whereas in England we had to create it. It didn't exist... punk didn't really exist in England... so the whole riot grrrl thing was kind of like, alright, we have to build this whole culture, it's not just the thing of building another facet

British riot grrrl map drawn by Karren Ablaze for the
***Bad Girls* exhibition at the ICA, 1993.**

of culture. We have to find venues so we can put on shows where like 14-year-old's can go to them. And we have to write fanzines and write to each other and create a network.[80]

News of American riot grrrl also ignited the imagination of music journalists Everett True and Sally Margaret Joy who both wrote for the music weekly *Melody Maker*. They kept their ears close to the ground for the reverberations of British riot grrrl. Unknown to Everett, his own house-mates would create the band that would act as the heartbeat of the British riot grrrl scene: Huggy Bear.

HUGGY BEAR: THIS IS HAPPENING WITHOUT YOUR PERMISSION

Huggy Bear was originally a project conceived by Jon Slade and Chris Rowley in which Jon created music on a 4-track and Chris would overdub his vocals. At the time Chris was going out with Niki Elliot and she began adding her vocals to Jon's tapes as well. Jon wasn't expecting Niki's involvement and decided that if Chris was going to get his girlfriend involved in their band then he would get his girlfriend, Jo Johnson, involved as well. The four collaborated together producing various demo tapes throughout 1991, which drew upon DIY 4-track productions, indie-pop aesthetics, and various samples. Mathew Fletcher, the original drummer, left due to their refusal to practice a song more than once and Karen Hill, an old school friend of Jo's, began drumming in Huggy Bear when the time came to play live gigs. Huggy Bear played just two gigs in 1991, the first in September with Heavenly at a hotel in Oxford and the second at the Heavenly Christmas party in December 1991. Chris and Niki were frequent customers of the Rough Trade shop in Covent Garden, and subsequently became interested in K Records, Beat Happening and American zines like *Maximum Rock 'n' Roll*. It was from talking to Gary Walker, who worked in Rough Trade as well as being a gig promoter and founder of Wiiija records, which he ran from the Rough Trade shop, that the Huggies found out that Gary was bringing over a band called the Action Swingers. They had heard that Julie Cafritz, former guitarist for Pussy Galore, was in the band and they became ever more excited about the new group. They wanted to impress Gary with a demo tape that would ensure that they get the support slot for the Action Swingers London gig. Huggy Bear set about consciously making a tape that was more in keeping with the punk sound of the Action Swingers. Unfortunately, they ended up not getting the gig, but it marked a significant shift in the musical style of Huggy Bear and the evolution of what British riot grrrl would look and sound like. This tape, highlights of which were released by Wiiija as the *We Bitched* demo tape, became the critical link between Huggy Bear and American riot grrrl culture. Huggy Bear decided to give Everett some tapes to

Top: The Raincoats performing live in the 1980s.
Image courtesy of Shirley O'Loughlin.
Bottom: Huggy Bear performing at Subterania in the 1990s. © Erica Echenberg/Redferns
www.musicpictures.com.

hand out to the people he met in the American punk underground, and the reaction was more than the
Huggies expected.

The third Huggy Bear gig in the Spring of 1992 saw the new punk direction in sound really take off; gigs that year started small in the Bull and Gate, Rough Trade shop and the Dome. Jon finally persuaded the initially reluctant Everett True to check out his band and although he was impressed, he didn't feel it was appropriate to write about Huggy Bear himself and enlisted Sally Margaret Joy to write a gig review. This review didn't make it into the published version of *Melody Maker*. In the summer of 1992, Everett and Sally interviewed Huggy Bear and they began to put their own spin on riot grrrl: Huggy Nation. Drawing on their own working class backgrounds, past British youth subcultures and Chris' youth work experience, a decentralised youth network of girl/boy resistance bent on cultural agitation was proposed.

> We want new playgrounds for the kids. New places where they can write, new places where they can hang out, nice new music they can listen to... what Huggy Nation want aren't martyrs, but prime movers—people who can be seen, but aren't standing for everybody else. Prime movers can be any one of the five of us—the seven of us. It can be people who we meet, who paint, or write or smash up bank windows. Prime movers doesn't imply hierarchy. It's people going out to do stuff and networking and letting us know about it. We have this big wide net of like, unrest.[81]

Huggy Bear began playing larger venues in London supporting bands like Stereolab, Tindersticks, and Pavement. Wiiija released their first single "Rubbing the Impossible to Burst" in September and immediately sold out, John Peel invited them to do a session in October, and a second single "Kiss Curl for the Kids Liberation" emerged around Christmas to coincide with their support slot with Sonic Youth and Pavement at Brixton Academy. Huggy Bear became the central resource for information about British riot grrrl, producing the zines *Reggae Chicken, Huggy Nation* and various bullet-teens, putting on their own gigs and events and fostering connections between isolated girls, as Layla Gibbon described, "in England I just remember like everyone would write to Huggy Bear, and Huggy Bear would kind of match people up. Like they gave me the address of this girl who lived in a small village in Wales, to write to when I first wrote to them".[82] Spurred on by what available information there was on riot grrrl, a girl-orientated DIY culture began to emerge. 1992 and 1993 saw the development of tape labels like Slampt Underground Organisation in Newcastle and Spazoom in Cardiff; zines like Natasha's *My Little Fanzine*, Layla Gibbon's *Drop Babies*, and Bidisha's *Girl Pride*; bands like Linus, Pussycat Trash, Skinned Teen, Mambo Taxi, Delicate Vomit and Coping Saw; riot grrrl meetings began to gather across Britain in Leeds, Bradford, Portsmouth and London. Girl positive manifestos began to emerge as riot grrrl was applied to the situations and lives of British girls and young women.

> My interpretation of RIOT GRRRL
> * It's about AUTONOMY: gaining more and more control over my life. Creating the stuff, music, porn, writing, I want to hear and read instead of waiting and consuming and being bored and unsatisfied. Girl autonomy means we need our own fanzines/ magazines/ music/ films/ books/ venues... the things boys can take for granted.
> * it's about the UNDERGROUND: a community of people sharing their art, challenging and encouraging each other through their network of fanzines, letters, meetings, shows, etc.
> * it's PUNK ROCK: Pissing everyone off. Being a loud mouth. Noise. Ugly aesthetic. Looking for the bullshit in even the most respected works of feminism, etc, duh. No heroes. Fuck the rules. Yeah a stripper can be a feminist.

* it's about <u>feminism</u>: girls talking to each other about how their lives are different to boys' lives. Why is that? What can we do to change it?

* it's about GIRL-LOVE: valuing friendships with girls, loving girls, supporting each other through shit and encouraging each other to get on and do stuff.[83]

Here lies in your hands the first fanzine from riot grrrl. Read it and scream with joy girl, this is the start of the New Feminism, we've got lots to say about this 'man's world' we live in, and I bet you do to! This belongs to all us girls, a way to say what you feel without editing, without censorship. Get together with some friends and write your own fanzine, get your thoughts down on paper and spread the word GIRL POWER REVOLUTION. You are strong girl, you are bad and beautiful, you can do anything you want to do. And you can do it now. THE FUTURE BELONGS TO US GO FORTH AND RIOT GRRRL!![84]

Remember: right now is the most important time in the history of the world, right now is the most exciting time of anyone's life. So why are you worrying about tomorrow? Why were you standing still at that gig when you desperately wanted to dance? Pussycat Trash, our first local girlpunk explosion, kicking out distorted pop over primal drums, fuzz guitar and minimalistic songs... this is punk pop! Who says your friends can't be your heroines and heroes? I'm sick of having to buy imported records from The States to hear good music, let's create our own scenes! Punk is happening in pub backrooms all over the country, so why are you waiting for the London music press to tell you what to like? Form your own band, release your own cassettes and records, DO IT YOURSELF. It's easy, a lot easier than you probably think.... All you need is imagination, passion and honesty, and a sense of belief in what you're doing.[85]

Top: Flyer for early American Huggy Bear gig in St Paul, Minnesota.
Opposite: Huggy Bear Guitar Mania Nation Poster, Image courtesy of Susan Corrigan.

On Friday 12 February 1993, Huggy Bear appeared on *The Word* and performed "Her Jazz" live. The performance ended without a hitch, but eager to disrupt the live TV show, members of Huggy Bear and Riot Grrrl London began protesting at the Barbie Girls feature aired immediately after Huggy Bear's performance. *The Word* was taken off the air as the protesters were ejected from the building. This event rocketed Huggy Bear's notoriety and forced riot grrrl into the mainstream gaze. Huggy Bear hit the cover of *Melody Maker* on the 27 February with an insiders report by Sally Margaret Joy.

MEDIA HEAT

Networks of encouragement and support started to spread across Britain, however the nationalised media attention became the main focus and threatened to distract the vital network building required to build this new girl DIY infrastructure. The involvement of Sally Margaret Joy in Riot Grrrl London particularly became controversial. As Karren Ablaze! commented on the London riot grrrl scene, "I think that a lot of their energies went into fending off media interference, due to people coming in just because they wanted to document it as part of some media related work."[86] Although there was no blanket media blackout, those involved with riot grrrl and Huggy Bear began to distance themselves from any involvement or association with the media. Subsequently it didn't take long for a media backlash to hit the British riot grrrl scene. The movement regularly found its way into the pages of the *Daily Mail, NME, Melody Maker, Evening Standard, Guardian, Independent, Every Woman*, and *Daily Star*. The tabloid's moral panic rhetoric cast riot grrrl as an anarchic girl gang bent on inflicting revenge against men;

> They screech, they spit, they snarl, they swear. Every word they scream through the microphone is a prayer against men. When their music stops, you are left with a pounding head, buzzing eardrums and no doubt that men are 'the enemy'. Meet the riot grrrls, the latest, the nastiest phenomenon to enter the British music scene.[87]

> They are the toughest, meanest group of feminists since women began burning their bras back in the swinging sixties. The so-called riot girls play rough 'n' ready rock music and they list MAN-HATING among their favourite hobbies.... And so a scorching Saturday evening finds me outside the Dome, a premier London rock venue.... To steady my nerves, I have an ice-cold beer in the bar next door.... A gang of teenage girl bruisers has followed me into the pub. A shiver goes down my spine as an incredibly scruffy girl spits: "Oh no! It's the Daily Star".... I scurry away in a cab. The chilling

punk rock feminism

My interpretation of RIOT GRRRL:

it's about AUTONOMY: gaining more and more control
over my life. Creating the stuff, music, porn,
writing, I want to hear and read instead of
waiting and consuming and being bored and
unsatisfied. Girl autonomy means we need our own
fanzines/magazines/music/films/books/venues...the
things boys can take for granted.

it's about the UNDERGROUND: a community of people
sharing their art, challenging and encouraging
each other through their network of fanzines,
letters, meetings, shows, etc.,

it's PUNK ROCK: Pissing everyone off. Being a
loud mouth. Noise. Ugly aesthetic. Looking for
the bullshit in even the most respected works
of feminism, etc., duh. No heroes. Fuck the rules.
yeah a stripper can be a feminist.

it's about feminism: girls talking to each other
about how their lives are different to boys'
lives. Why is that? What can we do to change it?

it's about GIRL-LOVE: valuing friendships with
girls, loving girls, supporting each other
through shit and encouraging each other to get
on and do stuff.

screams are ringing in my ears and I'm just thankful I wasn't stripped naked and hung from the nearest lamp-post.[88]

Music critics began picking apart Huggy Bear and riot grrrl, "your Skinned Teens and your Huggy Bears and yeah the whole damn lot of you are as rigid and formulaic as the boy noise that you so right(eous)ly criticise"[89] scolded Sarra Manning in *Melody Maker*. Huggy Bear were attacked for manipulating the media and riot grrrl was characterised as elitist and contrived, even guilty for *creating* the problem of gender inequality in music culture;

> We'd almost won the battle. A year ago we'd almost reached the stage where it wasn't an issue whether a musician had a penis or a clitoris.... Suddenly it's an issue again. We're back to square one. Thanks to riot grrrl, female musicians are, once again, a novelty.... I smell a secret fear of actually connecting with anyone outside their elitist fanzine culture (This is an elite. Most of you don't get to share flats with ET or Nation of Ulysses.... Or get invited to the riot grrrl "cabinet meetings").[90]

This put the task of building a riot grrrl underground infrastructure under significant strain. One national project was realised at the Institute of Contemporary Art (ICA) in London on 4 December 1993. The Grrrlstyle Revolution Day was coordinated by Riot Grrrl London and incorporated a day of discussion, poster art, zine-making and art installations. Huggy Bear went on to tour America and Japan and the British DIY girl underground struggled to maintain zines, record and tape labels, bands, gigs and events now fledgling outside of the public eye.

LEGACY

> Society hasn't really changed that drastically for women in the last ten years... the thing that's really tired is that misogyny is constantly recycled as the new hip product and what's cutting edge. I happen to think that resistance is really cutting edge.[91]

> Talking about waves of feminism is weird for me.... I understand that there are pushes and times where it gets more prominent at least in the mainstream. But to me it just seems that as long as sexism exists so must feminism.[92]

Riot grrrl experienced its own 'false feminist death syndrome' as the media declared riot grrrl a political failure, a genre of bad music and a simplistic reinvention of (male) punk.'[93] Ironically the American youth markets became flooded with girl-powered commodities whilst a new generation of angry yet acceptable singer songwriters like Fiona Apple, Lisa Loeb and Alanis Morrisette became the new faces of 'women in rock'.[94] In Britain, acts like Shampoo and the Spice Girls epitomised the cleaned up major-label friendly version of riot grrrl.

1996 saw the single "Wannabe" from the new all-girl group Spice Girls debut at number one. Signed to Virgin records, the group embraced merchandising and marketed products to young girls and women under the slogan 'girl power'. This form of girl power, however, rewarded young girls for providing the financial support that ensured the Spice Girls success. Instead of directly encouraging girls to create their own art, music, writing and culture, the Spice Girls rhetoric ensured that Spice-mania would be the focus of their adoration. 'Personalised' messages on products such as, "The Spice Girls say: 'Thank you for making us the number one act in the world. And thanks for buying this officially licensed product. Girl Power forever!"[95] indicate the consumerist terms and conditions within which

"Punk Rock Feminism" manifesto.
Image courtesy of Susan Corrigan.

the Spice Girls version of girl power operated.

The mid to late 1990s also witnessed a massive shift in the independent music scene as punk and grunge moved overground and male indie, rock and punk bands like Blur, Oasis, Nirvana, REM and Green Day achieved commercial success and mainstream popularity. To those involved in the movement during this era it felt like, "there had been a roll-back, a regression".[96] Many key riot grrrl bands broke-up during the decade: starting with Huggy Bear, Pussycat Trash, Bratmobile, Heavens to Betsy and eventually, Bikini Kill disbanded in 1998. Internal conflicts raged in riot grrrl communities, energy and spirit declined, and the need to change terms became evident as Slim Moon argued, "the media has changed what riot grrrl means, so they have to find a new name for their ideas".[97] Feminist cultural activism burned away within new terms and projects, to embrace race, class, sexualities, size, queer and trans issues and communities to produce a more sophisticated politicised cultural assault on gender binaries and boundaries.

An example of this is the *Free to Fight!* project which was set up by Anna Lo Bianco, Staci Cotler and Jody Blyele. Based in Portland, Oregon, the group of self-defence trainers created a record and workbook, which was distributed through Blyele's Candyass independent record label.[98] Incorporating survival stories, spoken word, self-defence instruction, and music. The project, which later expanded into a tour with Team Dresch and self-defence demonstrator Alice Stagg, introduced the possibilities and opportunities for women to incorporate self-defence into their everyday lives.

In 1995, Ed Varga began putting on queer community building shows under the name Homocore Minneapolis, which eventually morphed into a series of large-scale festivals in Olympia called Homo-a-go-go held in 2002, 2004 and 2006. The DIY queer festival Queeruption began in South London in 1998 and has since been held annually at various locations worldwide, for instance in New York City, Tel Aviv, Barcelona and Vancouver.[99] In other areas the first Rock 'n' Roll Camp for Girls was founded in 2000 as a summer day camp in Portland, providing young girls with access, inspiration and technical training to express themselves through music. Frustrated film-maker Miranda July set up the Big Miss Moviola video-letter project to provide other women filmmakers with opportunities for networking and having their work screened. New bands like Le Tigre, Sleater Kinney, The Gossip and The Butchies emerged and records labels like Mr Lady, Candyass, Kill Rock Stars, Slampt, Spazoom and Chainsaw continued to support music created by women and queers. The availability of new technologies of music production and expansion of musical styles enabled bands like Le Tigre, Scream Club and Chicks on Speed to explore the possibilities of feminist music crossing over hip hop and electro boundaries. Post-punk and hip hop women of colour bands like The New Bloods, Yo Majesty and Siren's Echo are questioning and challenging the boundaries of sexuality and gender.

LADYFEST AND CONTEMPORARY DIY FEMINIST CULTURAL ACTIVISM

In 1999 the EMP in Seattle was looking for music scenes to document for its exhibitions and contacted Allison Wolfe to gather people together for a retrospective on riot grrrl.[100] It had been the first time that these women had come together to reflect on riot grrrl since its decline, the chemistry between these women was still present and the encounter inevitably enabled a new idea to be realised;

> It was kind of cool, it was really touching and I think it was really emotional for a lot of us
> too. It was really cool to all be together again and realise that we were all still musicians
> or artists and doing things but kind of really separately and in a way we missed that sense

Programme for the ICA's *Bad Girls* exhibition, 1993.

ICA EDUCATION

Institute of
Contemporary Arts
The Mall
London SW1Y 5AH

For further details
please contact Kim
Sweet, ICA Education
Officer

Tel: 071 930 0493
Fax: 071 873 0051

BAD GIRLS

September - December 1993

After the backlash the whiplash. **Bad Girls** is a programme of film, performance, exhibitions and talks in which women artists move beyond the political to create personal and often fiercly explicit art.

Grrrlstyle Revolution at the ICA
4 December 1993

Comprising of writers, musicians, artists and performers, **Riot Grrrl** takes a feminist message to younger women and teenaged girls. With origins in the US and UK new punk rock underground, **Riot Grrrl** began as an imperative for young women to control their own lives using creativity and self-expression.

12.00 - 01.00 hrs
Fly Grrrl Posters and Polar Opposites
Installation in public areas of the ICA with poster art depicting Grrrls and their own corresponding artwork, twinned with two pincushion poles depicting Heroines and Queen Bees. Nominate your own goddesses or stick it to the enemy within!

14.00 hrs
Incen - diaries
Riot Grrrl answer the media using the media.
Discussion relating to punk rock feminism, the way music feeds into the Grrrls representation and screening of Grrrls video diaries. Open to men, women, girls and boys.

16.00 hrs
Girl Love and Girl Action
Feminism and activism: Putting priorities in order.
Discussion open to women and girls only.

16.30 hrs
Something for the Weekend
Partcipate in the creation of a women and Grrrls only quick-zine fagzine. Written, spoken and drawn contributions welcome.

ICA Bar and Cafe
Its a dirty Job, but someone's got to do it
Waitress service with a difference.

Admission to all **Riot Grrrl** events is free with ICA day membership, £1.50, £1.00 concs.

of community and networking. In the aftermath of that or during that I had been talking to
Corin [Tucker] and Sharon Cheslow just being like what do you think if we did something?
My original idea was a Lollapalooza girl tour but it seemed like way too much work so then it
eventually it became like why don't we do this single event, a festival, year 2000, bring in the
new millennium and just re-announce that there's something politicised and feminist and girl-
orientated that's still here.... Also I'd been frustrated with the state of music, all these macho
boy music festivals that were so corporate and mainstream at that point. Kids paying 50
bucks to get in to some stupid festival where girls get told to take their shirts off or they get
grabbed or even raped.... The purpose of Ladyfest was to be like "NO we need to take back
our alternative culture, we need to all be responsible for being creators and participants in our
communities and in our culture... don't just let it happen to you, make it happen."[101]

In 2000, the first Ladyfest was held in Olympia, described as, "a non-profit, community-
based event designed by and for women to showcase, celebrate and encourage the artistic,
organisational and political work and talents of women". The idea of Ladyfest was a
deliberate and conscious move away from the pitfalls associated with an identity-centred
movement like riot grrrl, towards a more action-orientated form of feminist activism. As
Tobi Vail explained:

Ladyfest was deliberately created... with strategy in mind. Reflecting on riot grrrl, which was
so immersed in identity, we wanted to come up with something that was action based... it
became clear that we should try to create something that could be reproduced by women
in their own communities, hoping that we wouldn't be imposing a universal idea of what
feminism is. We tried to develop a method that would foster localism. This was in response
to what I saw as some of the failures of riot grrrl, and a means to prevent us from repeating
those mistakes. Hoping that we wouldn't just be inspiring girls to copy a certain haircut or
feel they weren't feminists if they didn't dress or talk like 'us', we were hoping to develop
a decentralised means of organisation that would enable women to create an event that
reflected their particular needs and desires.

The initial four-day event encompassed workshops, discussions, bands, art and film and
attracted 2,000 attendees from around the world and managed to raise $30,000 for local
women's charities. In a move that strongly echoed riot grrrl, the term 'Ladyfest' sought
to reclaim and politicise the culturally disparaged term 'lady' and positioned Ladyfest as
an idea without copyright, which was encouraged to be taken away by other women and
applied to their own communities.

The Ladyfest ethos took off, since 2000 over a hundred Ladyfests have been held across
the world.[102] Ladyfest represents an important facet of contemporary action-orientated
feminist cultural resistance, open to multiple interpretations and change. Allison Wolfe
gives her take on the strengths of Ladyfest, "I love that people are taking it to their own
communities and own towns and making it what makes sense to them in their scenes and their
communities."[103] The feminist politicised possibilities and experiences that Ladyfest created
sparked off a new era of feminist cultural activism.

The beginning of this decade really felt like the start of something, I guess with the whole
riot grrrl thing, it just felt like, it was our turn now to do something new and continue on this
tradition of feminism and punk rock and it just happened at the right time in our lives.[104]

Since the first Ladyfest in Glasgow in 2001, alongside Queeruption and Queer Mutiny

Bikini Kill no 2, produced by Bikini Kill members
Tobi Vail, Kathi Wilcox and Kathleen Hanna.
Image courtesy of Julia Downes.

BIKINIKILL

#2

GirlPower

events, a new feminist and queer politicised DIY punk underground community began re-emerging as collectives began networking and organising across Britain including Local Kid (Bristol), FAG club (Cardiff), Homocrime (London), Manifesta (Leeds), Female Trouble (Manchester), Lola and the Cartwheels (Sheffield), The Bakery (London), Kaffequeeria (Manchester), Magical Girl (Dublin). Bands like Party Weirdo, Drunk Granny, the Corey O's, the Battys, Valerie, Vile Vile Creatures, Lesbo Pig, Peepholes, Jean Genet and Hooker infuse punk sounds and performances with feminist and queer politics. Club nights and gigs seek to provide safe and friendly spaces for, as FAG club describes QUAGS (Queers Of All Genders and Sexualities), that is, people who feel marginalised or outside of the norm. On the fringes of commercial culture, these spaces embrace the legacy of cultural resistance created by women, feminists and queers. The feminist-orientated DIY punk underground heart beats on. As Tobi Vail concluded her EMP interview in 1999, "Bikini Kill started something, but it isn't finished yet."[105]

Flyer for the Free to Fight project, set up by Lo Bianco, Staci Cotler and Jody Blyele.

1 Vail, Tobi. "EMP Riot Grrrl Retrospective Interview", 1999
2 Vaneigem, Raoul. *The Revolution Of Everyday Life*, London: Left Bank Books and Rebel Press, 1983
3 Debord, Guy. Cited in Marcus, Greil, *Lipstick Traces: A Secret History of the Twentieth Century*, London: Faber & Faber, 2001, pp.415
4 McClure, Nikki. "EMP Riot Grrrl Retrospective Interview", 1999, p.8
5 Maffeo, Lois. cited in Juno, Andrea. *Angry Women in Rock* vol 1., New York: Juno books, 1996, pp.122
6 Riot Grrrl Panel #1, EMP Riot Grrrl Retrospective, 1999, pp.2
7 Moon, Slim. EMP Riot Grrrl Retrospective Interview, 1999
8 Pavitt, Bruce cited in Azzerad, Michael, *Our Band Could Be Your Life*. New York/Boston: Little, Brown and company, 2001, pp.468
9 Smith, Erin. EMP Riot Grrrl Retrospective Interview, 1999
10 Neuman, Molly. "EMP Riot Grrrl Retrospective Interview", 1999
11 Cheslow, Sharon."EMP Riot Grrrl Retrospective Interview", 1999, pp.4
12 Cheslow, Sharon."EMP Riot Grrrl Retrospective Interview", 1999, pp.5
13 Cheslow, Sharon."EMP Riot Grrrl Retrospective Interview", 1999, pp.6
14 Riot Grrrl Panel. EMP Riot Grrrl Retrospective, 1999, pp.2
15 Riot Grrrl Panel. EMP Riot Grrrl Retrospective, 1999, pp.2
16 Vail, Tobi. EMP Riot Grrrl Retrospective Interview, 1999, pp. 6
17 Dresch, Donna. *Chainsaw* #2
18 Vail, Tobi. *Jigsaw* #2, 1990
19 Smith, Erin. "EMP Riot Grrrl Retrospective Interview", 1999, pp.8
20 Wilcox, Kathi. cited in Schilt, Kristin. "*Riot Grrrl is...*": The Contestation over meaning in a Music Scene", *Music Scenes: Local, Translocal and Virtual*, Nashville: Vanderbilt University Press, 2004, pp.118
21 Hanna, Kathleen. cited in Juno, Andrea. *Angry Women in Rock*, vol. 1, New York: Juno Books, 1996, pp.97
22 Nation of Ulysses, *Ulysses Speaks* #9, 1991
23 Vail, Tobi. "EMP Riot Grrrl Retrospective Interview", 1999, pp.9
24 *Bikini Kill #1: A Color and Activity Book*, 1991
25 Wolfe, Allison. "EMP Riot Grrrl Retrospective Interview", 1999, pp. 1-2
26 Hanna, Kathleen. "Gen X Survivor: From Riot Grrrl Rock Star to Feminist Artist", *Sisterhood is Forever* edited by Robin Morgan. New York: Washington Square Press, 2003, pp.132
27 Wolfe, Allison, "EMP Riot Grrrl Retrospective Interview", 1999, pp.3
28 *Riot Grrrl Manifesto*, 1991
29 Cheslow, Sharon. "EMP Riot Grrrl Retrospective Panel", 1999, pp.4
30 Neuman, Molly. "EMP Riot Grrrl Retrospective Interview", 1999,
31 Neuman, Molly. "EMP Riot Grrrl Retrospective Interview", 1999
32 Hanna, Kathleen. *Angry Women in Rock*, vol. 1. edited by Juno, Andrea. New York: Juno Books, 1996, pp.99
33 Klein, Melissa. "Duality and Redefinition: Young Feminism and the Alternative Music Community". *Third Wave Agenda: Being Feminist, Doing Feminism*, edited by Heywood, Leslie and Drake, Jennifer. Minneapolis/London: University of Minnesota Press, 1997, pp.212-213
34 Cheslow, Sharon. *Don't Need You: The Herstory of Riot Grrrl* directed by Koch, Kerri. Urban Cowgirl Productions, 2006
35 Tucker, Corin. "EMP Riot Grrrl Retrospective Interview", 1999, pp.6
36 Wolfe, Allison. Personal oral history, 2007
37 Tucker, Corin. *Don't Need You: The Herstory of Riot Grrrl* directed by Koch, Kerri. Urban Cowgirl Productions, 2006
38 EMP Riot Grrrl Retrospective Panel #3, 1999, pp.1-2
39 EMP Riot Grrrl Retrospective Panel, 1999, pp.7
40 Shive, Madigan, *Don't Need You: The Herstory of Riot Grrrl* directed by Koch, Kerri. Urban Cowgirl Productions, 2006
41 Neuman, Molly. "EMP Riot Grrrl Retrospective Interview", 1999
42 Rebecca "girl" in *Girl Germs* #4, 1991
43 Tucker, Corin. "EMP Riot Grrrl Retrospective Interview", 1999, pp.3
44 Smith, Erin. "EMP Riot Grrrl Retrospective Interview", 1999
45 McClure, Nikki. "EMP Riot Grrrl Retrospective Interview", 1999
46 Wolfe, Allison. *Don't Need You: The Herstory of Riot Grrrl* directed by Koch, Kerri. Urban Cowgirl Productions, 2006
47 Wolfe, Allison. *Girl Germs* #3, 1991
48 Carns, Rachel. EMP Riot Grrrl Retrospective Interview, 1999, pp.2
49 Snead, Elizabeth. "Feminist Riot Grrls Don't Just Wanna Have Fun", *USA Today*, August 1992
50 France, Kim. "Grrrls at War", *Rolling Stone*, 8-22 July 1993, pp.23-24
51 Spencer, Lauren. "Grrrls Only; From the Youngest, Toughest Daughters of Feminism—Self Respect You Can Rock To", *The Washington Post*, 3 January 1993
52 Spencer, Lauren. *The Washington Post*, 3 January 1993
53 Chideya, Farai. "Revolution, Girl Style" *Newsweek*, November 23rd 1992, pp.84
54 Spencer, Lauren. *The Washington Post*, 3 January 1993
55 Snead, Elizabeth. "Feminist Riot Grrls don't Just Wanna Have Fun", *USA Today*, 7 August 1992
56 Snead, Elizabeth. *USA Today*, 7 August 1992
57 Spencer, Lauren. *The Washington Post*, 3 January 1993
58 Cheslow, Sharon. "EMP Riot Grrrl Retrospective Interview" with Tobi Vail, 1999, p.1
59 Hanna, Kathleen. *Don't Need You: The Herstory of Riot Grrrl* directed by Koch, Kerri. Urban Cowgirl Productions, 2006
60 Wolfe, Allison. Don't Need You: The Herstory of Riot Grrrl directed by Koch, Kerri. Urban Cowgirl Productions, 2006
61 Tucker, Corin. "EMP Riot Grrrl Retrospective Interview", 1999, pp.6
62 McClure, Nikki. "EMP Riot Grrrl Retrospective Interview", 1999, pp.6
63 Wolfe, Allison. "EMP Riot Grrrl Retrospective Interview", 1999, pp.4
64 Wolfe, Allison. "EMP Riot Grrrl Retrospective Interview", 1999, pp.3
65 Neuman, Molly. "EMP Riot Grrrl Retrospective Interview", 1999, pp.9
66 Tucker, Corin. *Don't Need You: The Herstory of Riot Grrrl* directed by Koch, Kerri. Urban Cowgirl Productions, 2006
67 Lamm, Nomi. "EMP Riot Grrrl Retrospective Interview", 1999, pp. 7
68 Although it is worth noting that many involved in riot grrrl also came from working class and lower middle class backgrounds who experienced poverty. For more discussions of racism in riot grrrl see Kristen Schilt "The Punk-White Privilege Scene: The Construction of Whiteness in Riot Grrrl Zines." *Different Wavelengths: Studies of the Contemporary Women's Movement*, Ed Jo Reger. New York: Routledge, 2005. pp.39-56.
69 Bikceem, Ramdasha. *Don't Need You: The Herstory of Riot Grrrl* directed by Koch, Kerri. Urban Cowgirl Productions, 2006
70 Wolfe, Allison. *Don't Need You: The Herstory of Riot Grrrl* directed by Koch, Kerri. Urban Cowgirl Productions, 2006
71 Vail, Tobi. EMP Riot Grrrl Retrospective Interview, 1999, pp.9
72 Triggs, Teal. "Look Back in Anger: The Riot Grrrl Revolution in Britain" *Zed*, 5, 1998, pp.8-25
73 O'Brien, Lucy. *She-Bop II*, London/New York: Continuum, 2002
74 Nicky Wire cited in *Stanley* 2006
75 cited in *Bladh* 2005, p.4
76 White, Rachel. PhD thesis
77 Holborow, Rachel. personal oral history, 2006
78 Fletcher, Amelia. personal oral history, 2007
79 Johnson, Jo. Amy Raphael *Grrrls:Viva Rock Divas*. New York: St Martins Griffin 1995, pp.151
80 Gibbon, Layla. "EMP Riot Grrrl Retrospective Interview", 1999, pp. 6-7
81 Rowley, Chris. full transcript of *Melody Maker* interview with Everett True and Sally Margaret Joy reproduced as a fanzine, 1992
82 Gibbon, Layla. "EMP Riot Grrrl Retrospective Interview", 1999
83 Elliot, Niki. writing as 'Mal-fille' Furball #1,1992
84 Joy, Sally. Margaret *Riot Grrrl* #1, 1992
85 Dale, Pete. *Head Shaved Smooth*: a slamptcore zine, 1993

86 Ablaze, Karren. personal oral history, 2006
87 Barrowclough, Anne. "Save the World? Not a Hope Grrrls", *Daily Mail*, 27 March 1993, pp.27
88 Poole, John. "I Brave the Riot Girls", *Daily Star*, 9 July 1993
89 Manning, Sarra. "Viewpoint", *Melody Maker*, 29 January 1994, pp.35
90 Price, Simon. "Rebel Grrrls", *Melody Maker*, 6 March 1993, pp.30
91 Hanna, Kathleen. *Don't Need You: The Herstory of Riot Grrrl* directed by Koch, Kerri. Urban Cowgirl Productions, 2006
92 Wolfe, Allison. personal oral history, 2007
93 Pozner, Jennifer L."The Big Lie: False Feminist Death Syndrome, Profit, and the Media" in *Catching a Wave: Reclaiming Feminism for the Twenty-First Century*, edited by Dicker, Rory, and Piepmeier, Alison. Boston: Northeaster University Press, 2003, pp. 31–56
94 Schilt, Kristen "A Little Too Ironic: The Appropriation and Packaging of Riot Grrrl Politics by Mainstream Female Musicians.", *Popular Music and Society*, 26 (1), pp.5-16
95 Text taken from the rearside of Spice Girls photo badge set, Spice Girls Ltd, 1997
96 Wolfe, Allison. personal oral history, 2007
97 Moon, Slim. "EMP Riot Grrrl Retrospective Interview", 1999
98 Free to Fight! is free to download from http://www.freetofight.org
99 See www.queeruption.org for more information
100 Online exhibit can be accessed at http://www.emplive.org/exhibits/index.asp?articleID=666
101 Wolfe, Allison. personal oral history, 2007
102 See www.ladyfest.org and www.myspace.com/ladyfesteurope for information on Ladyfests and related queer feminist DIY festivals worldwide
103 Wolfe, Allison, personal oral history, 2007
104 Cupid, Michal from Personal Video Diary Project at Ladyfest Cardiff, 2006
105 Vail, Tobi "EMP Riot Grrrl Retrospective Interview", 1999

POEMS ON THE UNDERGROUND

CAZZ BLAZE

BORED TEENAGERS: MOMENTS IN PUNK

Trying to define what is meant by the term 'punk' is rather like opening a can of worms. As Roger Sabin would have it, part of the problem faced by any writer seeking to write about punk is that there is already an orthodoxy, a prescribed view, one that is based on a narrow frame of reference and a tendency to romanticise.[1] In answering the inevitable question 'What is punk?' I would say the following: punk was a 1970s youth movement centred around music and fashion that flirted with politics at both extremes of the theoretical divide, with the likes of Skrewdriver and the Oi! faction representing the extreme right wing, and the likes of Crass and the anarcho-crust faction representing the extreme left. It promoted a DIY, independent approach to the production of cultural material such as records, fanzines, and clothes, and by implication helped to democratise how such products were created and consumed. At the same time, a number of individuals and groups founded their reputations and careers on punk—McLaren, Westwood, and Lydon to name but three—and haven't done too badly out of it financially. Punk rock was born in London with the birth of the Sex Pistols, or in New York with the birth of the New York Dolls, or even earlier, with the birth of garage rock bands such as the Flamin' Groovies, MC5 and The Stooges; depending on your point of view. The music was loud, fast, frequently parochial in its frame of references, but often with wider political targets in sight. It was angry, often nihilistic, with a strong distrust and disrespect of authority. Anarchy and chaos were to be celebrated, and punk bands were characterised by their spirit of defiance and antagonism, along with a desire to prioritise authenticity over musical talent. The musical culture in which bands played guitar in their bedrooms for years was replaced by groups who were, by and large, technically and musically inept, but who had the right attitude, learning how to play on stage and often splitting up after only a few gigs. Those that survived might develop musically and a significant number would go on to create some of the most inventive and startling music of the 1980s.

Punk garnered a loyal following in Britain and North America, fostered by the socio-political climate in both countries at the time.[2] In Britain, economic recession, youth unemployment, post-Second World War debt bondage, impending Thatcherism, widespread discontent and restlessness were the breeding ground, in America, punk was fed by the post-Vietnam era, characterised by the Watergate scandal, Reaganomics and general disenchantment. The early to mid-1970s are also frequently represented as being a stagnant period for music, and this has also been cited as a crucial factor by a number of writers when discussing the birth of punk.[3]

Perhaps the site of the most heated debate is when punk began and ended. Whereas most punk books take the split of the Sex Pistols in 1978 as the end, or beginning of the end, of punk and therefore of their stories, Simon Reynolds book *Rip It Up And Start Again* takes it as the beginning. In dealing with the post-punk period, a period he categorises as beginning in 1978 and ending in 1984, he begins his story in 1978, taking *Never Mind The Bollocks* as the end of punk, and Public Image LTD as the beginning of post-punk.[4] By doing this, Reynolds removes the idea of a clear ending for punk, and instead sees the repercussions of this so-called short-lived youth movement continuing for years to come. Reynolds is not alone in this: many writers have sought to draw a connection between the punk bands of the 1970s, such as the Sex Pistols and the Clash, and 1990s bands such as Nirvana and Green Day, but far fewer have sought to explore the lineage established by bands such as The Slits, Raincoats, Au Pairs, Kleenex and Delta 5, to name a few, and the riot grrrl bands of the early 1990s and beyond.

SHOUTING OUT LOUD: WOMEN AND PUNK

"Why was punk important?" For me it was like instead of going to university, I got all my education there, I had just come from this school in Maypole and didn't know anything much, but it was reading and talking and being in a band myself and what we learned at that time. We had the band (Fast Relief) for nearly two years and we played loads of gigs. And also there was so much mixing, people from different backgrounds and then with Rock Against Racism and the Anti-Nazi League, and all the politics around that, I was learning all the time.[5]

Young women are measured for their likeness or rather their positioning to mothers, whores, mistresses, spinsters and lesbians. Subcultures are not magically protected from these constructs, yet for some women in punk there was a place to be angry and to celebrate the illicit and clandestine—for some a means of seeing critically into the mirror and of challenging the reflection.[6]

Those of us who experienced that battleground have been shaped by it. We still find it difficult to shake off the questioning rigour that the scene demanded, and maybe we don't want to. That's the women punk made us.[7]

Summer 1976: According to those who were alive at the time, the summer of that year was unbearably hot in Britain, particularly in the south. In a 1984 interview with Janice Long, Siouxsie Sioux talked of people throwing themselves into the fountains at London's Centre Point that summer every night after punk gigs, "they just used to go wild" she said. The effect of the intense heat on the public throughout the summer of 1976 was also noted by Jon Savage: the weather gave people energy that they might otherwise lack, it made people stay up all night, and it made them stay out all night as well. Whilst seeing the influence of cheap speed in this phenomenon, Savage and his interviewees still believe the heat made a difference.[8] This is significant because, as well as possibly accounting for some of the skimpy attire worn by Sioux and her friends, the heat also helped to move things along from a sub-cultural point of view. 1976 can be seen, from a musical perspective, to be the first summer of punk. The Sex Pistols may have already formed by this point, and their infamous encounter with Bill Grundy might have been a full three months away, but it was on 20 September 1976 that the 100 Club Punk Festival took place. It was on this day that the first incarnation of Siouxsie and the Banshees—Siouxsie, Steve Severin, Marco Pirroni, and Sid Vicious—made their live debut, having blagged their way onto the bill prior to forming, and before actually learning to play. Once on stage, they performed a 20 minute set during which they mauled "The Lords Prayer" via "Knocking On Heavens Door", with bits of "Sister Ray" and "Smoke On The Water" thrown in for good measure.[9] Following the gig, the band promptly split up, yet, from this inauspicious beginning, both Sioux and Severin were to forge long-term careers.[10]

Many readers will no doubt be wondering why I have chosen this particular moment in punk as my starting point over, say, the Pistols and the infamous, and much rehashed, Bill Grundy encounter, but it is because the Bill Grundy incident is so often recalled that I have chosen to skim over it here. The 1976 Punk Festival is a better starting point, musically speaking, than the formation of the Pistols, Stooges, or New York Dolls because it marks a point when punk was beginning to reach a wider audience but is also pre-Grundy and thus took place before the ensuing tabloid hysteria that would dog punk for years to come. Similarly, the debut appearance of Siouxsie and the Banshees is worth mentioning because they were a band who not only blagged their first gig before they had actually formed, but are also a band who learned how to play on stage. Whilst this may have seemed an unusual way to form a band in 1976, the story of their formation has been repeated many times since, albeit minus the performance of "The Lords Prayer". Finally, the debut of Siouxsie and the Banshees is worth mentioning if only because Siouxsie is one of the very few female punk performers to have survived the punk period and who continues to have a viable musical career.

Jon Savage, writing in 1991, discusses the inner circle of punk performers who became connected with Westwood and McLaren's Kings Road shop, Sex. These mainly female performers gave the Sex Pistols a sexy kind of glamour, he argues, that the band lacked at that time.[11] In doing so, they "became part of the Sex Pistols and gave punk its Warholian edge".[12] Many of these performers, if they weren't already, soon became faces on the London punk scene, not necessarily through forming bands themselves, although some did, but most often simply by turning up and looking or being outrageous, much as Warhol's 'Superstars' had done ten years before. Of the women and girls who *did* form bands, punk—despite its perceived radicalism—could often be a disappointingly conventional ride.

The Adverts, for example, were comprised of four men and one woman, Gaye Advert, who played bass. They released their first single on the London independent label Stiff in 1977, and were shocked when the sleeve came back from the printers with a close-up

of Gaye's face on the front.[13] TV Smith told Savage that, as far as the band was concerned; the fact that the Adverts had a female bassist simply wasn't an issue, but that the sleeve had the impact of making them aware of it as an issue, and of cheapening things.[14]

By contrast, London band The Slits, who were comprised of four girls, toured with The Clash on the latter's 'White Riot' tour, and behaved rather badly by all accounts. Guitarist Viv Albertine pointed out to Savage that, had they been a male band, their bad behaviour would have been commended as being "like the Stones or the Pistols" but as it was, the coach driver had to be bribed to let the band on the coach every morning, singer Ari Up was banned from showing herself in hotel lobbies, and by all accounts the bands sexuality was perceived as threatening.[15] Viv Albertine has described some of the clothes The Slits wore as being a mixture of conflicting styles and signifiers; tutus with Doc Marten boots and leather jackets, for example and much has been made of the bands matted hair and singer Ari Up's jubilee knickers, worn over tights.[16] To begin with, the band played very hard, very fast, frequently out of tune speed punk, packed with fierce aggression. This musical period has only really been captured for posterity by their 1977 and 1978 Peel Sessions, which have been released a number of times on both LP and CD, and by the live compilation *In the Beginning*. By the time the Slits signed to Island, and released their debut album *Cut* in 1979, they had learned to play, and were exploring a more experimental reggae punk fusion that was equally as challenging as their earlier material, but, crucially, was less loud and in many ways less aggressive. In writing about the skittery, off-kilter experimental sound of The Slits and The Raincoats, Lucy O'Brien points out the tension between tentativeness and anger expressed by these bands.[17]

Left: Ari Up performing with The Slits, 1977.
© Ian Dickson/Redferns/musicpictures.com
Right: Front cover of The Slits *Cut* album, 2005
(original release 1979).
Opposite: Siouxsie and the Banshees performing
in London, 1977. © Ian Dickson/Redferns/
musicpictures.com.

These bands made an important contribution to rock in the early 1980s, investing it with an eerie, scratchy femininity. Less about shock tactics, guts and confrontation, their music was more a resolute expression of what it meant to be a woman at that time, in that particular culture.[18]

The Raincoats were themselves inspired by The Slits to form and Simon Reynolds has argued that the band bypassed traditional feminine pressures and stereotypes by projecting "ordinariness" whereas the Slits "turned unkemptness into style."[19] This 'ordinariness', he argues, was a radical gesture at the time, disassociating the band from the glamour and showbiz image of previous female performers.[20]

Whilst The Raincoats challenged the typical feminine image by projecting 'ordinariness', performers such as Siouxsie Sioux and Lydia Lunch, who had a more aggressively sexual image, were in the ironic position of challenging stereotypes of feminine beauty whilst themselves being adopted as punk pin-ups.[21] Siouxsie's image in particular, which revolved around the subversive use of S&M bondage gear, an homage to *Cabaret*, and a continuation of the Bowie/Roxy Music mid-1970s glam look, was particularly confrontational. Pictures of her from 1976 show her with short black hair, very pale, heavy pan-stick make-up, black eye shadow and eyeliner, culminating in a look that Radio 1 DJ Annie Nightingale later said was almost "like a mask".[22] There are a series of heavily bootlegged images of Sioux from this period, which show her at London's Screen On The Green, wearing a peephole bra, knickers, fishnets, suspenders and a swastika armband, have thrown up innumerable questions and contradictions as to what punk was really about.

Another regular hangout for Siouxsie, and for the group of Pistols fans that were to become known as the Bromley Contingent in the early days of the London punk scene, was the lesbian club Louise's on London's Poland Street. Whilst a number of writers have explored the London punk scene's links with the London gay scene at the time (particularly Jon Savage, and John Gill in his book *Queer Noises*) most agree that a tide of laddishness and uniform rules about what punk was, in many ways, swept away this link fairly early on. Nils and Ray Stevenson's book, *Vacant: A Diary Of The Punk Years*, for example, reveals that Nils, who is described by Savage as a "self-styled King's Road Casanova" celebrated the laddishness of the Sex Pistols scene and frequently made use of his privileged position within their entourage.[23] Although he appears to have been along for the ride, and for what he could get out of it financially, at times his diary reads like a prolonged exercise in getting his leg over, suggesting that he definitely exploited the punk scene sexually as well.[24]

Stevenson does not necessarily represent the norm: he happened to belong to a punk inner circle that probably bore little resemblance to the punk scenes outside London, but his approach is telling in other ways, as Lucy O'Brien writes:

> The punk scene itself, also, was not always one of halcyon acceptance. While there were men wrestling with questions of masculinity and feminism, there were just as many content to leave it unreconstructed. "A lot of the punk boys were just regular knobheads who happened to have spikey hair", remarks [Liz] Naylor.[25]

The relationship between punk and feminism has been discussed by a number of writers, it is a complex issue, and appears to be fuelled by almost as many contradictions as punk itself, as such, it is ultimately unresolved. Writer Lucy Toothpaste, whose fanzine *Jolt* was explicitly feminist, interviewed a number of punk women, none of whom would call themselves a feminist.[26] Toothpaste, who helped found Rock Against Sexism, and who later went on to write for the feminist magazine *Spare Rib*, told Jon Savage that she didn't believe punk challenged male sexuality or image, but that the early punk scene gave

The Raincoats performing in 1978.
Image courtesy of Shirley O'Loughlin.

women confidence.[27] Despite the refusal of many punk women to accept the feminist label, she does believe that the lyrics many of these women were writing were a challenge to perceived notions of femininity.[28] Both Cressida Miles and Lucy O'Brien would seem to reinforce this view, as both write of punk as, whilst being in no way egalitarian, at least providing a space in which women could explore anger, gender boundaries, and power.[29]

One of the punk bands who did explicitly explore sexual politics was the Birmingham band the Au Pairs, a mixed gender group whose *Playing With A Different Sex* LP is described by Angela McRobbie as injecting "traditional left and feminist politics" with "a sense of pleasure, mystery and eroticism".[30] McRobbie makes a convincing case for punk as an escape route for many frustrated young women in 1970s Britain, and the young women she focuses on in her essay were politicised by punk, and by the Au Pairs.[31] What her essay also reveals, however, is the girls' distrust of feminism, particularly radical feminism and separatism, and of what they perceived to be dictation as to how women should look and dress.[32] Having rejected the traditional roles of the working class Birmingham girl, none of the three were keen to embrace what they felt to be an equally restrictive set of 'rules'.[33] This could explain what Miles and O'Brien, amongst others, perceive to be a lack of solidarity between female punks. Miles, referring to a study by Roman, has pointed to the fact that many working class female punks felt more of an affinity with male punks of the same class, whilst O'Brien sees a solidarity amongst women in individual *bands*, such as The Slits and her own band (The Catholic Girls) but notes that this solidarity was undermined when bands were signed and had to contend with record companies who remained unreconstructed where sexual politics were concerned.[34] Possibly the most extensive study of the paradoxes invoked by the relationship between punk, gender, and feminism is Lauraine Leblanc's book, *Pretty In Punk: Girls' Gender Resistance in a Boys Subculture*, which explores gender resistance and relations in a wide range of punk communities in 1990s North America. Leblanc echoes the work of O'Brien and Miles, in that she identifies the key paradox as being the male dominated nature of the punk scene, a scene that is portrayed as equal and feminist, "but is actually far from being either".[35] Yet, this scene gave her, and her interviewees a space in which to be assertive, aggressive, and less feminine than their non-punk contemporaries.[36]

In becoming a punk, she argues, she was able to reject mainstream constraints but

Early shot of Viv Albertine performing with The Slits.
Image courtesy of Mick Mercer.

was, ironically, faced with a new set of pressures to conform to a stereotype of what it is to be a punk girl.[37] A stereotype she felt revolved around "masculine toughness and feminine compliance."[38] Whilst Leblanc's study takes place in a different location and time period to Miles, O'Brien's and McRobbie's work, and whilst it could be argued that the belief systems held by 1990s punks are not the same as those held by 1970s punks, her research is nonetheless uncomfortably telling on a number of levels. Leblanc's study took in a range of punk girls and women aged between 14 and 37, from a range of punk factions and sub groups, and from a range of Canadian and American regions. Having decided not to include riot grrrls within her field of study, Leblanc ends her book with a plea for "unity among punk girls".[39] She feels that, if united, the strength and creativity demonstrated by her interviewees could have a radical impact on punk, and could revolutionise it as a subculture, urging these girls and women to "make punk your own".[40]

Ironically, Angela McRobbie, writing in 1980, reached a similar conclusion in her feminist critique of subcultural theory:

> The working-class girl is encouraged to dress with stylish conventionality; she is taught to consider boyfriends more important than girlfriends and to abandon the youth club or disco for the honour of spending her evenings watching television in her boyfriend's house, saving money for an engagement ring. Most significantly, she is forced to relinquish youth for the premature middle age induced by childbirth and housework. It is not so much that girls do too much too young; rather, they have the opportunity of doing too little too late. To the extent that all-girl subcultures, where the commitment to the gang comes first, might forestall these processes and provide their members with a collective confidence which could transcend the need for 'boys', they could well signal an important progression in the politics of youth culture.[41]

Given that McRobbie has dismissed the freedom for girls to drink, take drugs and mooch about on street corners with the boys as essentially equally as oppressive as staying at home, it seems unlikely that what she was longing for in 1980 was the development of a binge drinking culture in which girls and young women are free to get lashed with the boys.[42] But they mustn't pass out on park benches with their knickers showing lest they invite passing rapists, censure and blame, or a culture in which the focus of adulation is the WAGS, the 'it' girls, the various size zero attention seekers, and pretty much anyone else who shouts and screams loudly enough for attention but ultimately has nothing to say, then it would appear that the important shift in feminine youth culture McRobbie was hoping for has yet to happen.[43] That is, unless the riot grrrls are allowed in from the subcultural cold.

LIKE WE NEVER EXISTED: PUNK AND RIOT GRRRL

"I don't know how many females in the music business have been influenced by The Slits, females around now. 'Cos I know there was this 10–15 year gap where it felt like we'd *never existed.*" Said Viv Albertine in 1996.[44]

As she told Lucy O'Brien: "The whole climate changed in the 1980s—music reverted back to a careerist option".[45] Here she touches on a process that Simon Reynolds has documented in full, sickening, detail in *Rip It Up And Start Again,* "but we were amazed that there was this void, with no one taking up the baton. There was a ten-year gap until riot grrrl and Elastica came along".[46]

Despite the fact that the preliminary research I carried out in preparation for writing this chapter has revealed a strong association in the minds of many between riot grrrl and punk bands such as The Slits and The Raincoats, the relationship between 1970s punk and 1990s riot grrrl has incited a certain amount of semantic argument between the few writers there are on the subject. Stewart Home, for example, has argued that riot grrrl is

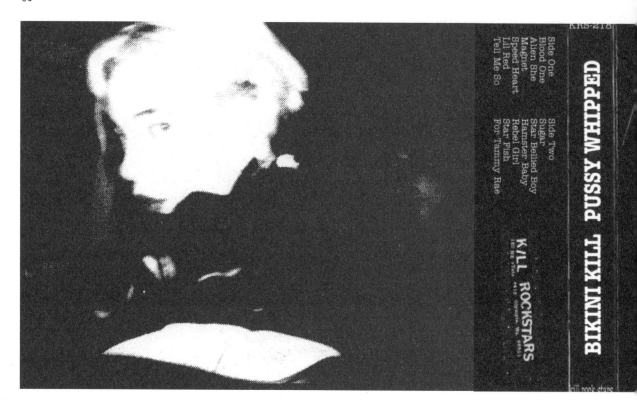

a "transformation" of punk; Lauraine Leblanc views it as a "break-away faction" whereas Lucy O'Brien, more kindly, refers to it as "the 1990s daughter of punk rock".[47] In effect, each of these writers are probably right: The relationship between punk and riot grrrl is a very under-researched area, and the case is not helped by the fact that a lot of punk writers seem to ignore riot grrrl altogether out of a combination of disinterest, suspicion, and embarrassed awkwardness.

"Before I was into riot grrrl bands I listened to a lot of mainstream punk, which was predominantly male (or so I was led to believe!)" wrote Angel, a fanzine writer from London in 1999.[48]

> I liked The Clash, Buzzcocks, Ramones, etc, and for a while I came to terms with the fact that this was as close to my way of thinking as music could be, but something didn't quite click. What riot grrrl did for me was to help fill in my missing history (by 'my' I mean women's) it helped me discover amazing bands practically ignored by the music magazines and rock family trees. Bands like X Ray Spex, The Au Pairs, Patti Smith, Joan Jett, The Slits and The Raincoats filled in those missing gaps and sang punk or rock 'n' roll from a female perspective, suddenly it all made much more sense, it put me as a female into the scene.[49]

She continued:

> I do see a very prominent link to 1970s bands like The Slits and riot grrrl, after all the basis of riot grrrl was girls creating music and unity and the Slits were making that music in the 1970s but they lacked the support of hundreds of other bands following suit like riot grrrl had and they had an even tougher male dominated music industry to convince.[51]

Angela, a fanzine writer from Glasgow, similarly discovered the female punk bands of the 1970s and 80s through riot grrrl: "I'd usually hear them through a friend making a mixtape with them on or something, or through someone saying 'Oh, if you like so-and-so (new riot grrrl band) you'd probably like so-and-so (old school grrrl band)' Not all the bands were

particularly punk either, but they all had that punk feel
to them."[52]

Two of the earliest riot grrrl bands to owe a clear musical
debt to punk bands such as X Ray Spex and The Slits were Bikini
Kill and Bratmobile. Whilst many of those I consulted about riot
grrrl while writing this chapter also mentioned bands such as
L7, Babes In Toyland, and Hole in conjunction with riot grrrl, there
was also a perception that these three bands were essentially
pre riot grrrl and, whilst they may have held an affinity with the
phrase, they weren't necessarily a part of it. As Sophy, author of
Sista Yes! Fanzine put it: "I never really considered Hole to be riot
grrrl. Some people did, which back then was quite reasonable,
but no, for me riot grrrl definitely began with Bikini Kill."[53]

Bikini Kill, and fellow Olympians Bratmobile, both formed in
1990. According to Mark Anderson and Mark Jenkins, the Olympia
punk scene has one of the more "gender balanced" punk scenes
in America, it is home to K Records and Beat Happening, and
as such there was room for a woman like Tobi Vail to write her
fanzine *Jigsaw*, in which she explicitly challenged the male
dominated nature of the many punk scenes she had been
involved with.[54] Vail was, at this point, playing drums in The
Go-Team. Kathleen Hanna, who would team up with Vail later
that year, was based in nearby Portland. Initially experimenting
with spoken word performances, something she would revisit
post-Bikini Kill under the name Julie Ruin, Hanna would turn
to music in order to make her feminist message accessible to
younger girls.[55] Her first band was Viva Kneievel, who completed
an American tour before splitting up, as Anderson and Jenkins

Left: Front cover of Bikini Kill's *Pussy Whipped* album,
(CD version) 1993.

Right: Front and back cover of Bikini Kill's *Pussy
Whipped* album (cassette version) 1993.

point out, at the time Hanna was working in a domestic violence shelter, and this had a strong influence on her work. The band had a number of songs about "gang rape and stuff"and after shows; girls would approach Hanna and tell her their own stories, causing her to fall back on her experience of crisis counselling.[56] Hanna acknowledges that there was, therefore, a strong link between the work she was doing at the shelter, and the work she was doing at gigs as part of Viva Kneievel.[57]

In forming Bikini Kill, Vail and Hanna had a clear image of the band as part of a punk feminist band, but were also keen to be "sexy and life-affirming" according to Anderson and Jenkins.[58] This approach drew criticism from feminists in some quarters when it was revealed that Hanna sometimes worked as a stripper, something Hanna defended on the grounds that being a stripper was only as exploitative as slinging burgers or waitressing. In the latter two cases, the exploitation may be less obvious, but the pay was also lower, she argued.[59] Similarly, it is ironic that a number of feminists in the British media in 1993 criticised bands such as Bikini Kill and Huggy Bear, not only for—in Hanna's case—their choice of work, but also for creating songs and fanzines for their audience rather than advocating an enforced reading list of approved feminist texts, given that both Hanna and Vail had studied the likes of bell hooks, Audre Lorde and Angela Davis, and were considerably well read.[60] This perceived lack of awareness of conventional feminist texts was a criticism that seemed to be conveniently forgotten when many of the same newspapers, music papers, and critics were admiring the Spice Girls a mere three years later.

The name Bikini Kill is reputed to come from a one off project singer/songwriter Lois Maffeo did with her friend Rebecca Gates, and was derived from a Frankie Avalon film, *The Million Eyes Of Sumaru*, in which a "female supervillian" recruits a number of beautiful women to become the wives or mistresses of all the worlds leaders, with the aim of eventually assassinating them all.[61] Hanna liked the name because it conjured up an image of girls with guns, and Anderson and Jenkins also point to the link between the name and Bikini Atoll, the island used to test American hydrogen bombs in the 1950s.[62] As a band, Bikini Kill played hard, thrashy fast punk, characterised from the start by Hanna's shrill, fierce shriek, which bore favourable resemblance to the vocals of Poly Styrene of the 1970s punk band X Ray Spex. Whereas X Ray Spex sang songs such as "The Day The World Turned Dayglo" and "Artificial", which touched on ideas of being swallowed by plastic and consumerism, Bikini Kill bore closest resemblance to X Ray Spex on the latter's debut single, "Oh Bondage Up Yours!" a rant against "all kinds of bondage" which was banned by the BBC. The refrain "buy me, tie me, chain me to the wall" is echoed in Bikini Kill's "Jigsaw Youth": "I can sell my body if I wanna—God knows you already sold your mind."[63] As a song, "Jigsaw Youth" is comparatively restrained in subject matter, for, unlike many of their punk predecessors, Bikini Kill's lyrics were explicitly feminist from day one. The self

Flyer for Bikini Kill gig at Huntridge Performing Arts Theatre. Image courtesy of Douglas Baptie.
Opposite: Bikini Kill, performing at the Rock for Choice concernt at the Sanctuary Theatre, Washington, DC, 4 April 1992. © Pat Graham photography www.patgraham.org.

titled *Bikini Kill* LP opens with "Double Dare Ya", which dares girls to do, and be, whatever, and whoever they want to be. Part way through the song, Hanna sings of the importance of women and girls being assertive, and of knowing what their rights are, before shouting, "RIGHTS, RIGHTS, YOU, DO, HAVE, RIGHTS!"[64]

As well as having a strong sense of feminism, Hanna was also very aware of the need for strong communities. "Everything's got to be a community," she told Kate Galactic in 1996 "or a scene, a lot of people doing stuff that relates back to it cuz then it keeps going cuz we don't live in a vacuum".[65]

> Having a community around you is really important and really helps. And knowing that there are record labels that will put out your music or your work even though you don't know what you're doing REALLY is inspirational. I thought records were created by these geniuses in some castle somewhere. I didn't realise for a really long time that it was just people making things. It seemed really far away from me.[66]

Her approach to music was marked, at that time, by lack of commercial ambition, rather a desire to play small clubs in order to make it easier for girls to see the band play, and to allow girls to see how easy it is to form bands.[67] The idea behind this tendency was to encourage people not to consume passively, and to convey this message in every aspect of the band, not just through the band's lyrics.

When the media backlash hit riot grrrl in 1993, Bikini Kill were one of the bands who caught most of the force of the blows. In an interview with Bill Savage of *Pamzine* in 2002, Hanna, by then a member of Le Tigre, described riot grrrl as:

> This thing that happened for like two and half minutes and then everyone was like "this is lasting too long, you need to stop". Then there was like this huge backlash and there were these really aggressive misogynist bands that were like "oh there's too many women around we have to do something about it", and it's like "we haven't even started, this hasn't even be-gun". But I know that my brain got really freaked out by people telling me to shut up, but they were saying shut up in terms of saying, "you're politically correct, you're putting men down" and even other women started saying that and it was making me nuts.[68]

Bikini Kill split up in 1999, with very little fuss or fanfare, following nine years of touring, releasing, and inspiring girls across the world. If the critics thought that they had seen the last of Hanna though, they were in for a rude awakening. Following the release of her spoken word *Julie Ruin* album, Hanna teamed up with Johanna Fateman and Sadie Benning to form Le Tigre, the feminist electro punk/pop ensemble who are still going today, albeit with some changes to their members.

Bratmobile, who formed in Eugene, Oregon around the same time as Bikini Kill were forming in Olympia had also made use of fanzines to explore and consolidate their own brand of new punk feminism.[69] Allison Wolfe (vocals) and Molly Neuman (drums) wrote the fanzine *Girl Germs* and, like Bikini Kill, were inspired by the DC band NOU.[70] Both bands were also more than ready for a girl revolution within punk, and they weren't afraid to say so.

This revolution, as you will have already read, coalesced and crystallised following the 1991 Mount Pleasant riots, and began to take shape just before the annual K Records International Pop Underground event, which that year included a 'Girl Day'. Those who appeared on the bill at 'Girl Day' included Bikini Kill, Mecca Normal, L7, and the Spinannes.[71]

Whilst Bratmobile are clearly a punk band, in many ways, their influences are harder to pin down than those of Bikini Kill. Both bands were inspired by NOU and Fugazi, and formed a mutual support network with these two bands (amongst others) but their sound had a sardonic edge to it that was not shared with them. The music of Bikini Kill reached Britain many months before the music of Bratmobile did, and for me, the bands early sound was expressed most vividly on their debut (and, unfortunately, only) Peel Session in 1993. Opening with a slowed down, sardonic cover of Blur's "There's No Other Way" marked by the menacing roll of Neuman's drums and the half breathed, half languidly drawled vocals of Allison Wolfe, they quickly segued into the fast, controlled punk of "No You Don't", which revealed the bands knack for rapid-fire lyrics and subversive bubblegum punk. This characteristic was perhaps most evident on the sarcastic, pounding "Make Me Miss America", a satire of American femininity that equated the myth of the beauty queen with bulimia, whilst also critiquing bitchy queen dialogue as expressed in Hollywood teen flicks. If Bikini Kill were a radical feminist critique of X Ray Spex, Bratmobile were The Go-Go's in their early days, revealing through their songs a gleeful feminist romp through bubblegum punk power pop that was sonically and visually exciting. Footage of Bratmobile and Bikini Kill gigs, collected together as part of the documentary film *Don't Need You,* pay testament to the electricity and sheer force of nature of both Hanna and Wolfe as performers. Hanna's performances reveal a force of will and strength of personality that is inspiring, whereas Wolfe's performances reveal a playfulness and slight teasing of the audience that imbue her performances with an almost otherworldly electricity.[72] Whilst Bratmobile took a hiatus in the mid-1990s, by 1998, they were back together, with the 2000 album Ladies, Women, And Girls cementing the reputation they had built up over the years.

In Britain, riot grrrl didn't really arrive until the summer of 1992. Amelia Fletcher, previously of C86/twee band Talulah Gosh and, then, singer/guitarist in Heavenly, is often credited with bringing riot grrrl to Britain, something she disputes: "It would have got here anyway." She told Jeanette Leach of *Kirby* fanzine in 2000.[73]

What actually happened was that I was over in Olympia, and I met Allison Wolfe and Erin Smith of Bratmobile, who actually coined the term 'riot grrrl'. I found it really inspirational, and I wrote a letter to Rachel from Slampt about it. I also talked to Huggy Bear, but after that

Top: Allison Wolfe performing with Bratmobile. Image courtesy of John W Stuart.
Bottom: Early Huggy Bear/Bikini Kill flyer, encouraging audience interaction and offering free American distribution of fanzines.

Since we can't talk to everyone after shows
(OR during!) due to time/energy/shyness factor
we ask that you write to us if you have some
thing to say:

BIKINI KILL
C/O KILL ROCK STARS
120 NE STATE #418
OLY WA 98501

Huggy Bear
C/O CATCALL
142ª St Pauls Rd
Islington, London, N1 2LL

☆ also: If you are a girl/woman who does a fanzine
and would like to have it printed and distribute
in the U.S. (For Free) Please write To:
RIOT GRRRL PRESS, PO BO☀ 11002, WDC 20008-0202 USA

it really had nothing to do with me. Heavenly were never considered riot grrrl, but I thought of them as such. It was funny—I used to go to Huggy Bear gigs, and people would say 'but you're not riot grrrl, you're indie pop'.[74]

Initially, Slampt's Rachel Holborow was unimpressed with Huggy Bear, the band who are one of the very few British bands to be universally associated with riot grrrl, "I'd seen them ages ago when they all wore maternity dresses. I think their first gig was at the Heavenly Christmas party in 1991. Matthew Heavenly was playing with them too, and they could hardly play at all".[75] By early 1992, the buzz around the Brighton band was growing. Pete Dale of Slampt takes up the story: "Friends in London told us that Huggy Bear (who we had seen the previous year when they sounded a lot like Talulah Gosh) had changed their sound into a mess of Pussy Galore-style genius, so we started making pilgrimages down south to see them play and we were entirely blown away by them at every single show."[76]

He continues, "Huggy Bear influenced me enormously—they were the most important British rock band of the 1990s. I quite enjoyed bands like Mambo Taxi, The Voodoo Queens and Linus at the time, but creatively Huggy Bear were the only British riot grrrl-affiliated band whose records continue to amaze and inspire me to the present day."[77]

"When I saw Huggy Bear at the Sausage Machine [in London] I was totally hooked", wrote Angel "never before had I witnessed a band with so much energy.[78] They sang about truth, injustices and love in such a cool way, the three girls in the band were so powerful and the two boys were on their side. I have never since seen a band live that have managed to move me as much as that first Huggy Bear gig did."[79]

Maxine, a DIY publisher from Bromley who, whilst studying at Leeds University, became involved with the Leeds And Bradford Riot Grrrl chapter, summed up the attraction of Huggy Bear for many when she wrote: "I loved Huggy Bear, really dug what they stood for. They were like The Smiths in that they could transcend just being a pop band and become a total philosophy."[80] She adds "The cool thing was though that most of the bands were putting out their own records/gigs/flyers etc so—to an extent—the mainstream couldn't touch it in a true sense."[81] Andy Roberts, guitarist in Linus, first saw Huggy Bear live in early 1992:

My friend Dale had been going on about the Huggies for a while (I pictured them as a disco band!) so I went to see them at the Rough Trade shop in Covent Garden. They were like a sort of teenage Sonic Youth, all hormones and laughter. The drum kit fell apart and Chris had to lie on the floor and hold it up while singing. I came back and raved about them to my bandmates Tammy and Jennifer, who were very cynical about the whole thing, shortly afterwards we were all converts. We made a Linus-zine to hand out and started our first run of gigs in front of real audiences (ie, people who were actually interested to hear us) Jen set up the Girlygig, which gave Sister George (among others) their first gig. Tam and Jen also set up the riot grrrl postal address, BM Nancee [which was used by the band Skinned Teen and the Piao! Distro/label, amongst others] the press called us a 'riot grrrl band' (and sometimes an 'all-girl band'!). That's pretty much the sum total of our involvement.[82]

Members of Linus were also present when Huggy Bear appeared on Channel 4's 'Yoof' programme, *The Word,* during which the band performed their single "Her Jazz", a call to arms which pressed for a "girl, boy, revolution" and included the much quoted line "This is happening without your permission."[83] Following their performance, the band joined the audience and it was shortly afterwards that what *The Guardian*'s Caroline Sullivan termed their "Bill Grundy moment" occurred.[84]

Andy Roberts, in a letter to the writer Sara Marcus, written in 2005, describes the "famous riot" as occurring when a few members of *The Word* audience heckled an item on the porn stars the Barbie Twins. Sarah from Wiiija, also present, was hassled by one of the bouncers, and was ejected, and the rest of the Linus and Huggy camp followed her out in disgust.[85] According to Roberts, *The Word* studio was not a pleasant place to be, and the security people were heavy-handed.[86] He also mentions that, earlier in the evening, his Linus bandmate Tammy had been told to "smile or get out".[87]

As a rock 'n' roll incident, the above simply does not compare to the furore caused by the Sex Pistols appearance on the Grundy show in December 1976. The Grundy show was aired on the BBC at teatime, not on late night Channel 4, it caused a mass of tabloid politicking and outrage that led to a full-scale moral panic about punk.

By contrast, whilst the Huggy Bear incident may have excited a few broadsheet journalists and the music press, the only front cover the band garnered as a result was the cover of the following weeks *Melody Maker*, which bore the headline "THIS IS HAPPENING WITHOUT YOUR PERMISSION" over a grainy still of Nicky Huggy. What is interesting though, by way of comparison, is that particular outrage was reserved for the Pistols Steve Jones in 1976 after he called presenter Bill Grundy a "Dirty sod," a "dirty old man" and "dirty fucker" in quick succession following Grundy's clumsy, allegedly drink-fuelled attempts to charm Siouxsie Sioux and Simone Thomas, who were stood behind the group alongside fellow Bromley Contingent members Steve Severin and Simon Barker.[88] Huggy Bear, by curious similarity, were thrown off *The Word* for daring to call presenter Terry Christian a sexist. The motivation behind each comment may have been different, yet it just goes to show the inflammatory effect accusations of sleazy or sexist behaviour can have when expressed in a light entertainment context.

Whether their appearance on *The Word* helped or hindered the band or not, Huggy Bear, like Bikini Kill, felt the full force of the riot grrrl backlash when it began in the British media. Unlike Bikini Kill, they seemed less able to cope with it, and performed their last gig at the Piao! Club at Camden's Laurel Tree in late 1994. By then, their work was, to an extent, complete, for in their wake they had inspired innumerable British girls to pick up the musical baton.

Skinned Teen, for example, were three teenage-girls from London who formed after a Huggy Bear/Bikini Kill all-girl show.[89] One of the girls, Flossie, had approached Kathleen Hanna after the show and told her that she was in a band, whereupon Hanna offered her a gig. As with the Banshees before them, Skinned Teen didn't actually exist at this point, but, with the incentive of a Bikini Kill support slot to focus them, Flossie, Esme, and Layla Gibbon (later to form Petty Crime), quickly got to work. The resulting sound was primitive and naïve, at times whimsical ("Pillowcase Kisser", "Nancy Drew") at other times strangely melodic ("C6H1005") and depended strongly—at least initially—on cardboard boxes for drums, accompanied by xylophones, recorders, and badly played guitar and bass. All three girls usually sang in tandem, creating a kind of jeering playground chant that was reminiscent of both the Slits and Swiss punk band Kleenex.

The teen girl harmonies belied a latent aggression that came out in the lyrics ("I face the front, always, always face the fucking front") and, over the years, a sly humour was to emerge, most evident on the bands split LP with the similarly young American band Rooul.[90] By the time this LP was recorded, the band were experimenting with new sounds, as is evident on the eerie "Black Cat", which made use of jazz-like rhythms and echo, and "Ex Boyfriend Beat", which had a low budget Saint Etienne-meets-Luscious Jackson feel to it. Despite splitting up not long afterwards, two of the girls (Layla and Esme) are still involved in music, Layla in the San Francisco band Modern Reveries, Esme in Headshoppe. Skinned Teen records can still also be heard occasionally playing at various modern-day British riot grrrl club nights.

The Glasgow band Lungleg, like the Olympia bands in America, considered themselves to be privileged in living in a city that was welcoming towards girls in bands. As they told Kate Galactic in 1996: "Nobody's really snobby in Glasgow about like musical ability or anything so you can be totally hopeless like us."[91] The Glasgow music scene, which, thanks to independent labels such as Postcard in the 1980s and bands such as Orange Juice,

MELODY·MAKER

TOMORROW'S RIOTS TODAY

'THIS IS HAPPENING WITHOUT YOUR PERMISSION!'

HUGGY BEAR

LIVE ON 'THE WORD'

Eye-witness report by Sally Margaret Joy

ALICE IN CHAINS ★ ST ETIENNE ★ BELLY ★ PULP
PM DAWN ★ SCREAMING TREES ★ THE CULT

ISSN 0025-9012

Back cover of Lung Leg's *Shag the Tiger* EP, 1995.
Opposite: Front cover of *Melody Maker*, February 1993, featuring Huggy Bear and their 'Bill Grundy' incident.

The Pastels, and The Shop Assistants, had a strong history of musical improvisation, so it was the perfect arena for Lungleg to try out their Raincoats-inspired punk pop. Taking inspiration from the bleached and hacked hair, heavy make-up and charity shop chic of punk equally as much as from the music, the band began by playing brief one minute or two minute songs, and are fondly remembered by Andy Roberts for attempting to cover The Raincoats "Fairytale In The Supermarket" without really being able to play it, or to remember any of the words beyond the chorus.[92]

By 1996, their songs were growing longer, and they had seen their peers (including Bis and Kenickie) go on to wider success without them. It was perhaps this sense of frustration that led guitarist Maureen Quim to remark:

> We used to have the attitude that we wouldn't sign to a big label—it was like we don't want to do that. But—what the fuck. People say don't sign to a big label or you'll sell out but it's like for someone that's working for £2.50 an hour, they're getting ripped off and like a big label isn't ripping you off paying for you to go on tour and travel. That's not being ripped off. Sure you can be fucked over a million times but you can just go back to where you started. It's better than working for £2.50.[93]

Aside from the argument behind Maureen's comments, that the punk ideology is frequently ethically opposed to a band 'selling out' by signing to a major label, what is interesting is the way in which Quim's comments seem to echo Kathleen Hanna's defence of her choice to strip to pay the bills rather than sling burgers or waitress. Whether working as a musician or as a stripper, the correlation both women make is that either profession—whether exploitative or not—is preferable to the low-waged exploitation that is frequently the only other employment option available to them.

Lungleg were to lose Maureen from their line-up a year later, but they continued for a while longer, releasing the Delta 5-esque "Maid To Minx" single in 1999 on Southern Records, which in addition to having an addictive bassline, took the odd pot shot at the Spice Girls and modern sexual and social mores. In the process of gigging around Britain, they inspired a number of bands, most notably The Yummy Fur, a band formed by John McKeown in 1992. McKeown now plays bass in indie band 1990s, but credits his sister Jane, Lungleg's bassist, with giving The Yummy Fur their name.[94] The two bands often gigged together and, like Lungleg, the band also attracted a lot of riot grrrls to their gigs, something that seemed, at times, to sit oddly with the sexually explicit nature of their lyrics. McKeown feels, however, that it was precisely this sexual frankness that attracted the riot grrrls to the group.[95] Instead of being whiny indie boys moaning about their girlfriends, the Yummy Fur wrote frequently very funny observational songs with titles such as "Theme From Ultrabra" (in which a boy tries on his girlfriends underwear and becomes strangely aroused), "Plastic Cowboy" (a gay cowboys and Indians homage) and "In The Company Of Women"; which namechecked Lungleg, amongst others.

Unlike Lungleg, the Yummy Fur, and Skinned Teen, Linus already existed as a band prior to the arrival of riot grrrl in Britain. They had, in fact, formed in 1989, but it wasn't until they saw Huggy Bear play in London that the band was able to find their own musical niche. A fan of 1970s and 80s punk, Roberts felt disenfranchised with what the late 1980s and early 90s British indie scene had to offer him. Linus were perhaps a rarity on the British riot grrrl scene in that they were a little older than many of its participants, and, unlike Skinned Teen and Lungleg, could actually play their instruments. Marked by a choppy guitar sound reminiscent of the Gang of Four, and by the drawling vocals of Tammy Denitto, a woman who had equally as intimidating a stage presence, in her own way, as Siouxsie Sioux, the Linus sound carried a polished post-punk menace that made them stand out from many of their contemporaries. This post-punk sound was later embraced by the Leeds band Coping Saw, a band who were more influenced by The Fall than Gang of Four, but who also, like Linus, made interesting music whilst being fronted by an antagonistic front woman (Karren Ablaze!). Linus' first release, *The Linus EP,* was put out by *Melody Maker* journalists, Jim Irwin and Sally Still, on their Bone label and it was quickly followed by some tracks for the Wiiija 7" compilation, *Some Hearts Paid To Lie*, which also featured the nascent Skinned Teen, Rachel Holborow and Pete Dale's Pussycat Trash, and the London band Comet Gain. Having gained a certain amount of airplay and positive press, things were going well for Linus until their label, Elemental, was bought out by One Little Indian in 1995, inevitably leading to the sacking of the entire Elemental roster.[96] By 1996, the band still was not signed, and was feeling depressed and alienated by the prevailing musical climate of Britpop and accompanying laddish behaviour. Founding member Jen Denitto left in 1996, and was replaced for a while by Charley Stone, formerly of Exeter band The Frantic Spiders, later of Salad, Gay Dad, Nightnurse, and Spy 51. Despite a number of releases for various labels, the band was considering splitting up when, in 2002, Ladyfest London re-inspired and re-invigorated them.[97]

It was thanks to Ladyfest that the band were able to become part of a network of supportive bands and individuals once more, and in 2003, the band played a stirring set at Ladyfest Manchester. By then, things were looking good for them, but the Linus renaissance was cut abruptly short with the death of founder member and guitarist Andy Roberts in July 2005.

Whilst Coping Saw were splitting up, and Linus were considering doing so, the late 1990s riot grrrl resurgence was led by Sleater-Kinney, an American band formed from the ashes of Heavens To Betsy and Excuse 17, in Portland, Oregon, in 1994. Singer/guitarists Corin Tucker and Carrie Brownstein had originally met in Bellingham, Washington, at a Heavens To Betsy gig, and, when their original bands had broken up, decided to work together.[98] They named themselves after Sleater-Kinney Road, a road in a neighbouring town and, in 1996 they met drummer Janet Weiss, who cemented the line-up.

The Sleater-Kinney sound was marked from the start by powerful vocals on the part of Tucker, dense, clipped guitar and bass, and crisp drums, marking them out as a band who were serious about music. Sleater-Kinney fired up the admiration of a second wave of riot grrrls on both sides of the Atlantic. They inspired genuine adulation in Britain, were followed on tour by innumerable fans of both sexes, and unwittingly inspired a series of riot grrrl picnics and meetings that would tentatively explore the idea of the riot grrrl legacy. Whilst many of these initiatives would ultimately falter, and fail, what they actually did was pre-empt the flurry of activity and inspiration created by Ladyfest a few years later. By the time they split up in 2005, they were beginning to be overshadowed by the likes of Le Tigre and the Arkansas band, The Gossip, but their timing in the late 1990s was immaculate.

By the end of the decade, the British riot grrrl bands, with the exception of Linus and Coping Saw, had all split up. Pale imitations of the Sunderland girl band Kenickie, who had

SLEATER-KINNEY IS:
Carrie Brownstein
Corin Tucker
Janet Weiss

Sleater Kinney's *The Hot Rock Album*, 1999, depicting Carrie Brownstein, Janet Weiss and Corin Tucker, the latter of which formerly headed-up influential riot grrrl band Heavens to Betsy.

also recently split up, abounded in the form of Chicks, Vyvyan and Mika Bomb. We may not have been aware of it at the time, but the next wave of British bands had already arrived: Valerie, Electrelane, Life Without Buildings, etc, with the exception of Electrelane—the most obviously musical of the three—they were to have little impact, but that was hardly to matter. By 2001, the debut Gossip album had been released, Ladyfest Olympia and Ladyfest Scotland had taken place, and all was right with the world.

"I don't [sic] if anyone was quite ready for The Gossip on the last night of Ladyfest Scotland" wrote Bill Savage in 2003.[99]

> Maybe that's why grown women were in tears of joy. Maybe that's why, as a slurring Ladyfest organiser told me later, the owner of the venue said they were the best band that has ever played there. A few months later I'm on the district line with a fellow Gossip witness "They're the next wave" she says wistfully in hushed tones, "Beth has so much charisma", then staring into the middle distance "… more charisma than Kathleen Hanna".… There are no certainties except the fact that the Gossip's set that night was legend in the making. The stuff revolutions are made of. A moment of pure clarity when you know: rock 'n' roll is the answer.[100]

Formed in Searcy, Arkansas, in 1999, the Gossip was influenced partly by riot grrrl, but apparently do not consider themselves to be a riot grrrl band. Their debut album, *That's Not What I Heard*, was released in 2001 on Kill Rock Stars, and showcased frontwoman Beth Ditto's bluesy hollar set against fierce garage punk songs of love, lust and life. "Swing Low" was reminiscent of a scuzzier Big Brother And The Holding Company, whilst "Where The Girls Are" and "Dressed In Black" ensured the band the undying love of queer identified riot grrrls everywhere. Initially, the bands live shows were as renowned for Ditto's fondness for stripping down to her underwear as they were for the bands incendiary performances.

A woman who describes herself as 'fat' with no hint of self depreciation, Ditto has claimed that by stripping off she reveals a normal looking body, rather than a size zero airbrushed babe, something that is comforting to other women rather than providing outright titillation.[101] By 2006's *Standing In The Way Of Control*, the band had honed their sound and given it a slick electro punk production that enhanced rather than compromised the raw emotion of their songs. An excited *NME* live review in the summer of 2006 compared Ditto's vocals favourably to Aretha Franklin, Janis Joplin, and Dusty Springfield, although it is worth adding that there is, on occasion, more than a hint of Etta James to her voice as well.[102] A word of mouth success, by the end of 2006, Ditto was being voted the *NME*'s 'Coolest Person In Rock', an award that had its meaning soured when the magazine reverted to its laddish reputation by putting Muse on the cover that week instead of a proposed cover featuring Ditto, ska-tinged popstar Lily Allen, and glam punk Kate Jackson.[103] The single "Standing In The Way Of Control", a comment on the Bush administration's decision to deny gay people the right to marriage, was also a runaway success. A staple of riot grrrl club nights from late 2005, it spread to indie clubs in 2006, and by 2007 it was re-entering the British Top 40 on downloads alone at number 13 and, later, number seven.[104]

Whether the band can continue to maintain this momentum remains to be seen. As a group, they have the good fortune to be fronted by a woman who is not only smart, but tough, meaning that when the inevitable Gossip backlash begins, a woman as strong as Beth Ditto should, hopefully, be able to ride out the storm.

Top: Front cover of The Gossip's *Standing in the Way of Control* album, 2005.
Bottom: Beth Ditto of The Gossip performing live on stage. Image courtesy of John W Stuart.

HERE COME THE GRRRLS: WHEN THE GIRL GROUP SOUND MET RIOT GRRRL

Just as many of the riot grrrl bands drew their initial inspiration from their contemporaries, and from the female punk bands who had gone before them, so there was also a particular brand of riot grrrl that found its roots in punk, but which sought to play around with 1960s garage rock influences, and with the girl group sound of the late 1950s and early 60s. Bands like Mambo Taxi, and the Voodoo Queens, who in addition to sharing band members also shared a love of 1960s garage rock compilations, such as the *Girls In The Garage* and *Pebbles* series, and the garage retro band Thee Headcoatees.

Four girls from the Medway towns, Kyra Rubella, Holly Golightly, Ludella Black, and Bongo Debbie were friends with Thee Headcoats, a garage punk band fronted by Billy Childish. The girls initially started out doing a few songs on stage with the band during Thee Headcoats set, before going on to record the album *Girlsville*.[105] Like the Pipettes years later, Thee Headcoatees sang but did not play instruments. They performed a mix of covers, such as Plastic Bertand's "Ca Plaine Pour Moi", and songs written by Childish, such as "Ballad of the Insolent Pup", but as with the Pipettes, image and attitude seemed to be more important than the extent to which the band wrote or played their own songs. Songs like "Headcoat Girl", which exuded cool girl gang exclusivity and "Young Blood", which revisited the snottiness of punk, sat side by side with the predatory girl garage rock of "Davey Crocket", "Jackie Chan Does Kung Fu" and "An Image of You", whereas "Spineless

Little Shit" and "Park It Up Yer Arse" achieved new levels of obnoxiousness. What both Mambo Taxi and the Voodoo Queens invariably took from Thee Headcoatees was the mix of garage rock and punk attitude, and a sound that mirrored the bands on the *Girls In The Garage* compilations, at one time the poor relations to the Shangri-La's and the Angels, whose back catalogues were given a new lease of life via the reissues industry. Whilst Thee Headcoatees exuded toughness, both bands would have looked elsewhere for the vulnerability and melodies that would lace through such songs as Mambo Taxi's "Insecure" and "Kiss, Kiss" and the Voodoo Queens "My Favourite Handbag" and "Summer Sun." For this, they would have looked to the Shirelles, the Chantels, and the Shangri-La's.

For Charlotte Greig, the appeal of the girl group sound was an honest, emotional intensity pouring out of the lead vocal, coupled with the use of intimate 'girl-talk' choruses in the form of call and response. Arlene Smith of The Chantels initially encapsulated this, and the Shirelles Shirley Owens was to take up the baton a few years later, whereas the Shangri-La's songs were full-on pop melodrama, displaying both a tough, hip independence and vulnerability on such classics as "Leader Of The Pack", "Out On The Streets", and "I Can Never Go Home Anymore".

Whilst Mambo Taxi, the Voodoo Queens, and later bands such as Kenickie, the Rondelles and The Pipettes all took a number of elements from this sound, all of them, without exception, updated these elements to suit their own particular sound. They eschewed the masochistic dirge of "He Hit Me And It Felt Like A Kiss", and instead fostered a style best encapsulated by the title of the Kenickie song, "Rough Boys and Modern Girls". Mambo Taxi formed in 1992 in Brighton, but they didn't actually release their first single until January 1993, though "Prom Queen", a clattering, crisp, up-tempo slice of spoiled teen kitschy punk was well worth the wait. It mercilessly lampooned the indulged, rich, American teen princess, the daughter of the business tycoon, who will never have to work because daddy will always provide. In a sense, it also lampooned the type of rich, aspirational lifestyle portrayed and celebrated on the popular late 1980s and early 90s American TV show *Beverley Hills 90210*, as well as pre-empting the Beverley Hills satire of *Clueless* a few years later. On the B Side of the 7" was a track called "Insecure", which contrasted sharply with the cheerful clatter of the A Side. A jangly guitar led homage to 1960s pop, it told a tale of feminine insecurity and fear in the face of a controlling boyfriend. At one point, the guitars dropped away, leaving the vocals exposed against minimal drums, as Lenie sang, "Oh they taught me that he's right, what if I find myself he's wrong?" with the guitars roaring back in on the word "wrong?" a sense of doubt was planted in the mind of the listener and, at that moment, Mambo Taxi perfectly evoked the vulnerability of bands such as the Chantels and the Shirelles.

The *Prom Queen* sleeve was designed by Anjali Bhatia, who was then the bands drummer, she and Ella Drouglis, the bands guitarist, were best friends and "still are to this day".[107] They first met as 18 year-olds on the London squat scene, and squatted together, meeting the rest of Mambo Taxi through going to gigs.

But by late 1992, Anjali was ready to leave the band behind.

> When I was in Mambo Taxi there were predominantly two songwriters in the band and I was basically writing my songs on the guitar and then the other two guitarists were sort of re-enacting the guitar parts, making up their own bits, and I'd go behind the drums and start singing them, so I kind of got a bit frustrated with being stuck behind the drums and also I was bloody knackered most of the time, like, singing and playing drums at the same time is pretty difficult.[108]

Bhatia had a "yearning" to go back to playing guitar, the first instrument she had learned, and to do something slightly different. The name for this new band came from

Huggy Bear, who Anjali had drummed for on a couple of occasions "when their drummer couldn't make it".[109] Impressed by her drumming skills, they had dubbed her "'the princess of the voodoo beats' or something like that", which stuck, and gave a name to the band (The Voodoo Queens) and to one of their earliest songs, "Princess of the voodoo beat".[110] Anjali was joined by her sister Rajni on keyboards, their cousin Anjula on bass, Anjali's friend and Mambo Taxi bandmate Ella on guitar, and Sunny on drums.

Front cover of Mambo Taxi's influential *Prom Queen* album, 1992.

Despite many of the band having never played before, the Voodoo Queens quickly set about writing songs, and quickly came to the attention of the Leicester band, Cornershop, who were writing agit-prop anthems such as "England's Dreaming", a track taken from their EP *Days Of The Ford Cortina*, which combined elements of punk-infused indie rock and Indian sitar. A meeting between the two bands at the Rough Trade shop led to an invitation for the band to play their first official gig at the Bull and Gate in Kentish Town, supporting Cornershop. Despite the fact that the Voodoo Queens only had three songs and, as such, were reluctant to do the show, Cornershop succeeded in persuading them. The evening of the show came around and, "We were like, absolutely shaking as it was," recalled Bhatia, "and then, like, Gary from Wiiija ran up to me and said, 'By the way, Peelie's here' and then that was it, I was like, uncontrollably shaking at that point, and the whole of us just got through the whole show really nervous at the fact that it was our first gig, and nervous that the great legend Peelie was there."[111] Despite their nerves, and the presence of the Radio 1 DJ, the band "had a really great time".[112] After the gig, there was a further surprise in store when Gary once again approached Anjali, this time on behalf of Peel. "Gary came up to me and said 'Peelie absolutely loved it but he's too shy to come over and talk to you'" laughed Bhatia, "So I just went and chatted to him, and he was just fantastic, and he absolutely loved it."[113] Spotting the bands potential, even at this early stage, Peel told Anjali that the bands set had "reminded him of the first time he'd seen the Slits" a comparison she still believes was "the zenith of compliments."[114]

Peel offered the band a Peel session, to which Anjali gave the same response that the band had given Cornershop: "We've only got three songs" Peel's response was much the same as the bands had been, "He was like, 'So what? Just come and do the three songs, we want you on there'."[115] By the time the band came to record their debut Peel session in January 1993, they had a fourth song—"Summer Sun"—which sat well alongside their three other songs: "Princess of the voodoo beat", "Supermodel, Superficial" and "Kenuwee Head", making for a classic session which was rightly released by Strange Fruit in 1994.

Although Mambo Taxi had formed prior to the Voodoo Queens, the buzz around the Voodoo Queens would essentially see them outstrip and eclipse Mambo Taxi in terms of attention and popularity.

Today, Bhatia admits that the Voodoo Queens were "totally hyped up," but adds, with a laugh, "with good reason, cos we were bloody good."[116] Whilst Mambo Taxi were free of this hype, the situation was not entirely detrimental in that what it did was ensure that the bands sound became stronger whilst at the same time freeing the band of the pressures of media scrutiny and, as a result, led to a number of understated garage pop gems such as "Poems On The Underground" (the bands second single) and the frivolously titled "Do You Always Dress Like That (In Front Of Other Peoples Boyfriends?)" (Their third single, and a subtitling nightmare for ITV's *Chart Show* in summer 1993) Their debut album, *In Love With*, was a mixture of girl group pop ("Kiss, Kiss"), garage rock ("Screaming In Public") and darker, more thought-provoking songs that dealt with insecurity ("Tom"), abuse ("Velvet Youth") and unwanted pregnancy ("Push That Pram (Under The Train)") They were also free to experiment with a number of side projects, such as the song they recorded for the Rugger Bugger *Gay Pride* 7" compilation in 1994, the hilarious yet filthy "Brett From Suede (it's about time you got laid) with a man", a satirical take on the Suede singers self-proclaimed bisexuality. They also recorded a version of the Shirelles "Foolish Little Girl" for the *Garden Of Delights* women's aid charity LP.

The Voodoo Queens were to achieve a certain amount of success in the indie chart with "Supermodel, Superficial", a robust, vitriolic rant directed at an industry of women whose only role, as the band saw it, was to encourage bulimia and anorexia in young women. "I'm really pleased that we caused a bit of a stir" says Bhatia today, "we made a really integral statement at the time, and affected a lot of people at the time as well, and no one else had really touched on those subjects, so I'm totally pleased about that."[117] "Supermodel, Superficial" was the bands first single for Too Pure, and the song also reached number six in the 1993 Peel show Festive 50 reflecting the support Peel had given the band.[118] They followed it up with "Kenuwee Head", an ode to the film star Keanu Reeves, before releasing their album *Chocolate Revenge* in early 1994. Despite having a good relationship with Too Pure, the band were dropped later that year, an experience Bhatia describes as "mutual".[119] "We wanted to do something different as well."[120] The band set up their own label, Voodoo, using the royalties they'd received from their earlier releases, but what seemed like a good idea at the time quickly became a financial disaster. The first single for the label, "Eat The Germs", was released in early 1995, but there were problems from the start, mainly due to a communication error with the pressing plant, which saw the band having to pay for 2,000 7"s instead of the proposed 1,000. The band "couldn't shift [the 7"s] at all" and, when a little while later, Anjali and Ella were evicted from their squat in Islington, Anjali was forced to dump a large number of the 7"s in a skip. By this time, things were souring.[121]

Although Bhatia can't recall a particular date when the Voodoo Queens split up, the one and a half month tour of Europe the band did in 1994 is remembered with a distinct lack of fondness. The experience of rattling around Germany in a "dirty, dilapidated van" for six weeks, living on cheese because the band were all vegetarian, made Bhatia feel jaded. "I was getting really bored with guitar music as well." She confessed.[122]

Feeling that they had taken the band as far as they could go, Anjali wanted to develop her song writing in a more electronic direction. She was also aware that the musical climate had shifted, and that a number of "pedestrian bands" such as Sleeper had emerged as part of Britpop, who held no truck with riot grrrl, or feminism. After playing an acoustic gig in early 1995 with the bands then drummer Steffy, Anjali was offered a solo record deal with Wiiija. She bought a sampler, and has since progressed to making computer-based music. Much of her work is used on adverts, in film, or on TV, and this is something she finds pleasing. 12 years after the Voodoo Queens Bhatia says "I kind've enjoy being in the background, the sort of music I really like is a lot of library music, labels like KPM, where a lot of music is very incidental and used as background music, so I do enjoy doing what I'm doing now."[123] She is also aware of being, once again, in a musical minority, "In all honesty, even to this day, there's not that many women who actually make music as producers, who

RIOT GRRRL   POEMS ON THE UNDERGROUND

actually sit behind a computer and make music," she explains, yet she finds the isolation of composing music on computer software comforting.[124] "I've always liked isolation, I always found it really daunting being thrown into the public eye with Voodoo Queens when I just wasn't expecting it at all", she concludes "I much prefer being how I am now and kind've like being in the background, whatever…."[125] Meteoric success doesn't interest her, and as long as she can pick up enough work to pay her rent, she doesn't really mind.[126]

By stark contrast to Bhatia are the Shampoo girls, Jacqui Blake and Carrie Askew, whose thirst for fame took them from Plumstead obscurity to superstar status in Japan via a series of bubblegum pop releases for EMI in the mid to late 1990s. Prior to their signing to EMI, the duo had made a name for themselves performing lo-fi punk pop songs such as "Pay Dirt", "Blisters And Bruises" and "Bouffant Headbutt", which were released on Bob Stanley's Icerink label in 1993.[127] Bhatia believes the band to be worth mentioning in relation to riot grrrl because, in addition to gigging with the likes of Mambo Taxi and Cornershop in 1993, she feels they were a part of the London riot grrrl scene, attending gigs and parties if not meetings. A band who firmly believed in the power of image, Jacqui and Carrie, who were 16 and 18 respectively when they first formed the band, created a look that was part 1960s dolly bird, part garish late 1980s kitsch.

Revolving around a love of bright colours, luxury fabrics, bleached blonde hair, piercings and heavy make-up, the girls image would, ironically, both acknowledge bands such as Lungleg whilst simultaneously inspiring bands like Kenickie. Musically speaking, Shampoo claimed to have been inspired by early Manic Street Preachers, Gary Numan, the Beastie Boys, and East 17. Yet their peculiar brand of girly pop and early punk, along with an image that has been described as part Johnny Rotten, part Lolita, part lipstick lesbian (much was made at the time of the fact that the girls held hands and frequently finished each others sentences) part sharp humour, cut a fine swathe through the contrived grey laddishness of the NWONW bands such as S*M*A*S*H and These Animal Men (who had a song entitled "Lady Love Your Cunt"), and the Camden new mod scene encapsulated, rightly or wrongly, by bands like Menswear.[128] Whilst Shampoo could be seen to have inspired the obnoxious yet infuriatingly catchy bratty pop of Daphne And Celeste a number of years later, it seems unfair to blame them entirely for songs such as "Ooh Stick You" and "UGLY", even if Shampoo's cover of East 17's "House Of Love" possibly inspired the New Jersey duo to take on Alice Cooper's "School's Out". Despite the mixed feelings Shampoo's image and music created amongst a number of my interviewees, the band were one of many mid-1990s groups who fused aspects of the 1960s with an appreciation of punk. 1995's "Girl Power" allegedly took inspiration from Helen Love's "Formula One Racing Girls", whereas tracks like "Bare Knuckle Girl" and "Don't Call Me Babe", on 1995's *Shampoo Or Nothing* album, do at least deserve credit for pre-empting the Spice Girls by a year.[129]

Whilst 1995 was the year that Shampoo discovered 'Girl Power', it was also the year that both Mambo Taxi and the Voodoo Queens split up, marking the end, in many ways, of the first wave of British riot grrrl bands. However, as the 1990s continued, it became clear that these two bands' amalgamation of 1960s pop and 70s punk had proved infectious and was, directly or indirectly, providing inspiration for a whole series of new guitar-led girl bands.

In the summer of 1994, Rachel Holborow of Slampt was approached at a party by an enthusiastic—not to mention very drunk—16 year old girl, Lauren Goften, who was talking excitedly about the band she had formed with her school friends Marie and Emma. The band, Holborow later learned, was called Kenickie, after the character in *Grease* and only existed in the girls' heads at this point. Nontheless Holborow was sufficiently interested

Top: Cornershop performing live at The Underworld,

London, in the early 1990s.

Image courtesy of Cornershop.

Bottom: Band shot of riot grrrl group Mambo Taxi.

Image courtesy of Cazz Blase.

to ask Goften for a demo tape the next day. Speaking in 1995 as part of Nick Allott and Deby Duke's *Slamptumentary* documentary, Goften, by then re-christened Lauren Laverne, and Marie Mixon (Marie Du Santiago) confessed that they were apprehensive, but despite being unable to play, they quickly set about writing the earliest Kenickie songs. They recorded their first tape, *Uglification*, when they could play just two chords, and played their first gig a fortnight later in Sunderland (supporting the Yummy Fur) by which point they had learned to play a grand total of three chords.[130] Largely dependent upon Goften's dad (himself a musician) for equipment, the band learned to play on stage, and were privileged to be adopted by Slampt early on and provided with a safe space in which to develop musically. Laverne recalls an episode early on at a gig when she managed to switch of her guitar part way through the band's set and, not knowing how to turn it back on again, was forced to sing her guitar solo instead.[131]

This period of the bands career was fairly short lived, in that the level of media and industry attention Kenickie were receiving (mainly, it has to be said at this point, as a result of the support they were getting from Slampt and from John Peel) soon began to gather momentum, leading to bizarre situations such as Creation Records boss Alan McGee taking a jet to Sunderland to visit the band, only to see his offer of a publishing deal turned down.[132] This industry attention put the band, who were studying for their A Levels at the time, in a tricky position, and it was also making DIY label Slampt very uncomfortable. This situation led to Kenickie leaving the Slampt fold, having fired off a solicitors letter banning the label from pressing up any more copies of the bands 7", *Catsuit City*,[133] and going on to record for Simon Williams' Fierce Panda label prior to signing to EMI. "Punka",

Left: Anjali Bhatia, formerly of Mambo Taxi, and later of the Voodoo Queens.
Image courtesy of Anjali Bhatia.
Right: Front cover of Shampoo's *Trouble* album, 1994.
Opposite: Kenickie performing live at Manchester Roadhouse, April 1996. Image courtesy of Cazz Blase.

the bands debut single for EMI, and possibly one of the most sarcastic songs ever written, mocked Slampt's ideology and ethos not only with its lyrics about bands that "never learn to play" but also with it's very title. "Viva La Punka" was the name of a Pussycat Trash album track, and many members of the Newcastle punk scene had the phrase tattooed on their arms.[134] Kenickie's use of the phrase suggested that they weren't thinking about whose feelings they hurt, yet for many fans the reference was obvious: painfully so.

Whilst Kenickie were not a riot grrrl band, they are worth mentioning because, not only did they emerge from a musical community that grew out of the movement, and was also instrumental in supporting and promoting riot grrrl bands, but the level of inspiration they provided for young girls was palpable. Helen Wray, for example, wrote in her fanzine *Dancing Chicks* of being turned off by the Spice Girls brand of 'Girl Power', whilst being utterly bewitched by the girl group flavoured punk pop of Kenickie.[135] Prolific and sophisticated songwriters, Kenickie's interest in the girl group sound is most evident on the band's second and third singles for EMI: "Millionaire Sweeper", a melancholy understated tale of teenage pregnancy and wasted opportunities, which made use of the drum pattern from the Ronettes "Be My Baby", and "In Your Car", an energy packed punk pop song that used call and response in a way that was reminiscent of the oft copied Shangri-La's song "Give Him A Great Big Kiss".

Despite their song writing abilities, Kenickie always seemed to be eclipsed by their onstage banter, love of glitter and luxury fabrics, and endearing personalities, which dominated interviews at the expense of their music. It could also be that, despite their talent, British girl guitar bands never seem to quite breakthrough to the mainstream without being somewhat tamed. When Kenickie split up in 1998, the letters pages of the *NME* and *Melody Maker* were awash with correspondence from distraught teenage girls for months afterwards, suggesting that, despite only achieving modest chart success, the band had served a vital function, and had plugged a much needed gap.

Post-Kenickie, a number of bands, such as the London band Vyvyan and Dublin's Chicks sought to fill the gap, but they were ultimately let down by their song writing. One band who came close to capturing a similar punk and girl group influenced sound, with good song writing, were the Albuquerque band The Rondelles, whose name evoked the Ronettes, and whose songs ("He's Outta Sight", "Fake Fight", "Do It For Me") strongly evoked bands such as the Shangri-La's or the Crystals. Their debut album, *Fiction Romance, Fast Machines*, was released in 1999, and was an infectious blend of pop sheen, catchy choruses, girl group harmonies, and punk guitars. It was immaculately performed and produced, and was described by Smells Like, the label who released it, as "The Shangri-Las meets Sleater-Kinney".[136] Like Kenickie, the band attracted the attention of an enthusiastic music industry, leading them to record for labels such as Teenbeat, K Records and Rhino and to tour with the likes of the Makeup, Sleater-Kinney, and Sonic Youth.[137] Though they made a grand entrance onto the scene, like Kenickie, they were not destined to enjoy a long career.

Next to pick up the baton of girl group punk on the post riot grrrl British punk scene were The Lollies, a Canadian/American/British band who were based in London, and whose keyboard-enhanced jangly garage pop was reminiscent of Mambo Taxi. They brandished a fully-formed sense of humour, which they indulged through songs like "Jonestown Mascara" and "Left My Heart In".

Their EP *Bang! Bang! Bang! Lookout! Lookout! Lookout!* was a knowing take on the Shangri-La's, with songs like "Bad Boyfriend" exploring what would have happened had the narrator of "Leader Of The Pack" shacked up with her motorcycle-riding boyfriend (tedium and domesticity) and "Dayjob Nightmare" exploring modern day feminine bondage through the eyes of a woman who is trapped in a low paid job she hates. At the end of the song, she walks into the office with a gun and shoots her boss, delivering the unforgettable line "in the future, you can make your own damn coffee."[138] The exact moment she shoots is echoed by the bands use of the phrase "Bang bang bang, lookout, lookout, lookout!" another nod to "Leader Of The Pack."

Whilst The Lollies garnered favourable reviews and a loyal fanbase, their brand of girl group punk pop has been overtaken in recent years by The Pipettes, a group of polka dot clad girls (and stripy topped boys: The Cassettes) who take the music of the late 1950s and early 60s and essentially re-write it for the modern age. Like the 1960s girl groups, they are an exercise in manufactured pop.[139] The band were inspired to form when former member Julia Clark-Lowes became inspired by Bill Drummond's book on the subject of how to get a number one single. The musical inspiration for the band came from Cassettes guitarist Bobby Pipette, a DJ who had been playing a lot of girl group records, including everything from Phil Spector-produced 1960s tracks, to Stock Aitken and Waterman-produced girl groups of the1980s, to Girls Aloud and the Sugababes, and was struck by the favourable reactions these records were getting.[140]

Rather than waiting to fall prey to a pop svengali, as a number of girl groups have, the Pipettes have effectively svengalied themselves. They write and arrange their own songs, treat their polka dot dresses as a uniform only to be worn on stage and have toured with bands such as Sleater-Kinney.[141]

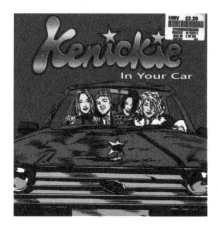

Top: Front cover of Kenickie's *In Your Car* album, 1996.
Bottom: Front cover of Kenickie's *Millionaire Sweeper* album, 1995.
Opposite left: Front cover of Strawberry Switchblade's *Since Yesterday* album, 1999.
Opposite right: Front cover of The Pipettes' *We are the Pipettes* album, 2006.

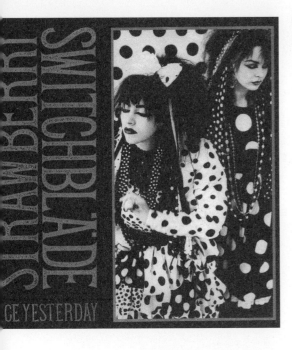

Whilst tracks such as "Sex" and "Tell Me What You Want" have a surprisingly innocent feel, "Judy", "Your Kisses Are Wasted On Me", and "One Night Stand" reveal a worldliness and range of subject matter that is more contemporary. An early Pipettes track, "I Like A Boy In Uniform (School Uniform)" could almost have been written for the modern day nostalgia fest that is the skool disco club night, suggesting an added level of cunning manufacturing. Whilst firmly entrenched in the girl group sound, there are sometimes glimpses of other influences scattered throughout the bands work, as the appreciation of Bill Drummond suggests, there is a subversive, almost punk quality to what they are doing, and it is also possible to see a link between the Pipettes and a number of post-punk female, or female-fronted, punk pop bands such as the Mo-dettes, Girls At Our Best, and Dolly Mixture. Many of these bands could be seen to lack the political charge of the original punk bands, but at the same time they also pre-empted the C86/twee pop scene of the mid-1980s, something a dismissive Sleater-Kinney fan at Manchester Academy must have picked up on in September 2005 when he dismissed the Pipettes as being "Very Norwich".

STRAIGHT AS AN ARROW: WHEN TWEE POP MET RIOT GRRRL

> The Indie pop mailing list is devoted to discussion of independently produced music, the kind that tends to come out on small-run 7" singles with handmade sleeves. They call it 'wimpy' and 'twee', but pop kids everywhere know that the true spirit of punk rock lives on not in the mass-marketed 'alternative' scene, or the sub-metal caterwauling of testosterone-poisoned grunge-rockers, but in the simple and pure efforts of kids banging out sweet delicious songs on cheap guitars.[142]

As 1970s punk gave way to 1980s post-punk, there emerged a series of punk pop bands in Britain, such as Altered Images, the Mo-dettes, Dolly Mixture, Strawberry Switchblade, and Girls At Our Best who, whilst generally (with the exception of Altered Images) only garnering cult appeal, would—along with post-punk bands such as the Marine Girls, Orange Juice, and Young Marble Giants—have a massive influence on the next wave of independent guitar-based music.

**Flyer for Punk at the National Film Theatre,
7–30 June 2002.**

According to Simon Reynolds, Orange Juice, in addition to being influenced by the Buzzcocks and Subway Sect, also owed a debt to the jangly guitar pop of the Byrds, and choppier rhythms of the Velvet Underground.[143] A series of influences that in turn inspired Primal Scream and the Jesus and Mary Chain, two other Scottish guitar bands, who Reynolds sees as the catalyst for what would become known as C86.[144]

The C86 scene got its name from a compilation tape compiled by NME writers Neil Taylor, Adrian Thrills and Roy Carr in 1986, which was available via mail order from the magazine.[145] Although the compilation reputedly contained a more varied selection of music than is generally thought, it featured Primal Scream's "Velocity Girl", alongside tracks by The Pastels, The Shop Assistants, The Soup Dragons, and Bogshed, amongst others. All bands who had been termed, at various times, 'shambling', or 'cutie', but who, after the tape was released, were inevitably dubbed 'C86'.[146]

According to Reynolds, the C86 bands also drew on post-punk, notably Postcard Records, Swell Maps, the Buzzcocks, Subway Sect, and The Fall, but, he argues that these bands purged post-punk of its most radical elements and replaced them with a 'cult of innocence'.[147] This aesthetic was characterised by the naïve names of the bands, and the hairslides, childish clothes, and oh-so-innocent lyrics that typified these groups at the time.[148] What is interesting about Reynolds brief discussion of C86 is that he is one of the very few writers, outside of the internet, to draw a clear link between this movement and riot grrrl, albeit superficially. Reynolds is right to point to the androgynous nature of many of the C86 bands, and what he sees as a sexual politics code of wimpy boys and "cute-but-tough girls" as influencing a perceived image of riot grrrls, but he is wrong to think that the influence stops there.[149] As we have already seen, the twee 'indie pop' band Heavenly, whose roots lay in the C86 band Talulah Gosh, were instrumental in introducing riot grrrl to the British scene, and in supporting many of the key bands and personalities who emerged during the first wave of British riot grrrl. This is doubly the case for K Records in Olympia, a label with a twee or 'love rock' roster long before 'Girl Day' took place at the annual International Pop Underground event of 1991.

What is often forgotten is that C86 was evolving itself by the early 1990s, so much so that it had cast off its C86 label altogether and had simply become twee pop. The second, or third, wave of twee bands were rather less dainty than some of their predecessors, with bands such as Rutland's Po!, Newcastle's Razorblade Smile, Oxford's Heavenly, Sydney's Even As We Speak, and Osaka's Nelories representing a range of differing styles and influences, as well as darker lyrical concerns. Po!, for example, sang of madness and despair, of bullying and abuse in songs like "Haunt You", "Little Stones", and "The Mad Girl", but they also sang songs of teenage small town boredom like "Bus Shelter In The Rain", and put a new twist on the childhood nostalgia of their predecessors by penning "Ever Been Had", a song which opened with the lines "I'm going into town, to watch my old school burning down."[150] Oxford's Heavenly, whilst starting out writing the distinctly coy "Cool Guitar Boy", by 1993 were penning the likes of "Atta Girl" an attitude packed slice of indie pop that featured a rapid fire exchange of vocals, and displayed a distinctly assertive attitude, whereas "Hearts And Crosses", the B Side to the inclusive "PUNK Girl," was about date rape. The scene wasn't just evolving lyrically either, Sydney's Even As We Speak would later go on to experiment with dance and techno, initially on the remix of their album track "Straight as an Arrow", as would one of the earlier C86 bands, The Field Mice, who began to experiment with ambient soundscapes in the early 1990s, and who would eventually transform into Northern Picture Library. Two labels at the heart of the British pre riot grrrl twee scene would be Oxford's Sarah Records, which was home to Heavenly and Even As We Speak, amongst others, and Port Sunlight's Sugarfrost, which released records by a mixture of largely obscure British twee bands (Razorblade Smile, Secret Shine, Pure) but tended to be known more for the bands it released from the Kansai region of Japan, namely The Nelories, B Flower, and the Jesus And Mary Chain-influenced White Kam Kam. It would be this scene, and these bands, along with bands such as Beat Happening and American labels such as K Records, that would have a latent influence on a number of the British riot grrrl bands, including Pussycat Trash, Helen Love, and Comet Gain. As Rachel Holborow of Slampt wrote in 1998:

> Pre-riot grrrl I was listening to indie women like The Breeders, PJ Harvey, Babes In Toyland, a bit of Sarah Records, a lot of old-school indie pop: Talulah Gosh, Brilliant Corners, Pastels and Beat Happening, K Records stuff. So musically it was pretty much something I could appreciate. But a lot of what I'd been into was about addressing, even inadvertently, gender issues. Like fey boys were better than butch, sexless girls were better than pouting pop sirens. I was trying to get to a point where my tits weren't an issue.[151]

The first Pussycat Trash 7" was the *Plink, Plonk, Pink, Punk,* which was released in 1993 on the London label Chocolate Narcotic. Whilst not especially representative of the bands later sound, this 7" is interesting in its own right because it pin-points very clearly the point where a love of twee pop met the punk ethic Holborow and Dale were to build on in establishing the Slampt Underground Organisation.

Opening track "Positive Bomb" begins with erratic drums and droning guitars, over which Holborow, singing in a style that owes a lot to Amelia Fletcher, plots a tentative plan for revolution. The second track, "Girlfriend", celebrates a simple tale of girl love, which can be read as platonic or erotic, depending on the listeners viewpoint, whereas "Hot Bed" is very C86, lyrically, but with a chaotic punk tune. The final track, "Squid Joke", sang by Dale, clumsily experiments with riot grrrl belligerence, and was probably inspired by Huggy Bear, including as it does the lines: "What can she do, with a guitar? She can explode, your fucking heart."[152] The bands second single "La La Ovular", which was released on Slampt in 1994, shows a progression towards the discordant jazz rhythms, punk noise and Crass-style politicising the band were to make their own, but still retains traces of twee pop on the strangely catchy "Stupid Nothing", where Holborow's vocal style is once more a mixture of snarled lyrics and Heavenly influenced twee.

Dale was to explore this synthesis of punk and twee further in Milky Wimpshake, a band who once introduced themselves live in Manchester by announcing, "Hello, we're Milky Wimpshake from Newcastle, and we're a Buzzcocks tribute band" (pause) "But we're in Manchester, so that's OK" and who had a sometimes drummer who had changed her name by deed poll to Joey Ramone.

Comet Gain also had its roots in riot grrrl but seemed to owe a debt to C86 as well, forming in 1993 they made their debut on the famed Wiiija compilation, *Some Hearts Paid To Lie.* A band that appeared to have a wide range of influences, ranging from twee, to punk, to 1960s Motown soul, Comet Gain's recording career was totally erratic but always interesting. Beginning with a series of garage punk songs that bore the mark of Huggy Bear, (Huggy Bear's Jon Slade was later a member) by 1995s *Casino Classics*, they were paying homage to northern soul (as the title suggests) and fey indie pop on the track "A Hundred And Nine". The contradictions of their musical influences were laid bare on 1995's *Gettin' Ready* EP, which saw the modish punk pop of "Baby's Alright" sit next to the wistful fey indie pop of "The Shining Path", whilst over on Side B, the mod flavoured "Charlie" sat next to "White Noise", a cover of the Pussy Galore classic.

The more obviously soul influenced "Say Yes To International Socialism" (possibly a nod to the 1980s politicising of Red Wedge) and brassy motown/northern soul influenced "Strength" were to follow, suggesting a new pop sensibility that was to come to an abrupt

Top: Front cover of Pussy Cat Trash's *Plink Plonk Pink Punk* album, 1993.
Bottom: Back cover of Pussycat Trash's *Lala* album, 1994.

Pussycat trash

Plink plonk pink punk

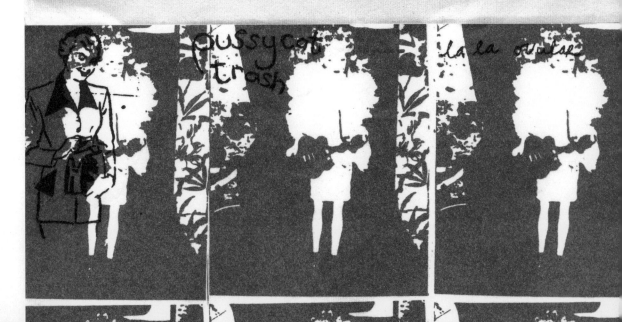

Pussycat
trash

la la oval al

end in 1997 when most of the band left to form the distinctly Sarah-esque Velocette.

If Pussycat Trash and Comet Gain owed a debt to Sarah Records and K Records, it is fair to say that Swansea's Helen Love and Glasgow's Bis owed a debt to the earlier sounds of The Fire Engines, Altered Images, and, once again, Talulah Gosh. Helen Love, who formed whilst the eponymous Helen, Roxy and Sheena were studying Art and Design at college during the first wave of riot grrrl, have always cited their main influence as the Ramones, whereas Bis, who formed about a year later, were interested in hip hop and bands such as Bikini Kill and (later) Sleater-Kinney.[153] The first Helen Love single, "Formula One Racing Girls," was released in 1993, a giddy race of casio keyboards, fairground organ, and buzzsaw guitars, the record has become justly famous in retrospect for name checking Huggy Bear, expressing a mild stroppiness (encapsulated by the narrator dumping her boyfriend) and for what is probably the first lyrical use of the phrase "Girl Power". Although, as Gill Neill, a former riot grrrl from Sheffield pointed out, "I remember going to see Huggy Bear and Bikini Kill when they toured together, and Huggy Bear's tour t-shirts said 'totally girl-powered' on the back, and I'm sure it was them who coined the term 'girl-power' long before Geri Halliwell co-opted it and made it mean doing back flips and sexually harassing the heir to the throne."[154] As Karren Ablaze also pointed out in 1998, Simone Ivatts, Coping Saw's bass player, was still wearing a homemade 'Girl Power' t-shirt she'd made in 1992, suggesting that a number of bands and individuals made use of the phrase.[155] It still seems likely that Helen Love were the first of these bands to incorporate the phrase into their lyrics though. Whilst Helen Love's early material made use of witty observation and social commentary ("You should put an advert in the music press, 'Sensitive boy needs a girl in a flowery dress'") they were later inspired by what Bis would term "Teen-C Power" and the Manchester band Valerie would term, more coherently, the "Disco Punk Resistance", a synthesis of disco and techno elements, basic punk pop, and punk-style lyrical call to arms, which, in Helen Love's case included keyboard riffs 2 Unlimited would have been proud of, and a healthy appreciation of digital hardcore acts such as Atari Teenage Riot and Lolita Storm. Two examples of this tendency would be 1997's "Does Your Heart Go Boom?" and "Long Live The UK Music Scene", both of which took broad swipes at an industry the band felt was dull and ripe for financial meltdown.

Bis, by comparison, lacked the cynicism of Helen Love. They were teenagers when they formed the band in 1994, and, whilst often criticised for making what many felt to be an amateurish, childish, cheaply produced racket, the band had varied and sophisticated musical tastes, which often outstripped their ability to write the songs they wanted to play. For example, "Team Theme", a track from the *Star Bright Boy* EP was allegedly inspired by the Special AKA's "Free Nelson Mandela".

Top: Front cover of Comet Gain's *The Getting Ready* album, 1995.

Bottom: Front cover of Bis' *Eurodisco* album, 1998.

Having released their debut EP, *Transmissions From The Teen-C Tip* on the Spanish label Elefant, Bis joined forces with the Glasgow label Chemikal Underground to release what would be their defining EP: *The Secret Vampires*, including a song that would sow the seeds of their fame whilst simultaneously sowing the seeds of their demonisation at the hands of the music press. It was called "Kandy Pop", and it would dog the band for years.

"I don't hate it", singer/keyboardist Manda Rin told *Fake It And Go Home* fanzine in July 2001 "but it gets annoying when people only know you for that song—which isn't our best. We sound nothing like that now, and the fans know that fortunately." "Kandy Pop", a song which sounded as though it was recorded in five minutes, and probably was, allegedly cost £10 to record, and, despite the throwaway nature of the track, it was to attract the attention of both *Top of the Pops*, who booked the band, making them the first (and most likely the last) unsigned band to appear on the show, and Radio 1, who playlisted the track. The Bis revolution was brief, beginning with the bands appearance on *Top of the Pops*, which led to a record label bidding war that the band largely ignored (signing to Wiiija instead), and concluding with what Wiiija termed "the most vicious press backlash in history" something the label believes the band handled very well, given their youth at the time.[156]

Stung by accusations about their musical competence and, frankly, vicious comments about singer/keyboardist Manda's physical appearance, the band roped in Gang of Four guitarist Andy Gill to produce their second album, Social Dancing, and promo pictures displayed a new slimline Manda, hair streaked and wearing revealing high fashion rather than the typical C86 hairslides, bracelets and t-shirts she had previously worn. Whilst claiming in her fanzine *Popgirls* that she had lost weight for her own reasons, polite doubt was expressed by a number of fans, leading to accusations that she had "sold out".[157]

If Bis were part of a British post-riot grrrl punk/twee synthesis, they were one of the last. Whilst Heavenly transformed into Marine Research (and later Tender Trap) following the suicide of Mathew Fletcher in 1996, the British twee bands that followed, whilst frequently numbering a significant number of riot grrrls within their fanbase, owed little or nothing to the movement. Examples would include Belle and Sebastian, Camera Obscura, Saloon, and, in America, the Aisler's Set. Many of these bands have gone on to be successful, and have rejected the twee tag outright, yet by listening to their records it is possible to trace the lineage of their songs, as Reynolds would have it, all the way back to the Buzzcocks, Subway Sect, the Velvet Underground, and The Byrds.

DO IT ANY WAY YOU WANNA: THE INDEPENDENT LEGACY

The principles of self publishing did not begin with punk, yet, despite the fact that the most high profile bands of the era all signed to major labels, the notion of the independent record label has become intrinsically linked with the punk ethic.

As Simon Reynolds has pointed out, The Buzzcocks *Spiral Scratch*, which was released on the bands own New Hormones label in January 1977 may not have been the first independently released record, but it was the first to make a polemical point out of what was, for the band, necessity.[158] Both Britain and America have histories of independent labels, and a number of music scenes both before and after punk have relied upon self-publishing, most notably the girl group sound of the early 1960s, house music in the 1980s and techno and drum 'n' bass in the 1990s.[159] But the punk period is important because it was at this point that independence became a virtue rather than simply a necessity.

As Reynolds would have it, *Spiral Scratch* sold 16,000 copies, and this wasn't simply because people were buying the record for the music, they were also buying it because of its sheer existence, and for what it signified: a revolutionary new way of doing things.[160]

Independence took on a new significance of purity of intention and desire on the part of the band to stay in control of their music and image, rather than become the latest playthings of a faceless record company executive. This purism didn't die with punk, it continued into the 1980s with labels such as Fast Product and Factory and, most importantly, Rough Trade.[161]

As a mark of disrespect for the prescribed way of doing things, many of these labels branched out into releasing things other than records. New Hormones and Fast Product, for example, both released art, whereas Factory took this approach to its logical conclusion by assigning a catalogue number to anything and everything, up to and including the Hacienda nightclub.[162] This approach was echoed in the 1990s by Slampt, who gave catalogue numbers to a variety of things, including the Slampt girl badge (Slampt 011), *Skin Swing Feel* fanzine (Slampt 009), *How To Get The Way You Are* comic (Slampt 036) and the *Slamptumentary* documentary (Slampt 037), and was, again, taken to its logical conclusion by Glasgow's Chemikal Underground, who named their recording studio Chem19.

By far and away the most important of the British independent labels throughout the 1980s was Rough Trade. As Reynolds has pointed out, Rough Trade became the chief coordinator and connector of the British independent movement.[163] It provided financial support to bands that wished to start their own labels, or to press up more copies of their releases.[164] It also organised the Cartel, which Reynolds describes as an independent distribution network built around an alliance of independent record shops, of which Rough Trade was one.[165]

In recognition of the burgeoning independent movement, Cherry Red boss Iain McNay started the first independent chart at the end of 1979, which was published in the trade magazine *Record Business*. At the time, independent meant independently produced, manufactured, marketed, distributed and retailed.[166] By all accounts a much stricter, and more honest, definition than is used today.

The American punk scene also stressed the importance of independence and, as in Britain; a number of indie labels grew up in the post punk period that would come to have long lasting importance and inspiration. Chief among these labels would be K Records, which was formed by Calvin Johnson in the summer of 1982.[167]

Initially starting life as a cassette only label, focusing on the nascent Olympia music scene, K Records recognised that they could keep their costs down by releasing on cassette, with most releases having a run of a hundred copies.[168] By 1983, Johnson, along with

Top: Front cover of the Buzzcock's *Spiral Scratch* album, 2000 (original release 1977).

Centre: Front cover of Built to Spill's *Marine Research* album, 1999.

Bottom: Back cover of Bis' *Heavenly's Keroleen* album, 1995.

Opposite: The Rough Trade shop on Talbot Road, London, featuring the postcode that would give Wiiija Records its name.

Heather Lewis, Laura Carter, and Bret Lunsford, had formed the group Beat Happening. K Records expanded its geographical outlook in 1987 by starting the International Pop Underground 7″ series, which continues to this day, and expanded again the same year with KNW-YR-OWN, which focused on music from the Anacurtes, Washington, area.[169] By 1991, the label was firmly established in Olympia, and was a crucial part of the scene that would support such bands as Bikini Kill and Bratmobile.

Another point of inspiration for riot grrrl, and for the labels who would become known for releasing riot grrrl records, certainly in Britain, would be the labels that sprang up around the C86/twee scene, particularly Sarah Records, which was formed in 1987 by Clare Wadd and Matt Haynes, and Rutland Records, which was run by Terri Lowe and Ruth Miller of the band Po!, and Sugarfrost from Port Sunlight. In fact, it has been argued, notably by Martin Whitehead, who ran the Subway label in the late 1980s, that C86, rather than punk, inspired women to promote gigs, write fanzines, and run record labels.[170] Sarah's Matt Haynes has also pointed out that Sarah Records had a policy of "not decorating record-sleeves with pictures of women (as boys have done since time immemorial)" and that "Claire was behind all that...."[171]

It was Wiiija records who, like K Records, provided support for many of the British riot grrrl bands, most notably by signing Huggy Bear, releasing the double 7″ pack *Some Hearts Paid To Lie*, and signing the likes of Comet Gain and Bis.[172] Whilst not tending to be as readily linked to riot grrrl as, for example, Kill Rock Stars, Slampt, Catcall, and even K Records, Wiijia support was, in many ways, vital. An independent label that already existed prior to riot grrrl, Wiijia was founded in 1988 by Pete, Nigel and Jude at the Talbot Road branch of Rough Trade, (the shops postcode being W11 1JA) and was inspired by the new, loud, exciting sounds coming out of America, typified by the Butthole Surfers, Swans, Sonic Youth and Big Black. The aim was to reflect a similar sound that was beginning to emerge in Britain through such bands as Therapy? and Silverfish.[173] The members of Huggy Bear were, apparently, regular customers at Rough Trade, and Delia (guitarist in Mambo Taxi) worked at the shop. When Huggy Bear dropped in a demo of their band, the label embraced them as a "breath of fresh air" in the wake of the depressing and ever-present grunge scene, and by the end of 1993, Wiiija were waving Huggy Bear off as they set sail for America and Japan.[174]

A much smaller, but equally crucial, London independent label around this time would be Chocolate Narcotic, a tiny label which released the first Pussycat Trash 7″, *Plink, Plonk, Pink, Punk*. Chocolate Narcotic was run by Chris Phillips and Rupert Cook, who also organised shows at the Camden Monarch under the name Chocolate Psychosis, they, along with Loretta Cubberly-Gomis, would go on to co-organise the Piao! Festival in February 1994 with members of Linus.[175] Held between the 26 and 27 February, this two day festival featured nearly 40 bands, and was held at Hammersmith Emerald Centre, a community hall which has since been flattened to make way for a bigger tube station and shopping centre.[176] The venue had no music license, and, according to Andy Roberts, "all tickets had to be sold in advance so we could make out it was a private party".[177]

The phrase "Pay In Advance Only" became abbreviated to "PIAO", which transformed into "Piao!", giving the festival its name, and leading Phillips and Cubberly-Gomis to launch further projects under the name, most notably a label, Piao! Records, which released the earliest Lungleg records, amongst others, and the Piao! Club, which put on gigs upstairs at the Laurel Tree pub in Camden, including the last ever Huggy Bear gig in late 1994.

Newcastle's Slampt Underground Organisation, who, as the name suggests, were always concerned with doing something more challenging than simply pushing product, explored this umbrella approach to music projects even further. "I used to buy everything which came out on K Records out of Olympia, Washington, because I had been obsessed for years with Beat Happening who ran the label." wrote Pete Dale in 1998.[178] He and Rachel Holborow started Slampt in the summer of 1992, taking K Records as their example, they planned to:

Front cover of Lung Leg's *Shag the Tiger* album. Opposite: Promotional flyer for The Slampt Underground, who promoted a range of musical and cultural events and products from the underground.

> Put out cassettes, fanzines and organise gigs. One of the ideas we took from K was that a) it didn't matter if you could/ couldn't play and b) Girls make good punk rock. We immediately put that into practice with Slampt, and pretty soon after we started doing stuff the *Melody Maker* (closely followed by the *NME*) started hyping a (at that point more-or-less non existent) British riot grrrl scene.[179]

The first release on Slampt was a fanzine, which quickly sold, providing Dale and Holborow with £100. With this £100 they released a series of tapes and, a year later, had graduated to releasing on vinyl. In 1994, John Peel booked Pussycat Trash for a session, and they apparently made "so much money out of it" that they were able to press Pussycat Trash's second single, "La La Ovular".[180]

The way Slampt worked was, in many ways, financially very simple: one project, essentially, financed the next, and, in their first year of operating they worked on a shoestring budget, releasing four tapes and several fanzines for just £100.[181] Despite being firmly committed to a fiercely independent left wing punk ideology that stressed sincerity and ideological commitment on the part of those they worked with, Slampt were able to maintain an average of 500 sales for each of their releases, with a number of their records, Pussycat Trash's *La La Ovular*, The Yummy Fur's Songs *For Walt Disney Played By Yuri Gurgaran*, and Kenickie's *Catsuit City*, selling considerably more.

This achievement was particularly impressive given that they were largely reliant on the fanzine networks for publicity, and that they refused to advertise in the music press. The music ucker up · Kiss us back · It's a dare · Yeah?

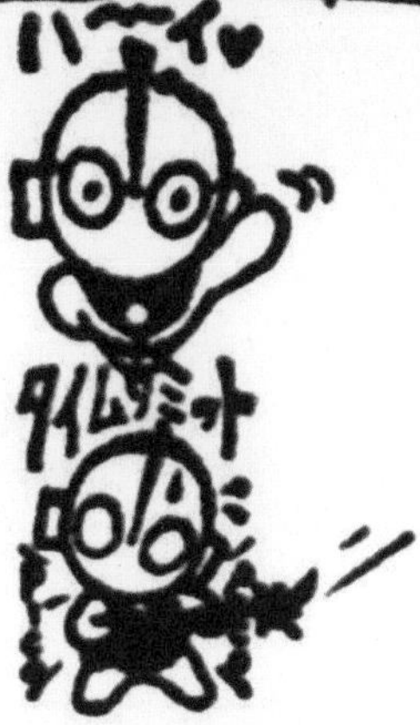

Unseen

"lo-fi is my fi"

Slampt 13 ·

those Morpeth Aliens stretch to snap Take A Rocket to their moon ★

two cassettes on Slampt: £1-50 each inc p+p

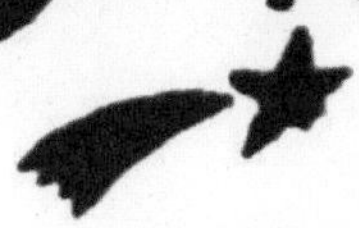

Slampt

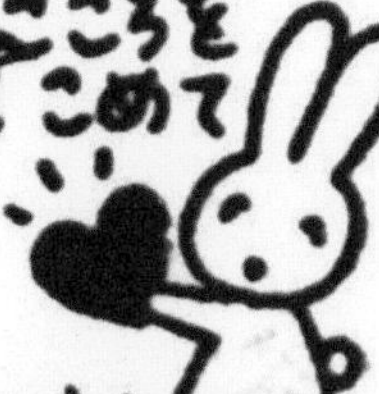

postal R-R-Romance limitless

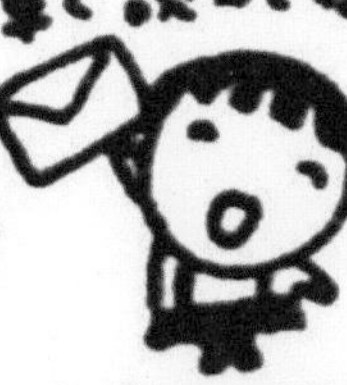

Slampt

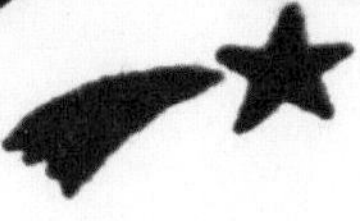

Slampt · 10 Meldon Tce · Heaton · Newcastle upon Tyne · NE6 5XP

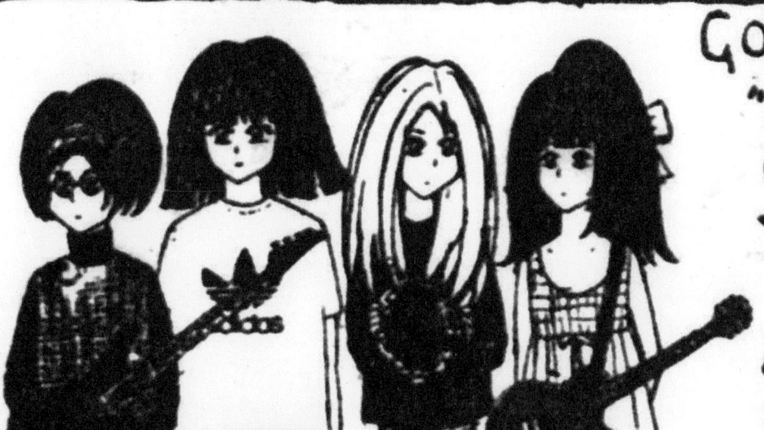

Golden Starlet

"Scarlet Harlot"

Slampt 14

scarey romance in a kitsh for blood sakes direction look out for your heart ♥

cheques payable "Slampt" · Eurocheques + IRCs ♥

weeklies were clearly aware of Slampt, in that they reviewed a number of the label's releases, it's also probable that they were aware, of some kind of new musical 'scene' developing in the northeast. Dale writes in the Slampt fanzine, *Fast Connection*, about an incident that occurred in the mid 1990s when a young female journalist approached Dave Bennun, editor of *Melody Maker*'s "Advance" section (which reported on new bands) about possibly doing an feature on Kenickie. Brennun's response is reputed to have been less than enthusiastic: "Oh great, another girl band from up north."[182] A comment Dale found intriguing as well as offensive, suggestive as it was of the idea that there was a large army of girls with guitars north of Watford, just waiting to colonise the south.[183]

In addition to releasing music and fanzines, and putting on gigs, Slampt also provided a vital distribution link for American labels such as K Records and Kill Rock Stars, and European labels such as Elefant, Candy Apple, and others, making it cheaper and easier for their releases to be purchased in Britain. By the time Holborow and Dale folded Slampt in 2000, they had not only issued over 70 releases, they had also marked out a space for riot grrrl and punk bands in the north east, supported that scene, and—in many ways—transformed it in the process. Like K Records, Slampt had fostered a community, the very thing Bikini Kill's Kathleen Hanna had stressed was so important back in 1996.

Post-riot grrrl, there was a resurgence of British independent labels, some of which were bedroom hobbies done on a shoestring which folded after one or two releases, some of which are still operational today. In Glasgow, labels such as Vesuvius and Flotsum and Jetsum helped support the thriving Glasgow punk scene, with Flotsum and Jetsum even joining forces with the club Nice 'n' Sleazy and the company Appollo Recordings to release the Club Beatroot singles series, a succession of live releases that were similar to, and possibly inspired by, the 'Live At The Roxy' recordings from the late 1970s.

Whilst many of these labels were set up by people barely older than the bands they were releasing, or—in the case of Slampt, Chemikal Underground, and a number of others—were run by some of the bands they were releasing, there were also a few labels in Glasgow owned and run by members of 1980s Scottish bands, for example Altered Images (Creeping Bent) and the Associates (Electric Honey) who were also supporting the next wave of bands coming up through the underground.

In America, the label most associated with riot grrrl is Kill Rock Stars, a label started in 1991 by Slim Moon and, like K Records, based in Olympia. [184] Initially, the label planned to release spoken word 7" singles, and the labels first release was a split 7" of spoken word work by Kathleen Hanna and Slim Moon.[185] However the labels next major release was a compilation of Olympia bands, including Bikini Kill, Bratmobile, Unwound and Nirvana, entitled *Kill Rock Stars*, which Moon was compelled to release because he recognised that bands like

Top: Front cover of *Club Beatroot* Part Three, released by Flotsum and Jetsum, Nice 'n' Sleazy and Apollo Recordings.
Bottom: Front cover of Kenickie's *Catsuit City* album, 1994.

Bikini Kill, Bratmobile and Unwound were too exciting to stay unsigned.[186] Throughout the 1990s, the label released work by the aforementioned artists, alongside Heavens To Betsy and Excuse 17, some of whose members would later join forces to form Sleater-Kinney, whose own (early) releases would also come out on Kill Rock Stars. The labels website describes Kill Rock Stars as being queer-positive, feminist, and artist friendly, and makes the point that—since the departure of Moon in 2006—Kill Rock Stars is one of the few female run indies in America, but the label has attracted criticism in recent years for growing (in the critics eyes) too close to the major music industry in America, a criticism confounded by Moon's decision to leave in order to become Senior Director of Nonesuch Records, a subsidiary of Warners.[187]

Whilst much has been made of the liberating impact of riot grrrl on the British and American music scenes, little attention tends to be given to the many European labels, bands, and chapters that have sprung up throughout the last 15 years, including the Spanish band Hello Cuca, Italian band Juicy Shoes, French label Mademoiselle, and the Polish "autonomous feminist anti-hierarchic group" Emancypunx.[189] In addition to fighting for women's rights and fighting against sexual discrimination, Warsaw-based Emancypunx, which is made up of women aged between approximately 16 and 28, produce fanzines and run a non-profit 'contribution' which distributes tapes, EPs and LPs by female bands and "anti-sexist bands".[190] They also distribute magazines, books, t-shirts, and postcards, as well as act as a catalyst for organisation and information-sharing.

The Riot Grrrl Europe site, meanwhile, which was set up to combat feelings of isolation amongst European riot grrrls, includes a list of labels and distributors which are run by a mix of English, Swedish, German, Polish, French, Finnish, and Italian grrrls.[191] All of which would seem to suggest that the echoes of punk, which (as in Britain and America) never entirely died out, paved the way for a riot grrrl scene across Europe that is rarely reported on, but which operates at a similar grassroots level to those in America and Britain. As in those countries, it has also led to a rebirth in small DIY independent labels, which, as Slampt, K Records and Emancypunx have all demonstrated, can be about a real sense of community and political activism, rather than simply pushing product.

A CONCLUSION, OF SORTS

What has been discussed in this chapter is a small selection of the music of riot grrrl, its roots, and its legacy. There are many more musical styles that have interacted with and been influenced by riot grrrl, but space does not permit me to discuss them. Some obvious examples would include acoustic singer/songwriters such as Mary Lou Lord, Lois Maffeo, Sarah Dougher, Rae Spoon, and Cat Power, to name a few. The anarcho-crust scene, which has interacted with a number of riot grrrl communities across Europe in a very deep way, only really threw up one riot grrrl band in Britain, namely Bradford's Witchknot, who included in their ranks future folk/electro influenced singer/songwriter Lianne Hall, and fanzine writer/performer Jane 'Shag Stamp' Graham, whilst the hardcore scene also had a slight but important impact, so much so that Rachel Holborow of Slampt said she often felt an affinity between Slampt and Subjegation, a British hardcore/emo label.[192] Rachel's former Pussycat Trash bandmate, Rosie, also went on to form the hardcore band Month Of Birthdays.

Aside from purely guitar-based music, Cornershop, a band who cut their teeth on the mid-1990s indie scene, sharing gigs and support with a number of the riot grrrl bands, most notably Mambo Taxi and the Voodoo Queens, have gone on to experiment with an increasingly sophisticated blend of guitar, sitar, and dance music, resulting in critical acclaim for 1995s *Woman's Gotta Have It* album, which included the "6am Julander Shere" single, an understated masterpiece which still sounds great today, and culminating in a number one single in 1997 ("Brimful Of Asha", as remixed by Big Beat DJ Norman

Cook) plus a run of low key classic singles, such as "Staging The Plaguing Of The Raised Platform" and "Lessons Learned From Rocky I to Rocky V". There was also the Birmingham rap crew Credit To The Nation, a short-lived outfit centred around 17 year-old rapper Matty Hansen, who penned a number of calls for racial and sexual respect and unity, such as the single "Call It What You Want" (which sampled Nirvana's "Teen Spirit" riff to great effect), album tracks such as "The Lady Needs Respect", written before the word 'respect' came to gather a series of emptier connotations, and "Sewing The Seeds Of Hatred", which directly challenged the BNP and Combat 18. Hansen also collaborated with a pre-"Tubthumping" Chumbawamba and, by the time he was interviewed in 1994 for Simone Ivatt's Sawtooth fanzine, was talking of playing a gig with Huggy Bear.[193] Riot grrrl has also made inroads into dance and electronica via such artists as Chicks On Speed, Le Tigre, Tracy + The Plastics, Peaches, and Anjali. All this is to say that as a stone thrown into a lake causes ripples on the surface of that lake long after the stone has sunk to the bottom, so the musical influence of riot grrrl has continued to have an impact on musicians and communities throughout North America, South America, Britain, and Europe long after riot grrrl vanished back underground.

EMANCYPUNX! WARSAW

Warsaw's Emancypunx! Logo, a group that releases zines, music and acts as an information-sharing hub for the contemporary European riot grrrl movement.

1 Sabin, Roger. "Introduction", *Punk Rock; So What? The cultural legacy of punk*, London/New York: Routledge, 1999. pp.2
2 Savage, Jon. *England's Dreaming: Sex Pistols and Punk Rock*, London: Faber&Faber, 1991. This is a theme that runs throughout the book as a whole.
3 Savage, J. *England's Dreaming: Sex Pistols and Punk Rock*, pp.123-124.
4 McRobbie, A. "Introduction", *Feminism And Youth Culture*, Hampshire and London: Macmillan Press LTD, 2000, pp. 9-10.
5 Miles, Cressida, "Spatial Politics: A Gendered Sense Of Place" in *Redhead*, Steve, Wynne, Derek and O'Connor, Justin, The Clubcultures Reader: Readings in Popular Cultural Studies, Oxford and Malden: Blackwell Publishers LTD, 1998. P53
6 O'Brien, L, "The Woman Punk Made Me", in Sabin, R., *Punk Rock; So What? The cultural legacy of punk*, London/New York: Routledge, 1999. pp.198
7 Siouxsie Sioux interview with Janice Long as part of the 'Who's That Girl?' series, Radio 1, 1984, broadcast date unknown. The fountains at Centre Point are situated between the Dominion 8 Theatre on Tottenham Court Road and Charing Cross Road in the West End.
9 Savage, J. *England's Dreaming: Sex Pistols and Punk Rock*. pp. 190-91
10 Savage, J. *England's Dreaming: Sex Pistols and Punk Rock*. pp. 219-220
11 Savage, J. *England's Dreaming: Sex Pistols and Punk Rock*. pp.183
12 Savage, J. *England's Dreaming: Sex Pistols and Punk Rock*. pp.183
13 Savage, J. *England's Dreaming: Sex Pistols and Punk Rock*. pp.332
14 Savage, J. *England's Dreaming: Sex Pistols and Punk Rock*. pp.332
15 Savage, J. *England's Dreaming: Sex Pistols and Punk Rock*. pp.335
16 Frischmann, J. "Women in Punk" part 2 of *Punk Fiction*, Radio 1, late 1996. Broadcast date unknown.
17 Savage, J. *England's Dreaming: Sex Pistols and Punk Rock*. pp.335
18 O'Brien, Lucy. *She Bop II: The definitive history of women in rock, pop, and soul*, London/New York: Continuum, 2002, pp.147
19 O'Brien, L. *She Bop II*, pp.146
20 O'Brien, L. *She Bop II*, pp.146
21 Reynolds, S. *Rip It Up And Start Again*, pp.214
22 Reynolds, S. *Rip It Up And Start Again*, pp.214
23 Miles, C. "Spatial Politics: A Gendered Sense Of Place" in *Redhead* et al, The Clubcultures Reader, pp.54
24 *Punk Fiction*, part 2
25 Stevenson worked for McLaren as the Sex Pistols road manager, before going on to manage Siouxsie and the Banshees.
26 Stevenson, N. and Stevenson, R. *Vacant: A Diary Of The Punk Years 1976–1979*, London: Thames and Hudson, 1999, pp.54 and pp.101
27 O'Brien, L. "The Woman Punk Made Me", in Sabin, *Punk Rock; So What?*, pp.141
28 Savage, J. *England's Dreaming: Sex Pistols and Punk Rock*, pp.418
29 Savage, J. *England's Dreaming: Sex Pistols and Punk Rock*, pp.418
30 Savage, J. *England's Dreaming: Sex Pistols and Punk Rock*, pp.418
31 O'Brien, L. *She Bop II*, p133, also O'Brien, "The Woman Punk Made Me" in Sabin, *Punk Rock; So What?*, pp.191, and Miles, "Spatial Politics: A Gendered Sense Of Place" in *Redhead* et al, The Clubcultures Reader, pp.53
32 McRobbie, "Introduction", *Feminism And Youth Culture*, pp.8
33 McRobbie, "Introduction", *Feminism And Youth Culture*, pp.6-7
34 McRobbie, "Introduction", *Feminism And Youth Culture*, pp.6-7
35 Miles, "Spatial Politics: A Gendered Sense Of Place" in *Redhead* et al, The Clubcultures Reader, pp.51–52
36 O'Brien, L. "The Woman Punk Made Me" in Sabin, *Punk Rock; So What?* pp.194
37 Leblanc, Lauraine, *Pretty In Punk: Girls' Gender Resistance in a Boys' Subculture*, New Brunswick, New Jersey, and London: Rutgers University Press, 1999, p6
38 Leblanc, *Pretty In Punk*, pp.6
39 Leblanc, *Pretty In Punk*, pp.6
40 Leblanc, *Pretty In Punk*, pp.6
41 Leblanc, *Pretty In Punk*, pp.231
42 McRobbie, Angela. "Settling Accounts with Subcultures: A Feminist Critique", *Feminism And Youth Culture*, Hampshire and London: Macmillan Press LTD, 2000, pp.42
43 McRobbie, "Settling Accounts with Subcultures: A Feminist Critique", *Feminism And Youth Culture*, pp.42
44 The phrase 'WAGS' used to refer to the wives and girlfriends of British footballers, in recent years it has come to mean the wives and girlfriends of any British sportsmen.
45 *Punk Fiction*, part 2
46 O'Brien, L. *She Bop II*, pp.160–161
47 O'Brien, L. *She Bop II*, pp.160–161
    Quoted in Miles, "Spatial Politics: A Gendered Sense Of Place" in *Redhead* et al, The Clubcultures Reader, pp.58
    Leblanc, *Pretty In Punk*, pp.64
48 Postal interview, 1999
49 Postal interview, 1999
50 Postal interview, 1999
51 Postal interview, 1999
52 Postal interview, 1999
53 Anderson, Mark and Jenkins, Mark, *Dance Of Days: Two decades of punk in the nation's capital*, New York: Soft Skull Press Inc, 2003, pp.309
54 Anderson and Jenkins, *Dance Of Days*, pp.309
55 Anderson and Jenkins, *Dance Of Days*, pp.309
56 Anderson and Jenkins, *Dance Of Days*, pp.309-10
57 Anderson and Jenkins, *Dance Of Days*, pp.310
58 Anderson and Jenkins, *Dance Of Days*, pp.310
59 Leonard, Marion. "'Rebel Girl, You Are The Queen Of My World' Feminism, 'Subculture' and grrrl power" in Whiteley, Sheila (ed.) *Sexing The Groove: Popular Music And Gender*, London/   New York: Routledge, 1997. pp.242-3
60 Anderson and Jenkins, *Dance Of Days*, pp.310
61 Anderson and Jenkins, *Dance Of Days*, pp.310
62 Anderson and Jenkins, *Dance Of Days*, pp.311
63 Bikini Kill, "Jigsaw Youth", Catcall, 1993.
64 Bikini Kill, "Double Dare Ya", *Kill Rock Stars*, 1991.
65 Kathleen Hanna interview, *Galactic* issue 2, pp.7, York, 1996
66 *Galactic* issue 2, pp.7
67 *Galactic* issue 2, pp.7
68 Savage, Bill. Le Tigre interview in *Pamzine*, Pamnibus edition, 2002
69 Anderson and Jenkins, *Dance Of Days*, pp.310
70 Anderson and Jenkins, *Dance Of Days*, pp.311–312
71 Anderson and Jenkins, *Dance Of Days*, pp.320–321
72 *Don't Need You*, Dir. Kerri Koch, USA, 2001
73 Marine Research interview, Kirby, Issue 4, London, 2000
74 Marine Research interview, Kirby, Issue 4, London, 2000
75 Postal interview, 1998
76 Postal interview, 1998
77 Postal interview, 1998
78 Postal interview, 1999
79 Postal interview, 1999
80 Postal interview, 1998

81 Postal interview, 1998
82 Postal interview, 1998
83 Huggy Bear, "Her Jazz", Wiiija, 1993
84 Sullivan, Caroline, "Angry Young Women", *The Guardian*, March 1993
85 "Andy's 1993" www.linusland.co.uk
86 "Andy's 1993" www.linusland.co.uk
87 "Andy's 1993" www.linusland.co.uk
88 Savage, J., *England's Dreaming: Sex Pistols and Punk Rock*, pp.257
89 www.roughtrade.com
90 Skinned Teen, "Straight Girl", from the compilation LP Elastic *Jet Mission*, Slampt, 1994
91 Lungleg interview, *Galactic*, Issue 2, York, 1996
92 "Andy's 1993" www.linusland.co.uk
93 Lungleg interview, *Galactic*, Issue 2
94 Interview with John McKeown, www.theyummyfur.co.uk
95 Interview with John McKeown, www.theyummyfur.co.uk
96 www.linusland.co.uk
97 www.linusland.co.uk
98 http://sleater-kinney.com
99 Gossip interview, *Pamzine* issue 6, London, Spring 2003
100 *Pamzine* issue 6, Spring 2003
101 *Pamzine*, issue 6, London, 2003
102 Review of The Gossip, Magnet Club, Berlin, Monday 19 June 2006. This review appeared in a late June/early July 2006 print edition of NME, but the online version has been edited, changing the author of the review and removing the references to Springfield, Joplin and Franklin.
103 Empire, Kitty "Finally it's girls on top", *Observer*, November 26 2006. This article can be read online at: http://music.guardian.co.uk/pop/story/0,,1956994,00.html
104 "The Gossip" in *Wikipedia: The Free Encyclopaedia*, available from http://en.wikipedia.org/wiki/The_Gossip retrieved 20/4/2007
105 www.damagedgoods.co.uk
106 Mambo Taxi, "Insecure", Clawfist, 1993
107 Author interview, London, 14/5/2007
108 Author interview
109 Author interview
110 Author interview
111 Author interview
112 Author interview
113 Author interview
114 Author interview
115 Author interview
116 Author interview
117 Author interview
118 Huggy Bear's "Her Jazz" was at number 3, beaten only by Madder Rose's "Swim" and the Chumbawamba and Credit To The Nation anti-fascist collaboration "Enough Is Enough." Peel Show Festive 50's past can be viewed by visiting the Keeping It Peel pages on the Radio 1 website: www.bbc.co.uk/radio1/johnpeel
119 Author interview
120 Author interview
121 Author interview
122 Author interview
123 Author interview
124 Author interview
125 "Shampoo (band)" in *Wikipedia: The Free Encyclopaedia*, available from http://en.wikipedia.org/wiki/Shampoo_%28band%29 retrieved   18/5/2007
126 Patterson, Sylvia "Sud Up And Prance", NME, 1994. Publishing date unknown.
127 "Shampoo (band)" in *Wikipedia: The Free Encyclopaedia*, available from http://en.wikipedia.org/wiki/Shampoo_%28band%29 retrieved 18/5/2007
128 Nick Allott and Deby Dukes, *Slamptumentary*, UK, 1995
129 Allott and Dukes, *Slamptumentary*, 1995
130 Allott and Dukes, *Slamptumentary*, 1995
131 Allot and Dukes, *Slamptumentary*, 1995
132 Allott and Dukes, *Slamptumentary*, 1995
133 *Dancing Chicks* issue 4, Leeds, 1999
134 www.smellslike.com/rondelles
135 www.smellslike.com/rondelles
136 The Lollies, "Dayjob Nightmare" from the EP *Bang! Bang! Bang! Lookout! Lookout! Lookout!*, Evil World, 2000
137 Barton, Laura, "Leaders Of The Pack," *The Guardian*, 1/11/2006. available at http://music.guardian.co.uk/pop/story/0,,1936461,00.html
138 Barton, "Leaders Of The Pack"
139 Barton, "Leaders Of The Pack"
140 www.twee.net/intro.html
141 Reynolds, *Rip It Up And Start Again*, pp.342–343
142 Reynolds, *Rip It Up And Start Again*, pp.522
143 "C86 (music)" in *Wikipedia: The Free Encyclopaedia*, available from http://en.wikipedia.org/wiki/C86_%28music%29 retrieved 20/4/2007
144 "C86 (music)" in *Wikipedia: The Free Encyclopaedia*, available from http://en.wikipedia.org/wiki/C86_%28music%29 retrieved 20/4/2007
145 Reynolds, *Rip It Up And Start Again*, pp.522
146 Reynolds, *Rip It Up And Start Again*, pp.522
147 Reynolds, *Rip It Up And Start Again*, pp.522
148 Po!, "Ever Been Had" from the album *Little Stones*, Rutland Records, 1989.
149 Postal Interview, 1998.
150 Pussycat Trash, "Squid Joke", from the EP *Plink, Plonk, Pink, Punk, Chocolate Narcotic*, 1993.
151 http://homepage.ntlworld.com/elizabeth.ercocklly/helen.htm
152 Manda Rin interview, *Fake It And Go Home*, issue 5, Lancaster, 2001.
153 Email interview, 17/4/2007
154 Helen Love, "Bubblegum", *Damaged Goods*, 1995
155 *Fake It And Go Home*, Issue 5
156 www.wiiija.com/history
157 *Popgirls* issue 2, Glasgow, 2002
158 Reynolds, *Rip It Up And Start Again*, pp.92
159 O'Brien, *She Bop II*, pp.66
160 Reynolds, *Rip It Up And Start Again*, pp.93
161 Reynolds, *Rip It Up And Start Again*, pp.93–95
162 Reynolds, *Rip It Up And Start Again*, pp.93–95
163 Reynolds, *Rip It Up And Start Again*, pp.102
164 Reynolds, *Rip It Up And Start Again*, pp.102
165 Reynolds, *Rip It Up And Start Again*, pp.102
166 Reynolds, *Rip It Up And Start Again*, pp.108
167 www.krecs.com

168 www.krecs.com

169 www.krecs.comvv

170 Whitehead, Martin in Hann, Michael, "Fey City Rollers", *The Guardian*, http://arts.guardian.co.uk/feature/story/0,11710,1325674,00.html quoted as part of "C86 (music)" in Wikipedia: The Free Encyclopaedia. Available from http://en.wikipedia.org/wikiC86_%28music%29 retrieved 20/4/2007

171 email correspondance, 20/6/2007

172 www.wiiija.com/history

173 www.wiiija.com/history

174 www.wiiija.com/history

175 "Andy's 1993" www.linusland.co.uk

176 "Andy's 1993" www.linusland.co.uk

176 "Andy's 1993" www.linusland.co.uk

177 Postal interview, 1998

178 Postal interview, 1998

179 Allott and Dukes, *Slamptumentary*

180 Allott and Dukes, *Slamptumentary*

181 Pete's column, *Fast Connection* issue 2, Newcastle-Upon-Tyne, 1996, pp.19

182 *Fast Connection* issue 2, pp.19

183 www.killrockstars.com

184 "Kill Rock Stars" in *Wikipedia: The Free Encyclopaedia*, available from http://en.wikipedia.org/wiki/Kill_Rock_Stars retrieved 26/4/2007

185 "Kill Rock Stars" in *Wikipedia: The Free Encyclopaedia*, available from http://en.wikipedia.org/wiki/Kill_Rock_Stars retrieved 26/4/2007

186 "Kill Rock Stars" in *Wikipedia: The Free Encyclopaedia*, available from http://en.wikipedia.org/wiki/Kill_Rock_Stars retrieved 26/4/2007

187 www.geocities.com/theloepa/emanz.html?200726

188 www.geocities.com/theloepa/emanz.html?200726

189 www.geocities.com/riotgrrrleurope

190 Allott and Dukes, *Slamptumentary*.

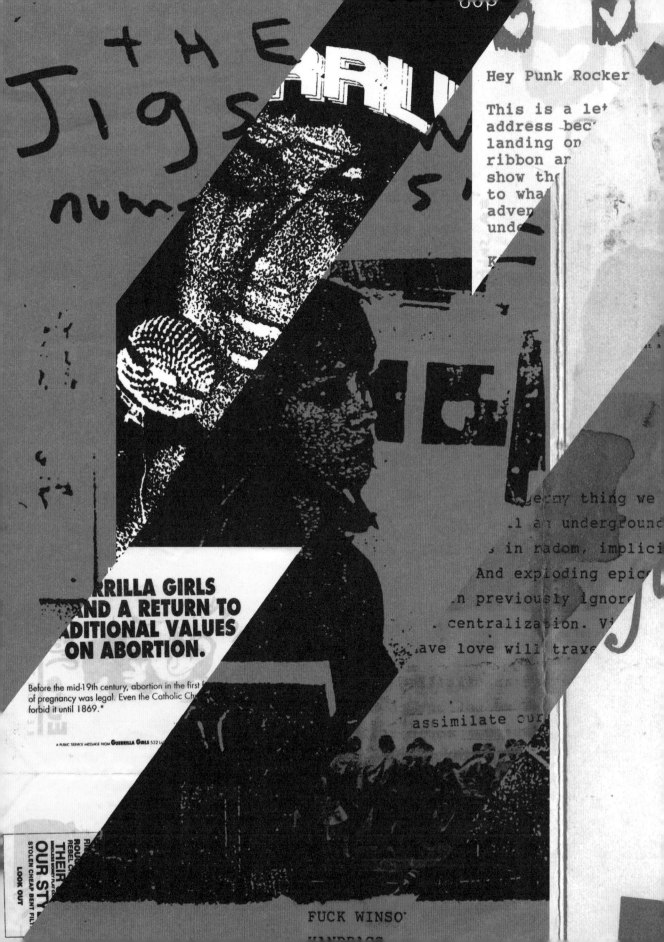

THE
Jigsaw
num

Hey Punk Rocker

This is a let
address bec
landing on
ribbon ar
show the
to wha
adven
unde

K.

RRILLA GIRLS
AND A RETURN TO
ADITIONAL VALUES
ON ABORTION.

Before the mid-19th century, abortion in the first
of pregnancy was legal. Even the Catholic Ch
forbid it until 1869.*

A PUBLIC SERVICE MESSAGE FROM **GUERRILLA GIRLS** 532 L

erny thing we
ll an underground
s in radom, implici
And exploding epic
n previously ignore
centralization. Vi
ave love will trave

assimilate cur

ROU
REBEL C
THEIR
OUR STY
STOLEN CHEAP BENT FILI
LOOK OUT

FUCK WINSO

RIOT GRRRL
WRITING

RED CHIDGEY

number
one

2001. Our grrrl culture emits radiation and inspiration. We X-ray society: pick out from the bones what we wanna keep + wot we're gonna discard//re-form. We've got power and alchemy + vision and humour and armies of us. xxx it's gonna change everything.[1]

I wrote these words in my zine *Varla's Passed Out Again* as a freshly graduated, ex-working class 21-year old girl who had just discovered riot grrrl. It was 2001 and my girl feministing had happened all backwards. I'd read rumours about riot grrrl in Hole and Nirvana biographies. I'd turned in a Cultural Studies paper about a 1990s grrrl subculture, which had spectacularly boomed then fizzled out. A friend had passed on a mix-tape of grrrl music which was all new to me; Heavens to Betsy, Sonic Youth, Bikini Kill. I wasn't even punk rock.

It was the internet that hooked me up. Riot Grrrl Europe led to Ladyfest, riot grrrl meets, Take Back the Night marches, zine-making, and illicit attacks on sexist bill-boards. "Graffiti was fun, with a sense of danger and sex. It was part of the feeling that I could do anything", reminiscences Caroline Hamer from the Central England Riot Grrrl chapter.[2] Full of girl energy and mischief, a bunch of us had taken to the streets during Ladyfest London, writing slogans like "Riot Don't Diet" on sexist adverts. We used the only tools to hand: lipstick and

Ladyfest Brighton flyer, 2005. Image courtesy of
Charlotte Procter.

Opposite: Graffiti at Ladyfest London, Carloline and
Bianca, 2001. Image courtesy of Red Chidgey.

marker pens. Riot grrrl was about creating the culture you wanted
to live in: making pro-girl spaces where it felt like there were gaps
in the mainstream, and showing your refusal to be defined by
the dominant society, even if that refusal was just a "fuck you"
written on a bill-board at a bus-stop on the way home.

Riot grrrl was also about taking risks with feminism, running
away with it. Dreaming up actions and gangs. As part of a
street action around Valentine's Day, I set up a mock dinner
table, each plate with a handwritten myth and reality of rape.
Streams of passers-by, male and female, stopped and worked
their way round the table, reading each plate carefully (the
power of unexpected words in the public sphere is a potent
thing). No one said I couldn't do these things, and even if they
had I probably wouldn't have listened. I was politicised in a way
that woke me up, creatively and expressively, and zines were a
large part of that. FingerBang Distro (2001–2004) was an 'anti-
business' distribution project that brought together European
riot grrrl resources. Under the name "riot grrrl" I wrote sex
zines, compilation zines, personal zines, feminist zines, and, in
so many other ways, found my voice.

Maybe riot grrrl was the first crush that led to heavier loves.
Ladyfest Brighton happened in 2005, a DIY queer feminist
arts, music and activism festival which raised £6,000 for
women's coalitions: The Revolutionary Association of Women
of Afghanistan, Truth About Rape, Threshold (a local mental
health advisory service threatened with closure), and the
Brighton Women's Centre. The much hyped Riot Grrrl History
discussion panel, with Tobi Vail (Bikini Kill, *Jigsaw*), Allison
Wolfe (Bratmobile, *Girl Germs*) and a screening of Kerri Koch's
documentary *Don't Need You*, marked riot grrrl as an event of
the past. The fact that we eventually had to turn people away
because we were over capacity suggests riot grrrl retains some
of its old allure and intrigue.[3]

DIY feminism inspires me as ever, but I no longer call myself
a riot grrrl. The girl gang energy leading me into activism has
left me wanting something else, something more threatening
to the status quo. But girls burn out, and when I do, I pick up
riot grrrl fanzines and reconnect with whatever it was that made
this happen; reconnect with girls who were loud and strong and
doing their feminist thing with few resources. I get reinvigorated
all over again and a special kind of adrenalin shot rushes to
that historical place of my brain where ideas turn into actions,
because well, why not?

Looking back, I'm amazed with what authority we claimed
riot grrrl, like it was ours all along, like we owned it. I didn't have
the same experiences as girls who went before, but each of ours
was valid. Riot grrrl became a signature every girl could forge
and no one would tell us we were cheating; we took a name and
made it our own, thereby changing its very reference.

So what is third wave feminism and how does it relate to
the grassroots literature produced within riot grrrl? "When we

started there wasn't anything such as a third wave, or any kind of feminism that would resemble one—it was solidly second wave", says Tobi Vail, drummer of Bikini Kill and author of the influential zine *Jigsaw*. "I don't know if that meant we invented it or what."[4] The term 'third-wave' has variously been described as a generational cohort; an ideology and a shared historical moment.

As an age cohort, 'third-wave' feminism refers to the Baby-Boom generation of 20 and 30-something women, a purview which resonates with riot grrrl's position as a youth feminist movement (from my personal experience as a riot grrrl in its 'second wave' in Britain, the youngest riot grrrl was 13 and the oldest, late 30s). Young women now are seen as the first generation to grow up with the successes of feminism so closely entwined in their lives. Third-wave attempts to fuse critical race theory, queer theory, postmodernism and anti-essentialism (often through the lens of popular culture) are negotiated within the polemic and intention of riot grrrl discourse, although few hard looks at race and class politics were delivered within the movement. In its own vernacular, riot grrrl insists on a 'no rules' anti-ideological credo that prompted self-empowerment and exploration:

> Clarity of agenda is not really something that is important to me—RIOT GRRRL is a total concept. There is no editor and there is no concrete vision or expectation, or there shouldn't be… we riot grrrls are not aligning ourselves with any one position or consensus, because in all likelihood we don't agree. One concrete thing we do agree on so far is that its cool/fun to have a place where we can express ourselves that can't be censored, and where we can feel safe to bring up issues that are important to us.[5]

As part of a shared historical condition shaped by new technologies such as the internet, cheap photocopiers, home computers, scanners, and so on—riot grrrl writers became the

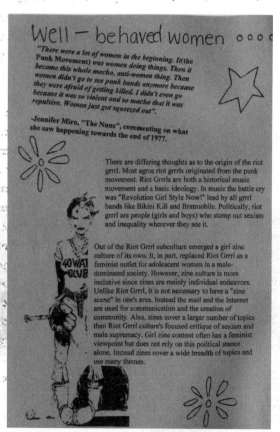

Well — behaved women °°°°

"There were a lot of women in the beginning. It(the Punk Movement) was women doing things. Then it became this whole macho, anti-women thing. Then women didn't go to see punk bands anymore because they were afraid of getting killed. I didn't even go because it was so violent and so macho that it was repulsive. Women just got squeezed out".

-Jennifer Miro, "The Nuns", commenting on what she saw happening towards the end of 1977.

There are differing thoughts as to the origin of the riot grrrl. Most agree riot grrrls originated from the punk movement. Riot Grrrls are both a historical music movement and a basic ideology. In music the battle cry was "Revolution Girl Style Now!" lead by all grrrl bands like Bikini Kill and Bratmobile. Politically, riot grrrl are people (girls and boys) who stomp out sexism and inequality wherever they see it.

Out of the Riot Grrrl subculture emerged a girl zine culture of its own. It, in part, replaced Riot Grrrl as a feminist outlet for adolescent women in a male-dominated society. However, zine culture is more inclusive since zines are mainly individual endeavors. Unlike Riot Grrrl, it is not necessary to have a "zine scene" in one's area. Instead the mail and the Internet are used for communication and the creation of community. Also, zines cover a larger number of topics than Riot Grrrl culture's focused critique of sexism and male supremacy. Girl zine content often has a feminist viewpoint but does not rely on this political stance alone. Instead zines cover a wide breadth of topics and use many themes.

FINGER_BANG DISTRO

I've decided its about time yours truly started her own distro…SO, if you would like to get your zines/ videos/ demos out and about into the world then send them to me. I'm interested in any project you've got up your sleeve, and even if you've just a vague idea and some passion, then write to me and I can try and hook you up with other like minded beans. The aim of FINGER_BANG is to spread the creative talents of the underground/unrecognised. It's about creating alternative medias and experiences, sharing information and skills, and getting people in touch on an international level. Also, I hope some money could be made to donate to a women's health organisation (even if its 10p off everything sold).
I am extra-excited about trying to distro all the riot grrrl zines that possibly exist so chapters, get in touch. And I'd like to promote the work of art collectives, poets, performers… it's perhaps possible that I can help in getting events filmed or that a little film-editing team can be created and videos put out. My ambitions run high…
Contact me at:

Photo: BY MY MUM xxx

Front cover of *Tiger Heart*, no 4, 2001. Image courtesy of Jessica Dainese.

Opposite left: "Well-Behaved Women Barely Make History", from *Rebel Queen*, 2003.

Right: Fingerbang Distro from *Varla's Passed Out Again*, no 3, 2001. Image courtesy of Red Chidgey.

first generation of feminist media producers to be totally DIY; grrrls could write, design, print and distribute their own work by themselves with little expense, skills or need for specialist equipment. This 'democratisation of communication', and the sheer haste with which amateur publications could be made, has led to zines being described as the most crucial form of expression and activism for third-wave feminists.[6]

While grrrl fanzines are messier, more individualistic and personal than their Women's Liberation pamphlet and magazine counterparts, a shared heritage is clear. "Like the feminist presses that sprang up in the 1970s, the girl zine network puts women in touch with each other on their own terms", writes Val Phoenix in her examination of grrrl and womyn activist communities. "Zines create and document culture: girl rage, resistance and love."[7] The chapter considers the goals and influences on early girl revolution rhetoric, the role of writing within riot grrrl cultures more broadly, and an overview of collectively produced riot grrrl zines from over 15 years of its self-publishing history.

HEARTS COVERED IN PAPER

It may seem like a small thing but so many girls only got the opportunity to express themselves in a relatively free way through riot grrrl and the bridges it built," says Natasha of *My Little Fanzine*. "We wrote fanzines about what we were thinking, picked up a guitar and began to play without having the first clue about how to hold the fucking thing, let alone what any of the notes were. For the first time our poetry was no longer confined to the bedroom. And we made friends. If riot grrrl was a movement full of geeks so be it."[8]

Riot grrrl writing was both tough and vulnerable. These feminist zines decanted myths of male artistic genius, standoffish standards of cool, adult-made codes of professionalism, and tame subject matter. They embodied both a utopian vision of I've-got-your-back grrrl politics ("Everygirl a riot grrrl") and the sometimes dystopian reality of girls' lives—as experienced through eating disorders, bullying, self-harm, racism, surviving sexual abuse, alcoholism, addiction, and so on.

They represented an unapologetic state of dipping into socialised girl identity and mixing it with unruliness, as the anonymous author of *Grrrls World* writes about her choice of title:

It's partly to do with Girl's World, those doll's heads with blue eyes and blond curly hair which summed up mid-1980s girliedom… but obviously it means much more than that. A declaration of grrrlspace- irony because it's so blatantly not a grrrl's world… I want to make my own. That's not meant

Front cover of *Ablaze!*, no 10, 1993.

Image courtesy of Karren Ablaze.

to be negative/separatist, but I want a different set of values and priorities, a grrrl-friendly attitude, a space where I can be myself and 'compete' on my own terms. That's what I aspire to be now, not conforming to an inanimate ideal of blonde hair and blue eyes; something strong and autonomous, not submissive and silent.[9]

Girls wrote and still write because they have fever. Whether it's a need to communicate, to express, to bitch or to purge, zines are about true love, which no amount of digital opportunities will dent, girls still write online but print zines are still being produced in their hundreds.

The whole process is intimate, from deciding it's okay to write your words and believe in them, to the moment you're stepping out of a copier shop hugging a batch of warm print to your chest. These DIY zine periodicals contain low production values, confrontational writing styles, and jarring illiteracies (slang, errors, swearing and illegible handwriting are common features). They are kind of motley and throw-away publications, but girls treat them as precious and will hold on to fanzine collections for years.

MANIFESTOS

2003. Riot grrrl is not something with mainstream appeal. It will not change society. But it's changing me. It's not the fullstop manifesto point of my politics—it's part, it's creative resistance, and it leads me further than its own boundaries.[10]

Whilst girl polemics were rushed off and disseminated both in America and Britain there was no official statement or plan linking the two scenes together. "The thing about riot grrrl is that there is no one manifesto," commented Catcall records grrrl Liz Naylor to the *NME* in 1993, "people are expecting some organised front for riot grrrl, but I think that would detract from it".[11] Instead, music, zines, hanging out, and animated letter-writing networks forged the friendships and communities needed for riot grrrl to develop an infrastructure. Connections between grrrl groups and projects were made philosophically and practically through shared goals and ways of working. "WE CAN DO ANY STUFF", asserts the British *Right Now. Riot Grrrl* manifesto, "It's an idea that links Huggy Bear and Simple Machines and Nation of Ulysses and *Ablaze!*".[12]

GIRL REVOLUTION RHETORIC

Reading an early version of the *Right Now. Riot Grrrl* manifesto called *Girlspeak*, Tobi Vail recorded the cross-pollination of ideas in her 1993 fanzine *Jigsaw*:

Stay tuned for more after I get back from the United Kingdom cuz from what they keep telling me there seems to be some kind of girl activity going on thereabouts too right now… a little while ago I read a fanzine or a column in a fanzine called *Girlspeak* from the United Kingdom that was truly wild and seemed to merge the Ulyssess things once again with the girl revolution rhetoric and talked about doing things like passing out chocolate to girls only at shows to encourage more of them to come out and also mentioned strategies for dealing with the misogynist asshole who undoubtedly would rise to the occasion.[13]

Girlspeak was a draft newsletter disseminated in the fanzine world as "The Organ of GIRL POWER INTERNATIONAL (GP): a worldwide network of Girl Revolutionaries." Written by Karren Ablaze during the spring of 1992, *Girlspeak* was influenced by the inflammatory situationist polemic of the Washington DC punk band NOU. "It's the most exciting and electrifying anti-parent culture thing been seen round here. No mystifying marketing, just liberationary literature adding a new dimension to our flailing indie-culture- write your own manifestos", wrote Karren after interviewing the band.[14]

In *Jigsaw #5*, vocalist Ian Svenonius demonstrates the NOU "art terrorist" style, which influenced some early riot grrrl writers:

NOU declares the monster metaphor as the most useful in disseminating our role as terrorist-role-MODels for the children who share our hatred for the three prongs of the triumvirate against the P-Power of NOU, being the Pigs on the street, the Parent Culture sound, and the PTA (Natch). The Young Tiger…is forever concerned with transformation, metamorphosis, from the murderous mundane. Symptomatic are: uniforms, name changing, gang-forming, sartorials, alien obsession, Drag-Queening, Terrorism, Monster Kids. Monsters are all about wrecking the despicable, repressed, and the square.[15]

Impressed, Ablaze took on NOU doctrines of youth rebellion, but reworked them with a stronger girl style. The NOU's militaristic stance, with its slogans and insignia, bores girls who are less inclined to be excited by the traditional trappings of war. We do not deny that a war is being fought, but for NOU and GP the targets are different, thus the strategies varied as well. "They fight the adult world, and we fight the man-world," runs the intro to Ablaze's manifesto.[16]

DEATH TO THE PARENTCORE WORLD

A disjointed track, *Girlspeak* calls for 'girl love' (through making friends with girls at gigs), 'unmarriage' (breaking out from monogamous relationships), "working to fuck things up at every opportunity" (shop-lifting and work-place sabotage), and straight-edge lifestyles ("the drinking of orange juice and coffee rather than brain rotting fluid"), amongst other things. Whilst no mention of riot grrrl is directly made, it's there implicit in the appeal to girl solidarity and autonomy.

"I wrote my girl power manifesto, alone. For six months I held onto this, too scared to print it, fearing for my own sanity," writes Karren in her 'herstory' of the British riot grrrl movement.[17] "These ideals, these waking dreams, didn't fit into British culture, except for cases like Greenham Common [long-term women's peace camp]. And I couldn't live there—where would I plug in my word processor?"[18] Karren was the founder and writer of the then five-year old fanzine *Ablaze!*.

On first glance, *Ablaze!* looks more like a magazine then the usual rushed off, photocopied rag zines. Designed to formal grids, it carried adverts, ran for a word-jammed 50 pages, and had a subscription base—albeit a slightly rocky one. "In order that you can cope with the spontaneous appearance of *Ablaze!* we have put together special stress-free

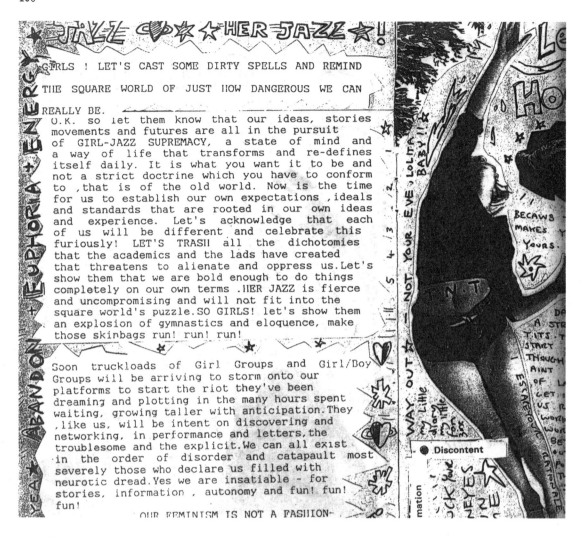

"Her Jazz" from *Huggy Nation*, no 4, 1992–1993.

two issue subscriptions," announces the intro to issue ten. "As usual, we also guarantee that if for any reason we cease to publish, you'll be fully refunded for the magazines you don't receive. Get your *Ablaze!* the smart kid's way."[19]

In approach, writing style and coverage it was still the stuff of fringe publishers: "*Ablaze!* is a fanzine because we are fanz, fanatics, zealots, extremists, we are wild for stuff we're wild for and that fact can't change, except these passions are so real they have sell-by dates, determined entirely by my own chemistry" says Ablaze in her own indomitable style. "Money off the government and money of the bank and bare hands made *Ablaze!* eight and nine. I wrote and designed most of them, without any qualification to do this," explains Karren about her DIY working practices. Like many zines, it was literally a homemade publication: "*Ablaze!* is based mostly in the living room, sometimes in the kitchen, occasionally in the bedroom or the bathroom."[20]

Karren collaborated mostly with guys on her magazine, as the independent publishing world was still a male dominated sphere in the late 1980s and early 90s. "I had a feeling of separateness from other girls, like mingled loneliness and fear," she recalls of the atmosphere. "Whenever I raised issues about sexism and put forward the feminism that came almost naturally to me, I was dismayed, really hurt, by the non-understanding of men around me."[21] Whilst the NOU gig provided a catalyst for action, Ablaze still wasn't confident about the ideas she was conjuring up. What she wanted and needed was a feminist rebellion which would take place in her everyday life, where girl gangs would run riot through all the things she loved: music, writing, and zines.

THE TROUBLESOME AND THE EXPLICIT

Huggy Bear had similar ideas. Their missive *Her Jazz*, also the name of the 1993 7" single, declares "Girls! Lets create some dirty spells and remind the square world just how dangerous we can really be."[22] Full of cryptic suggestions such as "Abandon and Euphoria and Energy=JAZZ—HER—JAZZ," it spurred girls on to "TRASH all the dichotomies that the academics and the lads have created that threaten to alienate and oppress us." *Her Jazz* envisioned a whole new scene emerging from Britpop apathy: "Soon truckloads of girl groups and girl/boy groups will be arriving to storm onto our platforms to start the riot they've been dreaming and plotting in the many hours spent waiting, growing taller with anticipation. They, like us, will be intent on discovering and networking, in performances and letters, the troublesome and the explicit."

Significantly, manifestos were a form of wish-fulfilment, conjuring up in words whatever the authors wanted to see happen in real life. This vision was crafted in different ways. What Ablaze labelled "Girl Power", the Huggies had termed "GIRL-JAZZ SUPREMACY": "OK so let them know that our ideas, stories, movements and futures are all in the pursuit of GIRL-JAZZ SUPREMACY, a state of mind and a way of life that transforms and re-defines itself daily." As with NOU "name-changing" and the Guerrilla Girls use of masks and pseudonyms, Karren Ablaze saw the potential in anonymity and multiple names: "we will confuse [the commercial press] by disseminating different pieces of literature under the same name, and there will be no sense in which any is more 'authentic' than the other".[23] What was to coalesce around the eventual name of riot grrrl was the need for a girl rebel consciousness rooted in constant transformation and action. "Riot grrrl was about inventing new titles", says Jo Huggy, "you think up some name for a fantasy revolutionary group of girls, spread the idea of it about and hope, for someone, it'll come true".[24]

Even when British riot grrrl did take grip, with press coverage, bands, fanzines, and chapters unfolding at a quick pace, alternative group names were still being bandied about. The TerrorZine was one example:

WHAT IS THE POINT OF A TERRORZINE?
To bring about a reign of terror in the areas we judge to need it.

WHY?
Because we are girls who will use any means necessary to achieve our goals.

WHAT ARE THESE GOALS?
To open people's eyes. To exert mental violence because we are not trained to exert physical violence, and violence is a weapon used to keep us scared.

WHO ARE YOU?
Girls who want to go to concerts and be involved in a new underground movement.

ARE YOU RIOT GIRLS?
We've never even seen any "riot girls". We like what they do but they're disorganised

and never answer any of the letters we sent to WIIIJA [Huggy Bear's record label] so we can't be bothered to wait for them to get their act together anymore. Just call us TERRORGIRLS if you like (saves you having to invent some cruddy name for us).[25]

The Terror Girls and the British riot grrrls held a few things in common, including a contempt for the mainstream music press that were seen as commodifiers of their scenes. "We make the British music press our first target", writes Ablaze in *Five Strategies for the Unleashing of Girl Power*, "kids will kick over the news stands and build their revolutionary methods of communication in the form of fanzines and messages in secret codes, meaningless to the newly abandoned square world that so depended on their blood".[26] In her energetic writing, Ablaze issues the warning, "The mutilation of the British music press" will serve as an interesting and enjoyable model for the total destruction of the male-parent culture."

PRICK TEAZE HEROINES

The principles of fun and danger were important elements for proto-girl rebels writing to find their communities. "Yes, we are insatiable—for stories, information, autonomy and FUN! FUN! FUN!" runs the *Her Jazz* missive. Part of this recreation was creating a new kind of language to pump through new ideas. "SO GIRLS! Let's show them an explosion of gymnastics and eloquence, make those skinbags RUN! RUN! RUN!" urges *Her Jazz* with poetic effect. Within Huggy discourse "skinbags" refers to anyone unallied with the new girl rebellion, but especially sexist authority figures and conservative/consumerist mindsetters:

> Are you faking it? Look at it this way…you're either a New Soul Kid or you ain't. You're a Skinbag if you ain't a New Soul Star. If you're a Skinbag, well, you can have anything written on you. A sell-by-date. A bar code. 'They' can carve that Indie Top 20 onto your bland brow for life!!? Look, DON'T LET THEM MANUFACTURE A T-SHIRT FROM YOUR DREAMS. The marketing devil is tapping his foot however begrudgingly to your pulse.[27]

There is something youth-violent literary about their slang—like Anthony Burgess' 1962 novel *Clockwork Orange* or Irvine Welsh's 1990s *Trainspotting*. But the Huggies message is creative and anti-doctrine: any metaphorical punches lay with rejecting the "square world's puzzle" and wanting to smash up the boy-system (although riot grrrl band members were assaulted regularly enough, as Kathleen Hanna testifies in her essay "Gen X Survivor: from riot grrrl rock star to feminist artist").[28]

Early British riot grrrl writing was combative, poetic, and often pretentious, the idea being to create a new kind of communication for girl revolutionaries (away from the adults, the academics, and

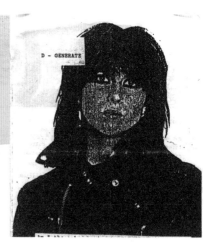

Top: Front cover of *Terrorzine*, 1993.
Bottom: Front cover of *D-Generate*, 1993, produced by Huggy Bear.

the "Neanderthal, Misogynist Assholes," as Karren Ablaze would pointedly write). Huggy Bear didn't flinch at accusations that their prose was alienating and affected, instead they embraced that nature as their own.

> "Part of our style has come from feeling like we're on our own", writes Jo Huggy. "Being hated and almost 'othered' has helped to liberate us from the mainstream. It's like: 'what can we do with the margins?' Any false sense of responsibility I may have felt towards an audience has disappeared."[29]

Accompanying Huggy Bear-made zines (such as *Huggy Nation, Parlez-Vous Code Fucker, Reggae Chicken,* and *D-Generate*) was a series of "PRICK TEAZE" flyers. These texts laid out the Huggies attitude to language and the need to mess it up. "Words change. We can change them. New words arrive. We can create them" run the flyers, giving a seeming nod to the power of 'grrrl' to redefine 'girl' and all its associations of passivity and obedience. Interestingly enough, feminists involved in the Women's Liberation Movement in the 1960s and 70s wrote manifestos denouncing men who called grown-women 'girls'. They recognised this as an act to infantilise them, akin to how black men would be called 'boy' by white supremacists. In defiance, the 1969 manifesto of the Women's International Terrorist Conspiracy from Hell (WITCH) outlined the 'weak' position of what a girl was, and declared that a liberated woman was not a girl:

> WITCH: HOW DOES A GIRL BECOME A WOMAN? When she defines her own life and stops being controlled by her family, her boyfriend, or her boss. When she learns to stand up and fight for herself and other women—because she has learned that her problems aren't just her own. *All over the world, girls are growing up...*[30]

When Kathleen Hanna wrote "BECAUSE we are angry at a society that tells us Girl=Dumb, Girl=Bad, Girl=Weak", she was writing against girls' themselves being treated as dumb, obedient, passive. She argued that a girl who was resisting was still a girl, and she was fierce. This standpoint was to later call into question the role of feminism as "*Women*'s Liberation" and the invisibility of girl activism.

VALERIE'S GIRLS

Valerie Solanas has been a figure both celebrated and rejected in feminist communities for her extreme writing and actions. An American artist and writer, she was abused by her father as a girl and worked the streets for income in her adulthood. She sold her body, her conversation, and her mimeographed *SCUM* Manifestos to survive. Maurice Girodias of The Olympian Press, publisher of William Burroughs and Henry Miller, met Solanas on one of her street watches. Impressed with her charisma and offbeat views, he offered her a contract to write a novel based on *SCUM*. Instead she submitted her Manifesto, printed by Girdoias in 1968. After shooting and maiming Warhol, whose Factory Crowd she had uncomfortably been hanging around with as a participant and a bystander, Solanas was sentenced to three years imprisonment before spending much of the 1970s under psychiatric observation. The day she shot Warhol the United States Senator, Robert Kennedy, was also assassinated.

"I know why Valerie Solanas shot Warhol and not the President", runs Kathleen Hanna's anti-celebrity zine *My Life with Evan Dando Popstar*, "cuz everyone knows politicians are corrupt BUT Warhol was trying to act like he was questioning notions of fine art (transcendence, biological determinism) through... mechanical reproduction (the destruction of the master artist via technology) ONLY Warhol was FOR REAL exploiting certain people (workers) and certain revolutionary conceptions IN ORDER TO buy himself $2,000 black mammy cookie jars. Valerie Solanas shot Warhol to stop co-option and also to be funny."[31]

Solanas' manifesto does declare, "SCUM will destroy all useless and harmful objects— cars, store windows, 'great art', etc." but Hanna's writing sums up a well-loved tendency in zines: to be provocative. In an article called "Manifesto Destiny", Voice *Literary Supplement* journalist B Ruby Rich muses on contemporary feminist expressions of violence.[32] "The 1990s is the decade of the riot grrrls, the Lesbian Avengers, Thelma and Louise, the Aileen Wuornos case, and Lorena Bobbitt. There's something intensely contemporary about Solanas, not just in her act but in her text as well" she suggests.[44] For riot grrrls, already marred by accusations of man-hate and violence in the press, writing was an act of revolt and irony rather than violence. Even Solanas complained of being misunderstood in a 1977 *Village Voice* article, "It's just a literary device. There's no organisation called SCUM… I thought of it as a state of mind."[33]

The *SCUM* manifesto is a tract full of sci-fi nihilism (where society will be fully automated, no one would breed anymore, and the human race will eventually peter out), anti-capitalism, and a destruction of gender roles. The manifesto ironically subverts the usual gender psycho-babble, which equates women with irrationality and physicality. Instead this is displaced onto the male sex: "women, in other words, don't have penis envy; men have pussy envy".[34] *SCUM* has echoes of Frances Swiney's *The Awakening of Women*, from the first-wave suffragette movement in 1899, where medical and biological evidence is called upon to assert the innate superiority of the female sex.[35] "The Y (male) gene is an incomplete X (female) gene", writes Solanas in *SCUM*, having previously completed a year of graduate work in psychology at Minnesota, "the male is an incomplete female, a walking abortion".[36]

Bam. *SCUM* is not an easy read, whiplashing from ironic humour to unsettling biological determinism. Yet, the essentialism in unstable and there's a definite sense of questioning gender roles and consciousness, rather than innate biological warfare. Under Solanas' radar, male-females (eg passive and serving females) are as much of a target of derision, if not more, than men. "The conflict, therefore, is not between females and males, but between SCUM—dominant, secure, self-confident, nasty, violent, selfish, independent, proud, thrill-seeking, free-wheeling, arrogant females—who consider themselves fit to rule the universe— and nice, passive, accepting, 'cultivated', polite, dignified, subdued, dependent, scared, mindless, insecure, approval-seeking daddy's girls."[37] The 1992 *Riot Grrrl London* zine set up a similar battle between grrrls and bimbos/lame girlfriends and trashed the "every grrrl a riot grrrl" credo: "Hi Bitchgurl—I've got your number. You might be 14, you might be 49. I hear you laughing (all brittle and false) at riot grrrl. You are so fuckin' indoctrinated into male culture + ideology, you can only view other girls as competition".[38]

RESPONSIBLE, THRILL-SEEKING FEMALES

"Life in this society being, at best, an utter bore, and no aspect of society being at all relevant to women, there remains to all civic minded, responsible, thrill-seeking females, only to overthrow the government, eliminate the money system, institute complete automation and destroy the male sex." This quote opens up both the *SCUM Manifesto* and the *Right Now. Riot Grrrl Manifesto*, Karren Ablaze's re-drafted version of "Girlspeak" expanded into a four-page article and printed in the 1993 issue of *Ablaze!* Ablaze, who rejected the boy-led rebellion of the NOU as "their imagery and ideas smacked of militarism, machismo," instead figured "a Solanas-style attack on patriarchy would be fucking wild".[39]

In the resulting *Girlspeak Manifesto*, Ablaze declares: "We have provisionally formulated a plan which includes specific methods of working, and new notions of time and space." Her

LORENA BOBBITT SAYS

HELLO BOYS.

THE ONE AND ONLY
Bobbittbra

THE ORIGINAL KNIFE - PACKING PLUNGE BRA.
AVAILABLE IN SHARP, EXTRA SHARP & FUCKING LETHAL
brought to you by Daisy & Havoc

"Bobbitbra" from *Bad Attitude,* no 7, 1995.
Image courtesy of Rosanne Rabinowitz.

targets, which we can compare to *SCUM*, are the intersection of capitalism and patriarchy:

> SCUM will become members of the unwork force, the fuck up force; they will get jobs of
> various kinds and unwork. For example, SCUM salesgirls will not charge for merchandise;
> SCUM telephone operators will not charge for calls, SCUM office and factory workers, in
> addition to fucking up their work, will secretly destroy equipment.[40]

> Fuck things up at every opportunity. Stealing from shops and, if you're unfortunate enough to
> have a job, sabotaging your place of work are currently are primary methods of dismantling
> things as they are.[41]

In practice, many girls used their employment to steal resources and use office
equipment to put out their zines. Ablaze's manifesto is however one of the more radical
manifestos circulated through riot grrrl networks, providing actual strategies and calls for
direct action resistance.

From reviewing women's independent publications over the past four decades, Solanas
holds a certain cachet or intrigue for grrrls and their anarcha-feminist allies. Extracts from
SCUM were published in Robin Morgan's Women's Liberation Movement anthology,
Sisterhood is Powerful; the Matriarchy Study Group, London reprinted *SCUM* in the 1980s;
and A K Press issues several *SCUM* versions on their catalogues. Feminist 1977 punk zine,

JOLT, has a page dedicated to Valerie in proto-riot grrrl style: over cut and paste extracts from the manifesto and a shot of Solanas, author Lucy Toothpaste scrawled "Great Punks in History". "She was the person who shot Andy Warhol and founded SCUM, the Society for Cutting Up Men. Too bad she didn't play the guitar", runs the handwritten commentary.[42]

Graphic designer Erica Smith, editor and creator of the successful British zine *GirlFrenzy*, featured regular Solanas updates under the strapline "We unearth a rag bag of rants, raves and demands from yesterday's women and today's girls." She also fondly referred to *GirlFrenzy* as having a "crazy-Solanas-feminist-activist-angle" in an interview with grrrl zine writer Rachel Slampt of *Fast Connection*.[43] Musing on the SCUM heritage, Smith says, "I think it would be wrong to raise Solanas to the level of Goddess of riot grrrl, but she's an intriguing figure, all the more so because she has been discarded into the loony-bin of history." In terms of radical polemic, she adds: "Solanas wrote great rhetoric, so if you're writing a new female manifesto, like Karren Ablaze did, she is bound to be a reference point." Understanding that the appeal of *SCUM* lay in the literary wit and fantasy of the tract rather than any descriptive form of behaviour, Smith offers an alternative reading strategy for the manifesto: "if you read the 'man-hating' as an attack on patriarchal/capitalist structures, her arguments make a lot more sense", she suggests.[44]

SOME HEARTS ARE PAID TO DIE

> BECAUSE we hate capitalism in all its forms and see our main goal as sharing information and staying alive, instead of making profits or being cool according to traditional standards.[45]

To put it simply, capitalism is the economic relation based upon a class of people owning capital and the means of production, and another class selling their labour and time. It is an unfair and exploitative system, with workers alienated from what they produce, and women usually doubly-burdened, being unpaid primary care givers responsible for domestic chores as well as wage-earners. Capitalism is also built on the premise of infinite expansion and the exploitation of natural resources.

In the last quarter of the twentieth century, the West has entered a period of late capitalism, supported by intricate infrastructures of advertising and consumer culture. Prices are dependent on market competition and often big-business multi-nationals price smaller, independent businesses out of the market, whilst pushing a commodity-driven 'mono-culture' of ideas and lifestyles. This has resulted in the diminishment of radical presses and local bookshops no longer able to compete financially with larger chains, and the upsurge of independent social movement media through zines and websites producing alternative accounts of social critique, reportage and culture.

Zine veteran V Vale describes zines as a "grassroots reaction

Top: Picture of Red Chidgey, Ladyfest London 2001.
Bottom: Riot grrrl graffiti figure, Riot Grrrl Essex, 2002.
Image courtesy of Red Chidgey.
Opposite: SCUM spin-offs, *Girl Frenzy*, no 2, 1992.
Image courtesy of Erica Smith.

to a crisis in the media landscape". With dissent quickly turned into commodity by the powers-that-be, and broadcasting saturated with celebrities and product placement, what "was formerly communication has become a fully implemented control process", he says soberly.[46] The flipside of this rise in the consumer lifestyle is a recent turn to the individualistic activism trends of 'lifestyle politics' or 'consumer citizenship'; people express what they believe in through the products they buy or boycott.

Within riot grrrl, capitalism is recognised primarily for its psychic effects. Kathleen Hanna's manifesto *Burn Down the Walls that Say You Can't* introduces these ideas:

> Resist the temptation to view those around you as
> objects + use them...
> Resist the internalisation of capitalism, the reducing of people + oneself to commodities,
> meant to be consumed...
> Resist psychic death...
> Figure out how the idea of competition fits into your intimate relationships...
> Recognise your connections to other people and species...
> Close your mind to the propaganda of the status quo by examining its effects on you, cell by
> artificial cell.[47]

Slogans like "Girl Love" and "Don't let the J Word Jealousy kill Girl Love" are poetic ways of expressing that it is not cool for girls to be suspicious of each other and compete for men, and that they themselves were not accessories or commodities within the boy-dominated punk rock scene.

"Riot grrrl tries to fight capitalism by creating alternatives to commercial/capitalist culture and by not participating in the mainstream music industry and press", explains Belgium riot grrrl Nina Nijsten. Organising events and putting out non-commercial media is also seen as a form of DIY activism. Nina adds: "This "not-participating, not buying/consuming and creating alternatives" is a very important and powerful kind of activism. It shows you can be independent.[48]

In their entrepreneurial communities, riot grrrl DIY cultural production was a way to make music, films, and publish on girl's own terms, with their own voices:

> BECAUSE we need to talk to each other. Communication/inclusion is key. We will never know
> if we don't break the code of silence...
>
> BECAUSE in every form of media I see us/myself slapped, decapitated, laughed at,
> objectified, raped, trivialised, pushed, ignored, stereotyped, kicked, scorned, molested,
> silenced, invalidated, knifed, shot, choked, and killed...
>
> BECAUSE every time we pick up a pen, or an instrument, or get anything done, we are
> creating the revolution. We ARE the revolution.[49]

One of the biggest shake-ups riot grrrl initiated was the influx of girls becoming cultural producers for the first time. This was generally a historical anomaly. Whether in media industries or feminist 'kid-lib' movements, conventional roles for girls have always included being talked down to and educated at (hence the Huggy Bear 1993 7" single "Kiss Curl for the Kid's Lib Guerrillas"). From teen-magazines to girls' advocacy projects, girls are constructed by adults as being pre-political, acquiescent, boy-crazy and unfailing fans of popular culture.[50]

"Society embraces the 'girl power' mantra but refuses to equip girls with the means to attain it", runs an un-signed and untitled piece in the 2002 riot grrrl *KW* zine.[51] "Textbooks pay tribute to war and violence, but schools won't suitably educate students about safe-sex, reproductive health, self-defence and abuse. Diversity is the new media buzz word, but laws

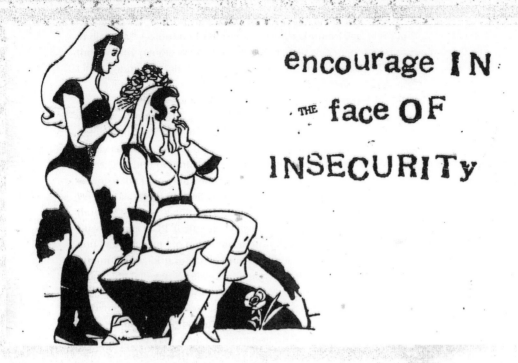

"Stop the J-Word", *Bikini Kill*, no 1, 1991.
Authored by Kathleen Hanna.

that maintain it are being dismantled while we watch BET. Young women are persuaded to follow instead of lead, and to become submissive consumers rather than involved creators of our culture and our destinies." Girls becoming involved creators and publishers contributed to what has been called the "girl zine explosion" of the early 1990s. It changed zine history forever.

GIRL ZINES

> 2002. I get a buzz when I receive letters and zines and music from girls I might never meet (and if you introduce yourself to a riot grrrl network, if you ask for help, information or whatever, you'll be acknowledged. There's no insider information or status); this recognition and mutual curiosity, this confidence I get from having allies, realising I'm not a freak for being a feminist like my society tries to make me/us believe; I'm so fucking alive and happy and inspired.[52]

Joining a radical history of self-publishing, zines are part of the "media for the misbegotten" stretching back to Thomas Paine and the pamphleteers of the eighteenth century.[53] Mail Art, Dada, Fluxus, and The Situationalist International anti-art movements of the twentieth century have all been heralded as precursors to zine cultures, alongside the chap-book produced poetry of the 1950s beat literary scene. As self-produced publications, riot grrrl zines have their own specific history within that of "fanzines", a term coined in 1941 by Russ Chauvenet for the new breed of science-fiction periodicals emerging from 1930s America. These science-fiction fanzines were produced on messy mimeograph machines—where typewrites created stencils on waxy paper which were then forced through with ink. With shifts in technology and the introduction of the photocopier, fanzines grew to encompass punk, football, TV and rap cultures, as cheap and democratic publications for the person on the street to convey their passions and interests.[54]

"Zine" entered into conversation alongside "fanzine" in the 1980s, as DIY cultures proliferated and moved away from the usual "fan" relation. Zine events, publications, review networks (such as resource guide *Factsheet Five*) and personal exchanges were growing, providing an infrastructure for a self-publishing boom. The tone also shifted. Whilst zines were always characterised by a certain personal voice, zine cultures in the mid-1980s turned towards more personal writing. This is in line with a greater push to the "autobiographical society". From *Oprah* to memoirs, reality TV shows to talk therapy, the confessional and the raw seemed to mark the cultural zeitgeist. Within girl zine cultures, the first-person experiences of growing up girl in a patriarchal society rocked the boat of what fanzine cultures had previously talked about. With zines about periods and sexual trauma starting to emerge through riot grrrl channels, "the girl zine revolution boiled over on the subcultural stove, occupying a unique intersection of art, protest, confession, and therapy", explains ex-riot grrrl zinester Jennifer Bleyer.[55]

Historically, fanzines are a male-dominated and straight (white) subculture. The 'angry grrrl' and 'homocore' zines of the late 1980s and early 1990s therefore marked a crucial turning point in fanzine history, with a rise in LGBTQ and girls authors taking their place and disrupting the usual order of things. "As to whether there was a queercore zine scene, I would say yes, and I have some awesome zines with rude names and way too many staples to back it up", says female comic artist Jeremy Dennis who published the queer and grrrl British zine listings zine *Qz* in the mid-1990s. In Britain, queercore came after riot grrrl (in America it preceded it with zines such as *JD, Sister Nobody*, and *Chainsaw*). "No-one really covered the DIY scene in the mainstream mags then, so the zines were where it was at," says Dennis. "In the days before the internet, zines were a crucial way for people who were into queercore, DIY, riot grrrl, whatever—but who didn't live in Brixton or Manchester—to actually meet enough of their own kind to have a good time."[56]

Front cover of *Promoting Queercore*, 1995.
Authored by Sister George.

NO RULES, NO LIMITS, NO CENSORSHIP

To understand the rise of girl zines in the early 1990s we need to think about what made them possible: machines. With the increasing availability of everyday technologies, such as photocopiers, home computers, and desktop publishing, more girls and young women started to self-publish. "Paper is easily accessible and requires no special skills," explains *Riot Girl London* zine editor Sophie Scarlet.[57] This is significant considering the usual limits on girl agency due to financial constraints—girls don't usually have money or access to resources (although of course this is determined by class position). As new technologies emerged, girls saw their chance to make use of the more defunct and cheaper modes to spread their words. "Make use of the most immediate and easy forms of communication. Those deemed obsolete", urged the

1992 London *Riot Grrrl* zine. "The Cassette. The Xerox. Quick dissemination of ideas and information."[58]

Nina Nijsten offers a definition of "zine" and how it is important within the riot grrrl movement:

> ZINE= self-made and self-published magazine or fanzine.
> Can contain anything, for example: reviews, interviews,
> political articles, stories, poetry, drawings, lyrics, profiles, etc.
> Most zines are sold very cheap at copy (+ postal) costs or
> given away for free at concerts, schools or in distros. Zines
> spread information. They are a revolutionary alternative to
> mainstream media. Every zine is a treasure. The personal
> is political. You decide what you write/make. No rules, no
> censorship, no limits.[59]

Grrrl art and poetry from *The Nerve*, 2001.
Image courtesy of Caroline Hamer.

"Why do i write zines? Cuz i believe that getting thru to ppl, getting yr opinions across, promoting good bands, talking about the 'underground', celebrating music and wimmin, talking about other ppl and cultures and scenes and not just yr own world is good (sic)" writes teenage zinester Linzey in her zine *Ornella*.[60]

Whilst each zine is ultimately a product of its creator's time, skill and agenda, common visuals occur within riot grrrl zines. Stock graphics include kid-photos (often the author as a young girl); reclamation of sexualised or soft porn images and sexual epithets (the marker pen use of 'BITCH', 'SLUT', and 'WHORE' on the page rather than the mid-drift); gig photos; cartoon imagery; pro (fat) girl drawings and comics; crossings out; and doodles of hearts, stars, anarchist As, and women's symbols. Images are ripped off from ephemerally sourced publications such as newspapers, magazines, store catalogues, old etiquette guides, and children's books.

It was a combination of punk meets girl feminism. "It was great to be part of a tradition I valued, which went back to *Sniffin' Glue* and beyond", says grrrl zine writer Rachel Kaye.[61] Punk fanzines were confrontational, messy and geared towards promoting bands and events within their own scene, with Mark Perry's *Sniffin' Glue* 1976–1977 and Jon Savage's *London Outrage,* 1976–1977 being influential trendsetters. Whilst riot grrrl zines share a common visual language with punk fanzines, such as cut 'n' paste amateurism and collage imagery, it was commonly translated through a girl vocabulary. "Through their appropriation of words and phrases traditionally used to disparage females yet avoided by many earlier feminists (eg *bitch, slag, hag, ladies, dyke, whore, just like a girl*) as well as their terms that connect females to anger (*mad, bitch, fierce, frenzy*), rebellion (*riot, revolution, war, trouble, Mohawk, cataclysm, homewrecking*), alienation (*nerdy, odd, geek, fiend, annoying, wrong*) and the taboo and perverse (*germs, pottymouth, cooties, pussy, rag, vampira*), grrrl zinesters demonstrate the strong influences of punk's unruly and insurgent aesthetics on many young feminists", writes riot grrrl feminist historian Mary Celeste Kearney.[62]

AN INTENSE WAY TO RESIST WHITE HETEROSEXUAL MALE HEGEMONY

Topics in grrrl zines run from the unspeakable to the pop cultural; from surviving incest to reclaiming 1980s pop stars. Coming out of girl's own lives, zines are a channel in which experiences of loneliness, abuse, and self-loathing are addressed in a safe environment. Studies show that most girls lose their self-esteem and confidence upon hitting adolescence, and instances of sexual abuse in female youth can be as high as effecting one in four girls.[63]

Girls have historically been encouraged to write diaries and letters, but these now turned up in their zines. Blurring the public and the private, young women published essays, dreams, diary extracts, childhood memories, interviews, factoids, rants, reviews, fiction, recipes, personal photographs, comixs, and re-printed letters. Frequent are the articles—often angry and painful—about body image worries, eating disorders, self-harm, abortion experiences, and acquiescing to sexual advances because it was just easier that way. Questions of sex and sexuality appear regularly within riot grrrl zines, as girls explore their hetero/homo/bi-sexuality and the ways in which to navigate the age-old sexual double standard that equates girls with sluts and guys as heroes if they sleep around or enjoy sex.

The feminist zine voice is both conversational and confessional. "And that stuff, the ways they made you feel so bad inside, if you say it to us we say yeah. It's true that that happened and they're shits and you, you are fine and you will come with us and we will grow", promises a riot grrrl call-to-arms.[64] One of the overwhelmingly emotional connections riot grrrl made to feminism was exposing patriarchy's effects on the psychic and sexual lives of girls, and refusing to be silent about sexual and emotional abuse.

"My friend Jenny, who does the zine *Not Sorry*, was the first person I heard use the term "political perzines", says Johanna of *YAWP!* and *Sisu* zines.

> I find it much more useful and interesting to read about politics, race, gender, and class, when it takes the form of an introspective personal essay. I hate zines that just reprint impersonal screeds about class war or whatever—even if I might agree with the viewpoint, I just can't make it through those articles. I really believe that change comes from interpersonal connections, not just reading theory.

An ex-riot grrrl, Johanna found about zines and grrrl culture through teen-magazines *Sassy* and *Seventeen*. She started making zines as a reaction to an abusive father and self-harming behaviours, and zines quickly become an important channel for her. "It's a powerful form of resistance: to say, I exist, I am this particular way, and my story is worth telling. I lay out these words and photocopy them and send them out because I think it's important for my stories to be heard, that I have something worth listening to. That's an intense way to resist white heterosexual male hegemony!" she says.[65]

For Karren Ablaze it was only with the onset of riot grrrl that she changed her writing style at *Ablaze*, allowing for the more personal and confrontational tone, that was the staple characteristic of riot grrrl personal zines (per-zines). It was a style which had to be pushed through: "If *Ablaze!* loses half its readership because of these changes, that's cool; the kind of kid who stops buying something because it's overtly feminist is not the kind of kid we wanna deal with" she says.[66]

BORING MEANINGLESS CRAP

A major site of struggle within riot grrrl zines was the 'beauty myth'; the valorisation and programming of thin, white, unachievable beauty standards which underpin the mainstream media and its advertising, and makes most girls feel ugly and alone (riot grrrl fights for fat liberation and the acceptance of all bodies and beauty types). To talk back to the mainstream society, images are stolen from magazines; cut up, collaged and detourened with slogans—a particularly popular way of clawing back at discourses presented in women's magazines and ads. Sometimes it's as simple as one *Riot Girl London* page; the background image is a fresh-faced blonde, hands held up to cheeks framing a perfectly red and white smile. Over this everyday, innocuous image—in deliberately singular, blocky, ransom-style newspaper cut-outs—are the letters "Boring Meaningless Crap". The tag-line reads "how many skinny airbrushed models can you stand?".[67]

Whilst sniper shots at the patriarchal consumer mainstream were a large part of the humour in riot grrrl zines, some participants quickly became frustrated with the formulaic agit-prop rants of grrrl zines. "I've had it up to here with all these zines I keep getting that just recycle and regurgitate the same one-dimensional ideas over and over" writes Anna Sin on her personal website in 1997 "I realise we all have to start somewhere (and believe me, my first efforts are completely embarrassing) but these zines are not even interesting, with really cliche articles like "Sexism Sucks" or "Girl Power Now", that offer nothing new to the discussion of feminism".[68]

Similarly, those who work within alternative literature and commix communities also regarded grrrl zines as lacking in sophistication or originality. Charlotte Copper, a long-term zine maker, author, and grrrl-ally, made acquaintance with riot grrrl at the 1996 Dirty Bird queer punk festival in San Francisco. She questions whether the riot grrrl agenda has become stifled by its own vibe. "I worry that riot grrrl is depressingly cliquey and faddish, and that if you are not part of the demographic, or don't represent the aesthetic, it can be nearly impossible to break in, or even to find it", she states.[69]

The mainstream media was also sceptical about these new grrrl zines. British music paper the *NME* alluded to them as a "load of biased ranting on some kind of new punk for women," and sister paper *Melody Maker* took a swipe at riot grrrl's apparent lack of feminist literacy through its publication stable.[70] "The best thing any riot grrrl could so is to go away and do some reading, and I don't mean a grubby little fanzine", it admonished.[71]

TWENTIETH CENTURY RIOT GRRRLS

> We need to learn about great woman in the past, because if we have come a long way we owe it to them, and they should not be forgotten. Knowing your past gives you more strength in the present and future. Knowledge is a powerful weapon… Male dominated society hides our history.[72]

Appreciating that one of the most radical ideas in history is 'a long memory', this section takes a look at proto riot grrrls from the past. Taking riot grrrl to broadly signify an attitude and a communication network, some direct parallels can be made between grrrl zines and the feminist fringe publications including the *Co-Operative Correspondence Club* magazine, *Cuntpower*, *JOLT*, *Shocking Pink*, *Girl Frenzy* and *Bad Attitude*.

THE COOPERATIVE CORRESPONDENCE CLUB 1935–1990

The first science-fiction fanzine *The Comet* may have been published by the Science Correspondence Club in 1930, but the first feminist zine was circulated by the all-female Cooperative Correspondence Club (CCC) a few years later. Never actually 'published', the *CCC* Magazine was set up as a means of group correspondence between women who met through the letters page of *Nursery World* magazine and were alienated in their roles as mothers and housewives. Adopting pen names, articles were handwritten and passed between members of the group, each woman adding a personal response before the issue was returned to the editor to be collated. The front covers were hand-stitched. This 'private magazine' served the proto-zine function of brining women out from isolation, enabling them to speak frankly about their lives, and exchanging ideas and support. Despite having

t. H.B.

C. C. C.

No. B. (VOL: III)

1ST JUNE.
1938.

an issue 'editor', like zines, no articles were ever altered. An ephemeral publication, most issues were dismantled after they were read. This magazine embodied a similar spirit to the secret 'girl lines of communication' which was to characterise riot grrrl publications and the girl zine explosion.

FEMALE ENERGY/CUNTPOWER *Oz* Magazine #29, July 1970

Developments in offset printing within the second half of the twentieth century made self-publishing an attractive option for anti-establishment thinkers. Publications such as *Oz, IT*, and *Frendz*, were put together by amateur writers with conscious misspellings, badly set articles, and hand-drawn headlines and graphics. Subject matter was confrontational and taboo, aiming to reach the new youth market emerging with the counter-culture. Germaine Greer, writing under the pseudonym Dr G, was a regular contributor to satirical magazine *Oz*, first published in Australia (1963–1969) by Richard Neville and Martin Sharp, and then transplanted to London (1967–1973). This publication was the subject of two obscenity cases. It was largely male-dominated and aesthetically misogynistic. With the rise of interest in *The Female Eunuch,* Greer was invited to guest edit the Female Energy issue of *Oz* (also known as the "Cuntpower" issue). Features include pieces by Kate Millet ("Sexual Politics: A Manifesto for Revolution"), "Conversations with Anais Nin", a male deodorant spray parody ad, DIY hand-knitted fashions for a "Cuntpower" bikini and "Cock Sock", and an editorial by Greer on "The Politics of Female Sexuality". The back cover featured a photo of a suffragette arrest. "Cunt is knowledge… skirts must be lifted, knickers… must come off forever. It is time to dig CUNT and women must dig it first" enthused Greer in a bout of female sexual pride and taboo-bashing which was also characteristic of later grrrl zines.[73]

JOLT, three issues, 1977

"But it's not really surprising if girls are still a bit uncertain about how to bust into rock. The very fact that rock, the so-called rebel culture, has always been completely male-dominated just goes to show once more that if there's one person more oppressed than a teenage boy it's a teenage girl."[74] Brainchild of the writer Lucy Toothpaste (aka Whitman), *JOLT* pre-empted riot grrrl concerns by over a decade with self-styled articles pressing for more girls in bands, diatribes against sexism and fascism in the punk scene, and cut 'n' paste revelry. Produced on photocopiers located in public libraries and department stores, *JOLT* sold for 25p and hoped to interrupt the male-dominated punk scene (such was the openness of punk culture then that members of The Slits went round to Toothpaste's house to introduce themselves after reading *JOLT*). Lucy was also an editorial member for the fanzine styled broadsheet *Temporary Hoarding*, the *Rock Against Racism* publication, and writer for *Spare Rib*, the national Women's Liberation Movement magazine. Toothpaste co-founded Rock Against Sexism (1979–1981), which shared riot grrrl goals of disrupting conventional gender stereotyping of female musicians and encouraging more women to learn instruments and join bands.

SHOCKING PINK 1981–1982 and 1987–1992

"Radical magazine for young women", launched as a reaction to the ageism in the Women's Liberation Movement. Described by ex-collective member and now *DIVA* journalist Louise Carolin as an "exploded publication", "part girl's magazine, part diary, part pen-pal correspondence" this was a professionally amateur magazine with a strong zine aesthetic.[87] Printed off-set onto newsprint, this magazine and had an irregular lay-out (part typeset, part hand-drawn) and a conversational, provocative writing style. Produced by a female youth collective, all under 25 years old, the 1981 editorial of the first issues

Front cover of *CCC* magazine, produced from 1935

—one of the first feminist zines ever made.

out now

PHIL GUY with the DE LUXE BLUES BAND

TEMPERANCE SEVEN
BOB DWYER'S HOT SIX
GEORGE WEBB DIXIELANDERS
CHARLIE CONNORS VINTAGE JAZZ
MONTY SUNSHINE   WALLY FAWKES

ROCKET 88

MAX COLLIE RHYTHM ACES

MICKY JUPP BAND

MONTY SUNSHINE JAZZBAND

GEORGE MELLY
with JOHN CHILTON'S FEETWARMERS

issue 8   90ᵖ

Shocking pink

- MAKING LOVE AND
MISCHIEF ★★

The Soho sisters . . . .

Top: Front cover of *Jolt*, no 2, 1977.
Image courtesy of Lucy Toothpaste.
Bottom: Front cover of *Girl Frenzy*, no 7, 1998.
Image courtesy of Erica Smith.
Opposite: Front cover of *Shocking Pink*, no 8. Image courtesy of Louise Carolin.

lays out its alternative status: "We feel like *Jackie Oh, Boy, Blue Jeans*, etc, don't give us a realistic impression of our lives. We want a magazine that looks at fashion, music, books, make-up, relationships, and all the usual subjects, but from an interesting and realistic viewpoint." *Shocking Pink* also combined proto-riot grrrl tactics of disinformation, sabotage, irony, and DIY advice, alongside a *Spare Rib* focus on news coverage and international politics. Teen-girl magazines, with their compulsory heterosexuality and talking down to girls, were primary targets of attack. Photo-stories were reworked for satirical effect and spoof advertisements warned, "Don't do it. *Jackie* isn't worth it." Published during Thatcher's prohibitive Section 28 Clause, *Shocking Pink* was a strong, visible image of lesbian youth and its allies.

GIRLFRENZY, seven issues, 1991–1998
GirlFrenzy emerged as a reaction to the lack of female comic artists in Britain and the staid status of the women's press. Creator Erica Smith described how a third way was needed between *Spare Rib* ("very po-faced and prescriptive") and *Cosmo* ("hypocritical consumption-fuelled rubbish").[75] Like *Ablaze!*, this publication sat more towards magazine than zine in terms of design and circulation (*GirlFrenzy* had an eventual print run of 3,000 copies per issue, was designed using PageMaker and Quark Xpress, and was printed off-set litho). In content it was off-beat and anarcha-feminist, "Made by women for people." Each issue featured an illustrated front cover and was compiled by an all-female contributor base of writers and comic strip artists. Regular features include manifestos, interviews with bands and comic artists, and "Sexist Shit of the Month columns". Existing pre-riot grrrl, *GirlFrenzy* was crucial in networking the emergent grrrl zine scene. Issue three was the first *GirlFrenzy* to cover riot grrrl, profiling K Records (who had been sending Smith release newsletters) and publishing Karren Ablaze's *Girlspeak* manifesto and Huggy Bear's *Her Jazz* missive before the *Melody Maker* cover story broke that autumn. Issue five contains a transcript of the ICA *Bad Girls* talk, which Karren Ablaze gave on British riot grrrl herstory. The "Demand the Supply" zine review pages of *GirlFrenzy* act as a barometer gauge of how girl zine and comix culture developed over the years. In an intersection of grrrl-core words, music and art, Smith also organised a series of events including spoken-word performances, art exhibitions and gigs for bands like Heavens to Betsy and Avocado Baby. The final issue of *GirlFrenzy* was published in book form by Slab-o-Concrete publishers. Sarah Dyer, creator of girl-zine directory *Action Girl Newsletter,* started her listings publication after picking up a copy of *GirlFrenzy#2* at a United Kingdom Comics Convention in 1992. As a tribute to Smith, Dyer also named her *Action Girl Comics* protagonist after the *GirlFrenzy* editor.

BAD ATTITUDE, eight issues, 1993–1997

"People told us we were mad to start a paper like this. After all, this is a time of 'backlash,' poverty, and world reaction when even the smallest gains of the last 20 years are threatened. But fuck it, there's enough pissed off women about to make this paper. As things go from bad to worse, its even more necessary to have a voice—to bring news of women fighting back internationally, a forum for suppressed ideas and struggles."[76] *Bad Attitude* was launched after radical publications *Shocking Pink* and *Feminaxe* folded. This anti-state, pro-fun, class struggle feminist newspaper was professionally printed and designed using desktop publishing technology. The *Bad Attitude* headquarters was an existing squat on Railton Road, London. Published in parallel to riot grrrl, *Bad Attitude* gave the movement regular coverage. Issue One features an article on riot grrrl: "riot grrrls are about creating a network/environment where women feel inspired enough to do something. And the confidence that comes from that. And unlike the traditional 'wimmins' music, unlike the passive consumerism associated with all these unmentionable les-fem record collection favourites... there are no rules to follow."[77] Grrrl punk music and fanzine reviews featured regularly, as well as an interview with Kathleen Hanna in issue three. In discussing the 1992 Washington DC Riot Grrrl Conference, the *Bad Attitude* interviewers draw attention to similar events throughout history. Comparisons were drawn to the Wild Wimmin's Weekend of 1990 where an old housing benefit office was squatted and workshops and events put on for the cost of donations. "Riot grrrl is just a new name—women have always been organising", declare the *Bad Attitude* girls.[78]

Front Cover of *Bad Attitude,* no 1, 1992–1993. Image courtesy of Rosanne Rabinowitz.

THE MAINSTREAM MEDIA

2003. Can we use the mainstream? Riot Girl London were recently approached by a film company making a documentary on the porn industry.... At first they wanted anti-porn voices, which we said we wouldn't provide, and they said okay come up with what you want—but the thing is, we all in the end felt too contrived, too reduced and too under threat of our views being ripped off to fit a nice package, that we didn't get involved. But I'm not totally against using the mainstream media. I think if we featured in something like J-17 it would be undoubtedly awful. I know I wouldn't be too happy with it as an accurate, politicised account of our aims. Yet I'm also weary of remaining subterranean. Riot grrrl would survive any media onslaught— it has in the past, it has now with sporadic press interest, and it will in the future. Cos it can't be grasped, destroyed. Used once and it keeps forever.[79]

Zines were crucial during the riot grrrl media black out and beyond to communicate, coordinate, and to empower girls individually and collectively. Zines "reflect the unfiltered personal and political voices of people from different backgrounds, countries and interests", says Austrian grrrl Elke Zobl, who runs the online zine culture archive project *GrrrlZines. Net*. "We don't get to hear those voices—especially those of girls and young women, women of colour, working class women, queer and transgender youth—in mainstream, adult-run media."[80]

As positive alternatives to music papers and teen-girl magazines, zines are a crucial way to bypass feminine stereotyping and misrepresentation. "I do fucking resent having to filter images of women, so I don't feel inadequate, ugly and wrong", writes an anonymous author in the 1992 *Riot Grrrl* London zine. "I never buy girls magazines as they are, in the main, like poison to me."[81] These DIY publications are important spaces for girls to showcase writing and art and to represent themselves, in a culture where 'experts' were taken off the pedestals and replaced by passion and DIY ethics. It doesn't matter if you are any good by traditional standards, 'just do it' is the unspoken motto of zine making. "Zines were also about control; control over image, content, and who they were distributed to", adds Rachel Kaye, editor of the eating disorder zine *Toast and Jam*.[82]

CUTTING THE TRIPWIRES OF ALIENATION

The zine scene was a semi-secret world between grrrls and their allies, and a space for healing, critique, outrage and bonding. "We're cutting the tripwires of alienation that separate girls from girls" declares the author of "Girl Power Explosion!" in the *Leeds & Bradford Riot Grrrl* zine, "we sneakily construct girl lines of communication". 'Grrrl love' was however put under some amount of stress as some girls talked to the media and others didn't. *Newsweek* is a case in point. Then 16 year-old Jessica Hopper, author of the long-running zine *Hit It or Quit It* and now professional journalist, collaborated with the press and felt the fall-out. "I started catching slag", Hopper told a *Seventeen* journalist, "I felt I was being personally attacked for talking to the media. I felt pushed out."[83]

In Britain, grrrls felt suspicious about dealing with the media. "We don't need them, we don't need the corporate press. We're truly independent, we'll pay our own way, we'll use our own channels. That's the whole point" argues Karren Ablaze's "Riot Grrrl. Right Now" manifesto. Attempts were made at collaboration. The *Leeds & Bradford Riot Grrrl* zine includes an article titled "What the NME didn't print" referring to a document supplied to journalist Liz Evans for the 6 March 1993 exposure feature on riot grrrl. "This article was written collectively by grrrls from Bradford and Leeds, at the request of a journalist from *NME*. It was written in a hurry to meet a deadline, but turned out to be waste of energy as they didn't print a word of it! They did include our PO Box address though and we have had around 40 letters so far…)", writes the grrrls in their zines, in testament to the ambivalent relationship riot grrrl had with the commercial press.

Riot grrrl fanzines record their communities and actions. They promote girl-core culture and cultural production with sincerity, not commercialisation. "So, for me, the educative function comes first, and the young tigress takes over", writes Karren in the *Leeds & Bradford Riot Grrrl* zine, "the path is so clear. I learned a load of stuff about publishing in a really informal way, and the thing for me to do is to pass on that power to the young women who want it".[84] As a point of comparison, the mainstream media is motivated by the need to sell copy. Fanzine cultures, and other social movement media and not-for-profit presses, exist for self-expression, communication, information-sharing, and entertainment. Fanzines usually only carry ads for DIY grassroots or independent projects, with flyers frequently traded between publications. Riot grrrl pitches its battle in the field of outsider grrrl culture, but has an uncomfortable relationship to the mainstream: part celebration, part rejection, part blatant theft.

ZINES AS CRITICAL PLACES

A REVOLUTIONARY PLAN

Michelle + me → inspired by riot grrrl fanzines → write own fanzine → read by those people who haven't already done fanzines → they do their own fanzines → creates underground movement unspoilt by the media → word is spread by word of mouth, fanzines, music, poetry, <u>action</u> → we become our own "pop stars", "authors", we are all "famous" → each individual's self-esteem improved by contact w/like minded people → we go out and inform others → new confidence improves all parts of our lives → no longer bow down to the whims of others → a new equality, etc.[85]

Whilst early grrrl zines called themselves 'fanzines', most rejected the conventional 'fan' status. Zines were seen as places where anyone could be an author and co-create riot grrrl through ideas and dialogue. "Lets get this writ at the start. Huggy Bear go with Kill Rock Stars + Kill Authors too. Non-passive reading—like a heckler with a brain as well as a tongue + a beer" declares 1993 Huggy Bear zine *Reggae Chicken* with characteristic word flair. "There is no proper, no real, no single meaning. Just ink + paper. This is the start of our conversation. Join in."[86]

Zines were flagged up as importance places where criticisms and exchange would take place, crucial if stagnation or cliques were to be avoided. "It is too easy for our doctrines to turn into dogma and RGSN [Revolution Grrrl Style Now] restrictions rather than as meaningful interactions" warns Tobi Vail in *Bikini Kill#2*, produced after the riot grrrl Summer of 1991. "We must not let the precedents we set ourselves distract us from the very things that drove us in the first place and it is with this in mind that I encourage girls everywhere to set forth their own place in the world, in relation to their own scenes or whatever, rather than to simply think about ours."[87]

THE HIVE-MIND THINKING OF MOST OTHER GRRRLS

This appeal was only partly met. Riot grrrl zines are characterised by multiple "riot grrrl is…" manifestos are earnest disclaimers that no one girl can speak for the movement. Yet, as already discussed, there was repetition within riot grrrl fanzines and quick rants failed to shape into sustained critiques or strategies. Early riot grrrl slogans were drawn upon without an understanding of the political aspects behind the refashioned "sisterhood" calls. As a political 'social movement' riot grrrl did not exist, but as an inspiration and incitement to politicisation and self-empowerment, especially amongst isolated female youth it was vital.

The problems of riot grrrl were played out in zines. Here, young women would exercise the voice they felt was being marginalised within riot grrrl networks: "I cruise the riot grrrl folder on AOL where I've been accused of "focusing too much on race" and otherwise disrupting the "race neutral" (ha ha) feminist illusions of many of the board's participants. It's slightly amusing, if almost most definitely disturbing: I mean, as resident race agitator, I'm cast in the role of an 'outsider' rocking the boat. Past discussions of race issues have been cut short as girls and women bemoaned the 'fighting' as bad for grrrl unity, meaning, racial difference is bad for grrrl unity" writes Mimi Nguyen in Punk *Planet#28*.[88]

Within the songs and zines of 'famous riot grrrls', racism was broached through the target of the domineering 'white boy'.[89] Lauren Martin wrote her reaction to these race politics in her zine *Might As Well Live*: "and yeah some of you say 'we are out to kill white boy mentality' but have you examined your own mentality? Your upper-middle class girl

"What the NME Didn't Print", *Leeds and Bradford Riot Grrrl*, 1993. Image courtesy of Karren Ablaze.

WHAT N.M.E. DID NOT PRINT...

IT'S A GRRRL!!!

The decision to write this was reached after much discussion and debate, we were scared of being misrepresented and exploited. However we realised if we didn't do it, that it would get done anyway, by people who don't know what's happening.We are sick of the Riot Grrrl thing being distorted.We want to set the record straight.We decided to submit this rather than do an interview so that we were the ones who were in control.We realised it was a chance to reach large numbers of isolated girls and hope this will give them the confidence to do something themselves.We don't want to be written about on a superficial level, or judged merely by our appearance.Whilst we don't want to ignore the debate on sexism in the music industry, we feel our energy is better spent on positive, practical, actual DOING stuff, rather than getting dragged down into bitching battles.If you don't see us talking theory all day it's because we're too busy out there in bands, doing fanzines and working behind the scenes for each other.Something practical and active rather than just passively reading what other women and girls are doing in the music press.We want to support and empower them in their ventures.

Riot Grrrl is not some shallow invented by consumerism fad which will disappear with the backlash.'Ironic sexism' may prevail in the music press, but excuses attempting to insult our intelligence won't wash with us.Only empty things happen fast, we're growing, we are underground and we're denying them power by not communicating.Riot Grrrl has no centre or leaders, for us the independent press has been more beneficial - our own 'zines, Maximum Rock & Roll and Profane Existence give grrrls space, an idea which has been fermenting and evolving for years.

GRRRL TALK!!!

Riot Grrrl was not created by a British music journalist, but grew out of the thriving punk/D.I.Y. underground in the U.S. Words to describe women's actions are always turned into derogatory terms, i.e. feminist and already the grrrl word is being distorted for us.The term Riot Grrrl has been useful to us so far.It has enabled us to form friendships and networks and take action where we feel it is necessary.We are aware that it is already in use and that people have pre-concieved ideas about its meaning.We are trying to make music, events and situations that fit in with our lives, experiences and politics, rather than us having to copromise to meet the standards of an industry.If that's a sin so be it!It's not just about gender, but power relationships based on gender, race, sexuality or abilities.We are just choosing to approach it from our own angles and the thing that most of us have in common is being female and into loud music!

GRRRLS JUST WANNA HAVE FUN!!!

Any girls can start gangs anywhere and you can also do stuff by yourself - challenging the gender roles that would strangle us.We are questioning the ideas we've been brought up with, but it's so obvious, so unthreatening to us.The threat is in the eyes of the threatened.The threatened are the power holders and they've got reason to be scared.Turning it around.Power to the powerless.Now that the press has got hold of the name and is trying to turn it into a movement in much the same way they tried to kill off Punk, our tactics may include changing our name to confuse those in power.Also to resist the temptation of creating scenes and personality cults, off which the mass

PROFANE EXISTENCE/c/o Active Distribution/BM Active/London WC1N 3XX.Bi-monthly/1 issue 90p ppd./make M.O.'s payable to J. Elliot.

mentality? what would you say if I said I wanted to kill that mentality too? Would you say: 'what about sisterhood'?!"[90]

Non-white girls were told race didn't matter (that to bring it up was divisive), and white and non-white girls alike told that their characters and ways were 'obnoxious' or 'loud' if they came from working class or poor backgrounds (a situation confronted by Erika Reinstein in her open letter "Dear Upper-Middle Class White Girl" in the zine *Channel Seven*).[91] Zine-making does require some social privileges: riot grrrl happened in leisure time. To make zines and write manifestos you need the time, confidence, and resources; attributes afforded to middle and upper class girls more than working class girls. Despite the rote list of oppressions riot grrrl manifestos and zines claim to protest against, including racism and classism, systems and structures of oppressions were rarely tackled in zines beyond the occasional grrrl admitting that she was white and privileged and working on it. It often fell to non-white people to act as confronters and educators within their communities, a problem with a long history within feminist movements, which are white-dominated. "When 'famous' riot grrrls got called out on racial bullshit, they were defended vociferously by the hive-mind thinking of most other grrrls. White privilege trumps Revolution Grrrl Style Now! I guess", reflects ex-riot grrrl Johanna.

HER HEROES AREN'T GONE

Yet even with hard critique, heroes don't die easily. *Her Heroes Aren't Gone: Letter to Kathleen Hanna*, an Australian zine produced in 2001, demonstrates the author's lasting impression of Hanna as a "real girlhood punk hero": "Kathleen, I KNOW you weren't the 'founder' of riot grrrl, I know there's no central spokesperson. But let's both be honest for just a minute and admit that you, in your desire for revolutionary change, somehow somewhat unwillingly become an unofficial spokesperson for riot grrrl.™"[92] *Her Heroes Aren't Gone* records the author's experience of riot grrrl ("I didn't find out about you from a DIY punk fanzine, Kathleen, it was from a story in a mainstream magazine") and the commodification of the culture's discourse in mass culture ("And now it's a meaningless marketing tool—I still can't believe it"). A common tactic within zine critique is to use the rhetorical device of an 'open letter'. In this vein, Kylie stages her criticism of some of the early strategies of riot grrrl, such as forming girl-only mosh pits, in a missive "directed" to Hanna herself. "But, I wasn't wearing rose-coloured glasses, that much is true. I mean, you made the boys stand to the back and that I could just never get cos 'feminine' doesn't necessarily have to mean peaceful, right?" she says.

In spring of 1996, Hanna issued *The Official Kathleen Hanna Newsletter* to the back-catalogue of people who had been posting her personal letters. "I wanna let you know that I do read absolutely every letter I get it's just kind of impossible for me to write each one personally any more", she writes in her introduction. "So my plan is to answer some of the most frequently asked questions from the letters I get and also to just pass on some stuff I think is really important."[93] The 'newsletter', actually a mini-zine, is both ironic towards the usual fan relation and sympathetic to the girls writing to her for advice. The cover image lays out the joke intended in the title; Hanna sits with bouffed up evening hair, lights trained on the fluff of the feather bower draped around her shoulders, and a quarter-turn pose favoured by studio photographers. Her eyes are half-closed, giving her a dopey, caught off guard look. There's no doubt about it, if this image was real, it would be a celebrity reject-photo for sure.

Through this image Hanna spoofs glamorous, 'perfect' stars. In the 16-page A5 newsletter, hand-written in a conversational style and including Hanna's illustrations, the author answers letters and questions she's been sent. She outlines the different ways to get help if you're an abuse survivor, lists resources for queer grrrls, issues the "riot grrrl is whatever each girl/woman/lady makes it out to be thru her own ideas and involvement" reminder (along with a image of a microphone-holding guy posing a question to a girl and a "power to the people" slogan), and passes on information about the racist (and, at that point, death-row) imprisonment of journalist and Black Panther radical Mumia Abu-Jamal.[94] Hanna suggests raising awareness and money for Mumia's Legal Defense Fund through resources and channels already at hand or accessible to girls—such as a "bake sale, a benefit show, a garage sale". Whilst direct action tactics are not usually discussed in riot grrrl zines, information and consciousness-raising are seen as vital.

INFORMATION PRIVILEGE

"You know how the zine/punk/activist community is always using the word 'privilege'? White privilege, male privilege, rich privilege, etc?" asks 2002 Chicago-based zine *Rebel Grrrl*. "That also refers to information. I've met girls who don't even know that there is such a word as 'feminism' forget the movements' history. Once you have information, get it out to people who don't know about it (information you receive is and becomes a personal responsibility, information privilege)."[95]

"Riot grrrl was instrumental in demonstrating to a new generation that you didn't have to know all the right words and to have read an approved booklist to call yourself a feminist", says Cazz Blase of *Aggamengmong Moggie*, "it gave the potential for girls/women to do feminist activism in a back to basics way".[96] Within zines practical tips were passed around on creating feminist girl cultures, such as making fanzines, recording music, sewing cloth menstrual pads, building websites, and booking shows. Feminist history and theory was not completely jettisoned. A strategy of sharing information and promoting feminism was to include book reviews and suggested reading in riot grrrl fanzines.[97] Feminist authors such as Kathy Acker, Karen Finlay, Dorothy Allison, Monique Wittig, Luce Irigary, Christine Brook, bell hooks, and Audre Lorde have been cited within grrrl zines as literary and ethical influences. 'Writing the body' or *l'écriture féminine* has also been cited by Kathleen Hanna and Huggy Bear members as influential strategies of feminist polemic, depending on foregrounding women's embodied lived experience and non-linear writing techniques.[98] This feminist literacy wasn't necessarily name-checked in the author's writing style, vocabulary or approach. "I used any language" says Caroline Hamer who was involved in riot grrrl between the ages of 14 to 18. "In later years I was influenced by Helene Cixious and Virginia Woolf's feminine ecriture but by that time I was institutionalised in university. Riot grrrl existed outside of that."[99]

TIME BOMBS DISGUISED AS THICK LETTERS

"Riot grrrl was a lifeline. When I was first exposed to riot grrrl [through a mix-tape of grrrl music a friend had given her at age 14] I was recovering from an eating disorder and it totally blew my mind", says riot grrrl zinester Rachel Kaye. "It was something that gave me courage and anger; it allowed me to see what I was doing to myself in a political/feminist way." From moving out of isolation, girls and young women then begin to self-organise and act against their oppression, often linking what they find through riot grrrl with broader social struggles. Rachel continues, "riot grrrl was a spiral of connections; music led to queer theory, led to civil rights, led to political feminism, led to animal rights, led to zines, led to films, led to friends".[100]

Behind the production and consumption of zines lay intricate webs of personal correspondences. As part of the 'sisterhood' sense of camaraderie, girls sent decorated parcels, letters, mix-tapes, flyers and friendship books (homemade pen-pal booklets) through the post to each other. Emily White, the *Chicago Reader* journalist who authored one of the most articulate and considered articles on riot grrrl in its early years, describes the crucial role of zines with riot grrrl networks: "girl fanzines, or zines, are time bombs disguised as thick letters" she says, speaking of both the personal and intimate style of the zines and their radical content.[101]

"I used to write to a lot of people, all grrrls", explains Sophie Scarlet, co-founder of the Riot Girl London chapter and now web-designer. "It was exciting knowing that there were all these girls out there in bands, writing zines. Plus realising I was bi and getting letters from a girl. It was pretty intense."[102] These postal-networks also helped girls who lived in more rural areas to feel part of the movement. With the rise of the networked society, on-line messaging has largely replaced paper forms of exchange, yet the importance of communication remains. "Email and website contact was essential", recalls Caroline Hamer, co-founder of the 2001 Central England Chapter and now teacher. "It opened my horizons and allowed for some incredible friendships. It let riot grrrl happen."[103]

Media exposure and informational communication technologies certainly accelerated the movement, but zine distros and review zines were crucial in the more general 'girl zine explosion' of the early 1990s, maintaining communication during the media blackout period, and ensuring the subsequent longevity of riot grrrl networks.

CORPORATE ZINE

By the mid-1990s, riot grrrl was pronounced dead in the commercial press. The movement continued to survive outside of the media gaze through its own momentum as fringe-lit feminism. Circulating on the margins of journalism, popular culture, autobiography and academia, this marginal position was chosen as an offensive tactic by riot grrrl authors and activists. "This is where the significance of riot grrrl comes in. It's not easy to infiltrate the system, take over the mainstream, and change society's attitudes towards women. So you start at a place where you are allowed control of yrself, yr music, yr attitude, yr words, yr opinions—a place where anyone with something to say can make their voice heard. You start underground."[104]

This underground was endorsed by American teen-girl magazine *Sassy*.[105] A pioneering magazine put out by a feminist editorial team, *Sassy* (1988–1994) addressed its young readers on a street level and dealt realistically with controversial issues such as abortion, rape, feminism, AIDS, same-sex desire, and birth control. The general aim was to shatter the model of consumer-based, boy-mad teenage rags that have defined girl-magazines since the beginning of the twentieth century. This left the magazine vulnerable to conservative advertisers

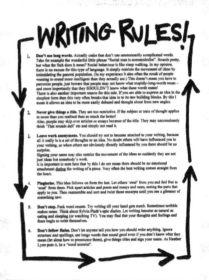

Top: "Educate", *Scratch the Surface*, 2002.
Image courtesy of Caroline Hamer.
Bottom: "Writing Rules", *Scratch the Surface*, 2002.
Image courtesy of Caroline Hamer.
Opposite: "Writers", *Tigerheart*, no. 4, 2001.
Image courtesy of Jessica Dainese.

Sylvia Plath

Go on now, go. Walk out the door. Don't turn around now, he's no use to you any more

Writers

"Nothing stinks like a pile of unpublished writing" (Sylvia plath)

"Most writers had unhappy childhoods" (Judith krantz)

"I walk down the street got the sun in my hair/ got my route laid out and my mind is clear/ got my pen and my pad, gonna get it all down/ 'cos words are a road that lead out of town" ("ain't no rules", transvision vamp)

"Writers are high on the charts when it comes to suicide, nervous breakdowns, pathological depression, and stomach ulcers. Years ago, I read a list of Nobel Prize-winning authors who died of alcoholism. Uncovering emotion so that the reader resonates demands a lot of digging on a writer's part, the removal of memory blocks inscribed "Do not remove". (···) And from Virginia Wolf, "I feel certain that I am going mad." Byron, Shelley, Melville, and Coleridge all suffered from various forms of manic depression and mood depression. Teutonic rage is usually that of an infant, which is why we call it infantile omnipotence. A wise person once told me that writer's block was mother sitting in the unconscious with a blue pencil. I'll buy that" (Nancy Friday. From *the Power of Beauty*)

withdrawing their revenue (Germaine Greer reports that "the magazine was in profit for only one of the seven years that [Christina] Kelly edited it, mainly because advertisers would not buy space in a magazine that was perceived as 'a repository of kiddie porn'").[106]

The magazine was influential on zine-makers at the time. "I was responding to the pleasure principle of *Sassy*", says Debbie Stoller who aimed for a "*Sassy* for grown-ups" in her third-wave feminist magazine *Bust*. "*Sassy* used language girls of all ages used, made the right cultural references, it made me laugh and feel good about being a girl."[107] Whilst *Sassy* offered a careful coverage of riot grrrl, its position as a mainstream magazine touting an underground culture was controversial. *Sassy*'s love affair with riot grrrl began when editor Christina Kelly hired Bratmobile guitarist Erin Smith as an intern in 1991, after picking up a copy of her zine *Teenage Gang Debs*.

Reviews of *Jigsaw, Girl Germs, Riot Grrrl*, and *Gunk* appeared in *Sassy*'s "Zine of the Month" column in the early 1990s, alongside the zine creator's full contact details. The magazine's readership was three million. The effect of spotlighting a grrrl DIY zine culture to a mass audience was overbearing. In an interview with Susan Corrigan for British style paper *i-D*, Kelly admitted, "I wasn't out to write about the riot grrrl movement. I knew the girls who were doing it and if they sent me their fanzine I would write about it, saying it was a riot grrrl fanzine. Or if a band had a riot grrrl 'message' I would say so. I really like their bands and their zines, and put them into my column knowing our readers would be into it, and they were."[108] Hundreds of girls seeking information about riot grrrl, especially those who were young, not already involved in a subculture, or who lived in isolated areas, flooded riot grrrl zine producers with their letters and requests.

Overwhelmed, Tobi Vail records the zinesters perspective in *Jigsaw #5*, "I didn't ask to be in their stupid magazine, I mean, I don't even know who sent them a copy. Secondly, I didn't make *Jigsaw* for the general public, I made it because I was going crazy and something had to be done." *Sassy* received negative feedback from girls within the scene who felt that the riot grrrl exposure was exploitative. The response of the popular teen-girl mag was to continue featuring the movement, but with a self-conscious edge; Erin Smith was asked to guest write the article "Co-Opting DC Scene Gossip for Our Own Profit" and the spine of the December 1992 issue of *Sassy* reads "Corporate Zine".[109]

Throughout riot grrrl, the idea of putting out a mainstream media production for female youth had been discussed by different groups. LA riot grrrls Dani and Sisi, of *Housewife Turned Assassin* zine and the Revolution Rising collective, were initially interested in putting together a public access cable show.[110] An advertisement ran in the British zine *Twinkle Eye Fizzy* trying to recruit girls to be part of a 'teen zine' project: "the anti-glossy magazine—it will be about honest stuff coming from real girls with a feminist slant that is easy to relate to… talk about feminism and riot grrrl, but we will not make it the focal point of the whole thing—the point is to write positive articles which will hopefully open minds and eyes, and not talk shit that's all so wrong, and bad for teens to feed into".[111] Nothing has yet come of these ideas and self-defined riot grrrl projects remain grassroots, although hundreds of grrrl-inspired media projects have taken place.

That there has never been an *official* periodical for the riot grrrl network is itself significant. In accordance with the riot grrrl ethos of decentralised organisation (creating a community without leaders or media stars), the importance of the network has always been for each girl to define what riot grrrl means to her, from her own place in the world. The *Riot Grrrl* zines of 1991, produced by Molly Neuman and Allison Wolfe as a weekly free mini-zine in Olympia, Washington, only inadvertently spawned the name of the movement when the press became involved. But the last issue of *Riot Grrrl* did come with a suggestion which was to be instrumental in the future of the movement: "Those of us who have been working on these issues might not do them again, but this name is not copyrighted. So take the ball and run with it!"

The left-field politics of anti-copyright is an important aspect of riot grrrl; visually, textually and philosophically. With anticopyright permissions frequently written into grrrl zines themselves, it's expected that zines will be disseminated by their information being copied and passed on. These tactics of poaching and dissemination are encouraged by the editor of Kablooie: "Fuck Copyrights. [We] deeply feel it is [our] obligation to convey important information to you. Whether this important information comes from a published author or your pet goldfish doesn't matter a bit. If bureaucracy did not exist and people could actually get things done, maybe we could meticulously contact each and every one of [our] sources. But probably not."[112]

British riot grrrl Caroline Hamer explains her working processes behind the Central England *Riot Grrrl* zine *The Nerve* and hints at some of the broader activist thinking behind the practice of plagiarism: "I used my computer and scanner, glue and scissors. I ignored any copyright and was hugely influenced by an essay on crimethinc about plagiarism—in other words I stole from a variety of sources."[113] Crimethinc (crime-think) are a situationalist influenced collective based in America, who produce information to inspire and provoke. They regularly encourage people to steal ideas in order to challenge intellectual property rights and to reorganise and revitalise thought by putting it into new contexts.[114] "And, as we stole ideas from numberless sources, there's no copyright on this manifesto—steal any or all of it for your own subversive purposes", wrote Karren Ablaze in "Girlspeak". Over ten years later this manifestos was still being circulated at the Ladyfest London event of 2002.

DISTRIBUTION & DISSEMINATION

2003. Zines are ephemeral objects: you can't buckle down exactly when they were made, maybe even who by; they are little pods and seed that circulate through bags, post, friends, space and they germinate. They get saved, traded, cut up, resourced and permeated. Sometimes a perfect zine will ooze out suggestions and hooks; my heart surges and I'm propelled to my desk to carry on.[115]

Riot grrrl literature slips "below critical radar" of the reading public, the mainstream press, and the academics.[116] As a product, riot grrrl writing is ephemeral and erratic.

"There is an organic, germy thing we can unsatisfactorily call an underground spreading tendrils in random, implicit, unnatural ways" writes a 1993 Huggy Bear zine *D-Generate*. "And exploding epicentres are blooming in previously ignored towns and cities. Fuck centralisation. Viva letter writing. Have love will travel."[117]

It is difficult to map the riot grrrl zine underground. Zine titles appear as serials for years or they end after one issue. Zines are left undated, unsigned, and unpaginated and the traditional notion of authorship is trashed. There's no market-approved barcode or slick glossy format to appraise. This writing doesn't come ready to consume in neat packages, digested thoughts, standard English, or with a regularised publishing schedule and subscriptions list. Issues were printed in low numbers, usually from ten to a 1,000 copies. Alternative and creative distribution channels are crucial to this broader fringe-lit scene; zine pages get blown up and wheatpasted over advertisements, slipped into teen-mags and diet books, and left in bathrooms and on bus-seats for chance readers to pick up. Grrrl zines were often communication by subterfuge.

THIS IS A RIOT GRRRL PRINTING PRESS

Soon girls realised that this network needed bringing together. A riot grrrl record and zine distribution service was first suggested in *Bikini Kill #2*, but with the band busy with tours, it wasn't until spring of 1993 that the Riot Grrrl Press launched. At the helm were Washington, DC, organisers, Erika Reinstein and May Summer (and the press re-located with the girls, from Washington to Olympia and finally, Chicago). A Riot Grrrl Press flyer, distributed at shows and through mail-outs, outlined the practical, historical and activist benefits of the project. These included; making the zine available to people outside of the punk rock scene, networking with other radical activist groups and feminists nationally and internationally, helping out young women who might not have the time and money to get their work printed and distributed, promoting works of fiction and poetry, providing access to back-issues of zines, and acting as a central place of information about different riot grrrl chapters. The idea was that a strictly "secret" communication network was elitist. "Hopefully networks would be created through Riot Grrrl Press which would encourage everyone not to be a passive consumer but an ACTIVE PARTICIPANT in the dialogue happening in our communities" writes Reinstein in *Channel Seven*. Her call seemed answered as a sister Riot Grrrl Press was also launched by Trish Kelly in Vancouver, Canada.[118] Zines were made from 'flats' sent in by zinesters, and catalogues produced to advertise their stock.

Several other national projects were also happening to connect girl writers. GERLL (Girls Empowered Resisting Labels and Limitations) was started by Sarah Wood in Chicago as a mail-order distribution service. Kristy Chan (of *Tennis and Violins* zine) put together the *Riot Grrrl Review*, faithfully reviewing zines she was sent printed with the creator's contact details. The motto of this project was "Queerpositive Progirl Boyfriendly". *Riot Grrrl Review* lasted five years from 1994 to 1999 before Chan stopped and archived issues on-line.[119] With the rise of grrrl zines, pioneering zine review zine *Factsheet Five*, then edited by R Seth Friedman, added a 'grrrl' entry to their classification system in 1993.[120] Sarah Dyer's *Action Girl Newsletter*, a girl-zine directory listing girl projects and resources, was also instrumental in networking girl zine authors. Starting as a one-page listing sheet in 1992, the project eventually grew so large after the "girl zine explosion" that Dyer was receiving up to 25 submissions each day. She quit publishing in 1996, reckoning her job at networking the emerging scene was well accomplished.[121] Grrrl-influenced zine projects proliferated in the years during and after riot grrrl, including non-profit zine distribution services such the American GrrrlStyle! Distro, (her)Riot of Sweden and the British Manifesta.

OUR WAY, OF COURSE: RIOT GRRRL PHILOSOPHY

Riot grrrl also migrated on-line in the role of archival and information centres, prompting a rash of European chapters meeting in real time. The riot grrrl Europe forum was launched in 2000 and serves as a site for geographically isolated women to converge and reclaim riot grrrl identity. Riot Grrrl Europe has been a central point for several European Ladyfests, co-founder Hilde states:

> What do we want to reach with riot grrrl here I mean, do we take the United States as an example, or are we doing it our way? OUR WAY, of course!! The situation riot grrrls were in, back in 1991 in the United States isn't comparable to the situation here at all. Europe consists of so many countries with so many cultures and languages (which of course, only enriches the scene), but I guess unity is an even bigger issue to us.[122]

As a way to communicate between chapters, a Riot Grrrl Europe message board was launched and the *Riot Grrrl World Newsletter* compiled; each issue a girl from a different country gathers and edits materials. Part of the new-millennium riot grrrl was the inclusion of boys, a greater turn to issues such as trans-visibility, and a greater exploration of allied social movement struggles such as anti-globalisation and environmentalism. The writers have turned from anger and poetry, to critique and exploration (building on the work riot grrrls had already done).

"Riot grrrl is for me a sort of autonomous updated feminism, located mostly in subcultures such as punk but directed at young girls, queers and women," explains Belgium grrrl Nina Nijsten about her involvement in European grrrl and Ladyfest projects. From reading about riot grrrl, Nina became active in the scene after Dutch riot grrrls from the Bunnies on Strike collective handed her a flyer at a gig. "Riot grrrls express their thoughts, stories and ideas freely. Other can relate to these writings, be influenced and start writing too. Riot grrrls pass on feminist ideas and anti-capitalist criticism in youth subcultures and empower others girls/queers/boys with their writings. You can hardly ever read about the topics addressed in riot grrrl writings in the mainstream press, certainly in such an honest personal way" she says. Zines also tackle issues for teenage-girls rarely addressed in the education system: "Riot grrrls fill a void of addressing contemporary feminist issues (for example, menstruation, abuse, street-harassment, self-defence, gender roles and homophobia) that aren't spoken about in other media or at schools", explains Nina. "The combination of DIY and feminism assures women and girls to be self-confident and start writing themselves, something that women/girls are usually not encouraged to do (at least not in a professional way). So a next generation of female writers can be born and develop."[123]

In 2001 Greta, a certified nursing assistant living in Tennessee, launched the Riot Grrrl Online site to help nurture the history of the movement. This site contains zines archives, message boards, download areas, and an interactive map where grrrls can pin-point their location to represent the geographical spread of the movement. The messageboard currently has over 1,300 subscribed members. "I don't believe in labels, but I really believe in the riot grrrl philosophy" says Greta about her long-term involvement in riot grrrl as a "girl positive movement". For her, riot grrrl is "about speaking out about women's issues and feeling good about yourself as a person".[124] Critics might wonder whether riot grrrl was an attempt at building a radical grrrls culture or individual self-empowerment. The answer

Top: "Let's Smash Patriarchy", *Flapper Gathering*, no 4, 2004.
Image courtesy of Nina Nijsten.
Bottom: Flyer for Riot Grrrl Press, outlining the importance of riot grrrl writing and distribution.

SiX reasons WHY RG Press is iMPortant

★ RIGHT ★ NOW! ★

bi, Marika may & erika

★ self representation. We need to make ourselves visible without using mainstream media as a tool. Under the guise of Helping us spread the word, corporate media has co-opted & trivialized a movement of angry girls that could be truly threatening & revolutionary. & even besides that it Has distorted our views of each other & created Hostility, tension, & jealousy in a movement supposedly about girl support & girl Love. In a time when riot grrrl Has Become the next Big trend, we need to take Back control & find our own voices again

xoxoxoxoxoxoxoxoxoxoxoxoxo

★ RG Press will make ♀'s zines available to people who wouldn't necessarily get them otherwise. Yeah, that's right. Networking. There are a lotta people in this world & there are probably several who would benefit from and/or enjoy reading our zines But Haven't had the opportunity. There are also a lot of radical activists & groups that we really need to network with NOW ok?

grrrlgrrrlgrrrlgrrrlgrrrlgrrrlriot

★ We will take the Burden off of (usually) young women who can't afford to distribute their zines or whose zines aren't well known. First it'll get the word out to everyone who gets the catalogue and thus we'll be doing all the shit work of copying and dealing with $
1993

★☆★☆★☆★☆★☆★☆★☆★☆

★ It's gonna Help feminist movement in general because it will create another vehicle of communication for ♀ nationally & internationally.

♀♀♀♀♀♀♀♀♀♀♀♀♀♀♀♀♀♀♀♀♀

★ It'll Be easier to get Back issues of zines. If you've ever tried to get a Back issue of Fantastic Fanzine from me (erika), you know what i'm talking about.

pleasepleasepleasepleasepleasepleaseplease

★ It will Help Riot grrrl Chapters have Better communication with each other By acting as a central place for obtaining addresses & such.

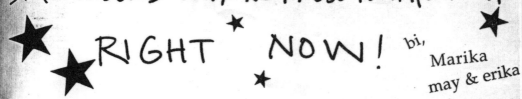

♥We HoPe You See OUR Point.☆

is probably both, one-girl at a time. "It depends on your definition of a social movement", muses Nina Nijsten. "Riot grrrl certainly is an attitude, but I think it is also more than that. It's not only an individual thing. Riot grrrl is something that unites a lot of people worldwide, inspires them, brings them together." Even after 15 years, the diffuse nature of the movement still stands strong. "Riot grrrls don't have one agenda, political program or fixed theory", affirms Nina, "That way it can evolve and adapt to contemporary needs".[125]

FRINGE FEMINISM

The rhetoric of "no rules" is a common motif within riot grrrl fanzines, as embedded in this *Bikini Kill* quote:

> We ARE what we think we are, what we feel we are when we wake up everyday:
> We are Feminist Slut Whore Virgins Psycho Tramp Hysterical Macho Mothers Protitutes With
> Heart of Gold Tearing Down Violent Hate Fuck Pornography and then Masturbating o Photos
> of Ourselves Sitting Reading A Book Alone Next to a Boy We Fuck But We Don't really like
> Falling in Love with Our Best Girlfriend Staking Of Our Clothes and Putting them Back On
> Being Quiet Yelling so Loud pushing the walls all down till they are sweating and bleeding
> FEMME butchs On motorscotter Harley carrying guns and bullet holsters full of lipstick
> hypocrobat that choose choose choose not to rule or makerules, okey? I am a feminist cuz
> the soul of every girl matters.[126]

"Like many forms of activism in the third wave, riot grrrl relies on the idea of contradiction as a definition", write the editors of *Third Wave Agenda: Being Feminist, Doing Feminism*.[127] Riot grrrl has been retrospectively claimed as an important element of "third wave feminism", a new generational model of feminism emerging out of America in the 1990s. Concerned with popular culture, pleasure, multiple alliances, and postmodern identity claims, the feminist zine has been declared a "crucial third-wave feminist tool for activism and expression".[128]

Riot grrrl discourse doesn't typically refer to feminism as an ideology or a movement but instead conveys it through an onslaught of pro-girl articles and aesthetics within fanzines. Self-defined labels include 'punk rock feminism', 'DIY feminism', 'underground feminism', 'creative feminism', and simply 'feminism'. "In the beginning American riot grrrls were trying to redefine feminism for the generation and its needs. "I think there are still doing this", reflects Nina Nijsten. "Today's feminist movement seems very institutionalised. Riot grrrl creates a kind of feminism that keeps its former rebellion and independence/autonomy and so can attract girls and women who feel they can't really access or be part of this institutionalised feminism."[129] When asked to describe their particular brand of feminism, grrrls are likely to pitch riot grrrl as a fun, imaginative alternative to 'political feminism', 'academic feminism' and 'mainstream feminism'.

"For me riot grrrl was more accessible, younger and more embracing of popular culture than the 'mainstream' feminist movement", says Rachel Kaye. "Riot grrrl acted as a gateway into mainstream feminism for a lot of young women who otherwise might not have been that interested."[130] As a youth-feminist network, Riot grrrl encourages feminist identification and grassroots activism (such as self-publishing, subvertising, forming bands and so on) away from the foundation of previous generation's ideologies: "riot grrrl is feminism, without the splintered factions of ecofeminism/liberal pro-feminism/conservative feminism, etc", argues Caroline Hamer. "It has enabled a new generation to inherit feminist ideals without taking the weight of a hundred years of dogma. And yet encouraging them to explore, revel in, educate themselves about the women that have gone before them."[131]

As fringe or underground feminists, riot grrrl participants create a counter-cultural

Dear Diary,

Things to do today:
1. get typewriter
2. find some recycled paper
3. look for my favourite pen
4. start an information riot

d.i.y.

zine workshops.

http://gzagg.org

GRRRL ZINES A-GO-GO
POB 33654
SAN DIEGO CA 92163

PuNK RocK
FeM-
inisM
rules
okay

BIKINI KILL

persona which thrives through an antagonistic relationship with the 'mainstream': from the punk feminism through which it defines itself (challenging previous generations of 'political' feminists), the language of emotion it carries as a weapon (a strike against rationality and the abstract postmodernism of the academy), the zine medium it hijacks (the Bikini Kill lyric "We Don't Need You" being a popular position with regards to the mainstream media), and the manner of DIY distribution it upholds (non-commercial circulation based on trades and informal exchange networks).

ML Fraser has labelled grrrl zines as a form of 'fringe feminism': "a fringe feminist is a feminist who resides on the fringes of culture. Women and girls who do not fall into any category of traditional feminism proclaim the ideals of feminism through the use of non-traditional media and ideology."[132] The grrrl zine legacy remains: "the grrrl zine movement is as strong as ever. There are zines telling women's private abortion stories, zines telling women's stories of abuse, zines fighting sexism and heterosexism, zines criticising the mainstream media, zines about body image, says Randie of *Media Whore* zine."[133] Publications that started life as photocopied rags and are now widely distributed magazines include *Bust, Bitch* and *Venus*. Zine culture is also reaching critical new masses through initiatives such as the Bookmobile touring zine library and the workshops by groups like Grrrl-Zines-A-Go-Go for high school girls.[134]

Top: Girl Zines A-Go-Go Flyer, 2004.
Image courtesy of Elke Zobl.
Bottom: "Punk Rock Feminism Rules Okay",
Bikini Kill, no 2. Authored by Kathleen Hanna.

WE LEARN OUR HISTORY LIKE LIES

> If we allow them to write the history it will teach girls that the revolution started in 1991 and ended in 1994 (or was that 1968 to 1972). Because they will convince us/them that we have ARRIVED, that we are already THERE, that IT has happened, that we are post-gay, post-feminist, post-riot grrrl, post-race, post-poor, post-oppressed. Because generation gaps are an invention of capitalism. Because we need to live in the place where we are truly alive, present, safe and accounted for. Because we refuse to allow our writing, songs, art, activism and political histories to be suppressed or stolen.
>
> –Tammy Rae Carter, *The New Women's Music Sampler liner notes*, 1999

In 2006 Leslie L Heywood compiled a comprehensive two-volume encyclopaedia called *The Women's Movement Today: An Encyclopedia of Third-Wave Feminism* which included a cover image of a riot grrrl type singer, microphone in heard, screaming. The first volume of the encylopedia is an A-Z running from "Abortion" to "Zine". This is the entry for "riot grrrl": "See Alt Culture; Bikini Kill; Music; Third-Wave Catch Phrases."[135] Even within a contemporary feminist text, the history of riot grrrl has been clipped and prematurely fossilised into a brand of music, a feminist sub-culture, and a footnote to "girl power" post-feminism/third wave feminism.

In defence, riot grrrl history isn't easy to recover. Grrrl zines are like snuff-publications, evading conventional notions of authorship and permanence (they 'kill authors' in their own particular way). Archival collections are starting to form to document these cultures. Built around the personal donations of girl zinesters, girl-zine depositories include: Sarah Dyer's Action Girl and Sarah Wood's *GERLL* Collections (Duke University), Tristan Taormino's *A Girls Guide to Taking Over the World* Collection (Smith College), Kim Nolan's Collection (DePaul University), and Ladyfest London Collection (The Women's Library).[136] These are primary source documents containing the stories and experiences of hundreds of girls, from different backgrounds, ages, and countries, coming into feminism on their own terms.

Riot grrrl zines didn't set out to change the world, or overthrow the patriarchy. They are small, enjoyable hand-made magazines through which girls communicated about their lives and discussed resistance in everyday terms. They were substitutes to music papers, teen-girl magazines, diaries and phone conversations. Thousands of girls have plugged into feminism as a result of grrrl zine cultures and messages, and hundreds more have developed careers as writers, journalists and artists from these "rehearsal room" zine spaces, as Erica Smith eloquently puts it.[137]

Of course, riot grrrl was never about conventional measures of success. If just one girl was positively affected by contact with pro-girl literature, then the victory was of a subtle kind. As a 'name' riot grrrl had a time limit, effective only as long as it inspired girls, continued to be re-made by each girl according to her belief and circumstances, and signified something empowering. The currency of riot grrrl was connection, fun, overcoming alienation, and creating. It was an attractive escape route within a social order that delimits the scripts of femininity, sexuality and girlhood available to young women and teenage girls. For some, it was a primer in feminism. Above all, riot grrrl was a collective wish and a kind of dare.

"Pretend You Like It", from *Tigerheart*, no 5, 2001.
Image courtesy of Jessica Dainese.

1 Chidgey, Red. *Varla's Passed Out Again* #2, Clacton-on-Sea, 2001
2 Hamer, Caroline. personal correspondence with author, 23 May 2007
3 "Ladyfest Brighton", Internet Archive, www.archive.org/details/FlatFourRadioLadyfestBrighton
4 Vail, Tobi. personal correspondence with the author, July 2007
5 Neuman, *Molly. Riot Grrrl* #4, Olympian WA
6 Marinucci, Mimi. "Zines", in Leslie L.Heywood (ed.), *The Women's Movement Today: An Encyclopedia of Third-Wave Feminism*, Vol.1, Greenwood Press: London, 2006, pp.374
7 Phoenix, Val. "From Womyn to Grrrls: Finding Sisterhood in Girl Style Revolution", *Deneuve*, February 1994, pp.41
8 Morris, Natasha. *My Little Fanzine*, Loughton, 1995
9 Anonymous, Grrrls World, Manchester, 1993
10 Chidgey, Red. a less intimate disappointment, Clacton, 2003
11 Naylor, Liz. cited in Liz Evans, "Rage Against the Man Machine", *NME*, 6 March 1993, pp.15
12 Ablaze, Karren. "Right Now. Riot Grrrl: The Expansion of Punk Rock, *Ablaze!*#10, Leeds, 1993, pp.15
13 Vail, Tobi. *Jigsaw* #5, Olympia WA, 1993.
14 Ablaze, Karren. "There's Only One Nation of Ulysses", *Ablaze!*#10, Leeds,1993
15 Svenonious, Ian. "The Monster Metaphor for Young Tigers", *Jigsaw*#5, Olympia WA, 1993
16 Ablaze, Karen. "Girlspeak", *GirlFrenzy* #3, London, 1992, pp.30
17 Ablaze, Karren. "Girl Love & Girl Action", *GirlFrenzy* #5, Hove, 1994. This "herstory" is a transcript of a speech Karren gave at the ICA "Bad Girls" event in December 1993.
18 Ablaze, Karren. "Girl Love & Girl Action", *GirlFrenzy* #5, Hove, 1994
19 Ablaze, Karren. "You Need Ablaze", *Ablaze!* #10, Leeds, 1993, pp.3
20 Ablaze, Karren. "Doing the Devil some Serious Damage", *Ablaze!* #10, Leeds, 1993, pp.50
21 Ablaze, Karren. "Girl Love & Girl Action", *GirlFrenzy* #5, Hove, 1994.
22 "Her Jazz", *GirlFrenzy* #3, London, 1992, pp.32
23 Ablaze, Karren. "Five Strategies for the Unleashing of Girl Power", Ablaze! #10, Leeds, 1993, pp.18
24 Johnson, Jo. "Huggy Bear" in Amy Raphael, Never Mind the Bollocks: Women Rewrite Rock, London: Virago, 1995, pp.151
25 Suki and friends, Terrorzine, London, 1993
26 Ablaze, Karren. "Five Strategies for the Unleashing of Girl Power", *Ablaze!* #10, Leeds, 1993, pp.18.
27 *Huggy Nation* #3, cited in Steven Wells, "Ready, Teddy, Go", *NME*, 6 March 1993, pp.12–13.
28 Hanna, Kathleen. "Gen X Survivor: From Riot Grrrl Rock Star to Feminist Artist", in Robin Morgan (ed.), *Sisterhood is Forever*, London: Washington Square Press, 2003, pp.131–137
29 Hill, Karen. "Huggy Bear" in Amy Raphael, *Never Mind the Bollocks: Women Rewrite Rock*, London: Virago, 1995, pp.167
30 WITCH manifesto in Robin Morgan (ed.), *Sisterhood is Powerful*, New York: Vintage, 1970, pp.617
31 Hanna, Kathleen. "Riot Grrrl Is…", *Bikini Kill* #2, Washington DC, 1991
32 Hanna, Kathleen. *My Life with Evan Dando Popstar*, Washington DC, 1991
33 Solanas, Valerie. *SCUM Manifesto*, Edinburgh: AK Press, 1996, pp.38
34 Rich, B.Ruby. "Manifesto Destiny" cited in Claire Dederer, "Cutting Remarks", *The Nation*, June 14 2004, www.thenation.com/doc/20040614/dederer
35 Solanas, Valerie. interviewed by Howard Smith, *Village Voice*, 25 July 1977, cited in SCUM Manifesto, pp.55
36 Solanas, Valerie. *SCUM Manifesto*, Edinburgh: AK Press, 1996, pp.4
37 Frances Swiney. discussed in Felski, Rita, *The Gender of Modernity*, London: Harvard University Press, 1995, pp.160
38 "Hey Lame Girlfriend", *Riot Grrrl*, London, 1992
39 Ablaze, Karren. "Right Now. Riot Grrrl: The Expansion of Punk Rock" (p.15), "Girlspeak" (pp.16-17), "Five strategies for the Unleashing of Girl Power", *Ablaze* #10, Leeds, 1993
40 Ablaze, Karren. "Girl Love & Girl Action", GirlFrenzy#5, Hove, pp.20
41 Solanas, Valerie. *SCUM Manifesto*, Edinburgh: AK Press, 1996, pp.38
42 Ablaze, Karren. "Five Strategies for the Unleashing of Girl Power", *Ablaze!* #10, Leeds, 1993, p.p18.
43 Toothpaste, Lucy. *JOLT* #1, London, March 1977
44 Smith, Erica. "GirlFrenzy" in Rachel Slampt's *Fast Connection* #5, Newcastle-Upon-Tyne,1999
45 Smith, Erica. personal correspondence with the author, 28 May 2007
46 Hanna, Kathleen. "Riot Grrrl Is…", *Bikini Kill* #2, Washington DC, 1991
47 Vale, V. "From the Editor", *Zines!* Vol.I, San Francisco: VSearch, 1996, pp.4
48 Hanna, Kathleen. "Burn Down the Walls that say you can't", *Bikini Kill* #2, Washington DC, 1991
49 Nijsten, Nina. personal correspondence with author, 19 May 2007, Reinstein, Erika. Fantastic Fanzine, Arlington VA, 1992
50 Ablaze, Karren. "Doing the Devil some Serious Damage", *Ablaze!* #10, Leeds, 1993, pp.50
51 Riot Grrrl KW, *In Spite of the Night* #1, Waterloo, Ontario, 2002
52 Chidgey, Red. a less intimate disappointment, Clacton, 2002
53 Duncombe, Stephen. *Zines: notes from underground and the politics of alternative culture*, London: Verso, 1997, pp. 15. A comprehensive history of zines is also provided by Nico Ordway, "History of Zines", Zines! Vol. I, V.Vale (ed.), San Francisco: V/Search, 1996; Zine Book, www.zinebook.com; and Amy Spencer, DIY: The rise of lo-fi culture, London: Marion Boyars, 2005
54 Spencer, Amy. *DIY: The rise of lo-fi culture*, London: Marion Boyars, 2005
55 Bleyer, Jennifer. "Cut-and-Paste Revolution: Notes from the Girl Zine Explosion", in Vivien Labaton and Dawn Lundy Martin (eds.), *The Fire This Time*, New York: Random House, 2004, pp.49
56 Dennis, Jeremy. personal correspondence with author, 26 May 2007
57 Scarlet, Sophie. personal correspondence with author, 16 May 2007
58 "Get Set.Go", *Riot Grrrl*, London, 1992
59 Nijsten, Nina, *Flapper Gathering* #3, Masmechelen, 2003
60 Linzy, Ornella. *Hornchurch*, 2001
61 Kaye, Rachel personal correspondence, 16 May 2007.
62 Kearney, Mary Celeste, *Girls Make Media*, London: Routledge, 2006, pp.163
63 See Harris, Anita (ed.), *All about the Girl: Culture, Power and Identity*, London: Routledge, 2004, for a discussion of the "girl at risk" approach to female youth.
64 Ablaze!, Karren. "Right Now. Riot Grrrl: The Expansion of Punk Rock", *Ablaze* #10, 1992, pp.15
65 Johanna, personal correspondence with author, 23 May 2007
66 Ablaze, Karren. "Doing the Devil Some Serious Damage", *Ablaze!* #10, Leeds, 1993, pp.50
67 *Riot Girl London* #3, London, 2003
68 Sin, Anna. "Ramblings about race, feminism, gender, privilege, blah blah blah", http://world.conk.com/world/vreject/dissertation.html (1997)
69 Cooper, Charlotte. personal correspondence with author, 16 May 2007
70 "Ready, Teddy, Go!" *The NME*, 6 March 1993, pp. 12
71 Manning, S. "Viewpoint", *Melody Maker*, 29 January 1994, pp.35
72 Bailey, Jenna. *Can Any Mother Help Me?: Fifty Years of Friendship Through a Secret Magazine*, London: Faber and Faber, 2007
73 Greer, Germaine cited in Lucy O'Brien, "The Woman Punk Made Me", *Punk Rock: So What?*, Roger Sabin (ed.), London: Routledge, 1999, pp.187
74 Toothpaste, Lucy. "Girl Bands", www.punk77.co.uk/groups/womeinpunjkoltarticle.htm
75 Caroline, Louise. interview with author, January 2005
76 Smith, Erica. Interview with Miss Amp, www.ampnet.co.uk/girlfrenzy.html
77 Unsigned editorial, *Bad Attitude* #1, London, U.K., Dec/Jan 1992/1993, pp.2
78 Taylor, Kathy. "Riot Grrrls", *Bad Attitude* #1, London, U.K., Dec/Jan 1992/1993, pp.24
79 RR, KW, VM, "riot grrrl", Interview with Kathleen Hanna, *Bad Attitude* #3, London, April/May 1993, pp.7.
80 Zobl, Elke in Amy Spencer, *DIY: The Rise of Lo-Fi Culture*, London: Marion Boyars, 2005, pp.38
81 *Riot grrrl*, London, 1992

82 Kaye, R. personal correspondence, 16 May 2007
83 Hopper, Jessica. in Nina Malkin, "It's a Grrrl Thing", *Seventeen*, May 1993
84 Ablaze, Karren. "Some of the things we have done in seven months of grrrl delight- A HERSTORY", *Leeds & Bradford Riot Grrrl*, Leeds, 1993
85 Muffled, 1992
86 Huggy Bear, *Reggae Chicken*, London, 1993
87 Vail, Tobi. "0069", *Bikini Kill* #2, Washington DC, 1991
88 Nguyen, Mimi. "it's (not) a white world: looking for race in punk", in *Slander*, www.worsethanqueer.com/slander/pprace.html
89 For a discussion of race politics/consciousness within Riot Grrrl see Kristen Schilt," "The Punk White Privilege Scene": Riot Grrrl, White Privilege, and Zines", in Different Wavelengths: Studies of the Contemporary Women's Movement, Jo Reger (ed.), New York: Routledge, 2005, pp.39–58
90 Martin, Lauren, *You Might As Well Live* #4, New York, 1997
91 Reinstein, Erika, *Channel Seven*, Olympia, WA, 1994
92 Kylie. *Her heroes aren't gone: Letter to Kathleen Hanna*, Brisbane, Australia, 2001
93 Hanna, Kathleen. *The Official Kathleen Hanna Newsletter*, Olympia, WA, 1996.
94 Mumia Abu-Jamal was convicted for the 1981 murder of Philadelphia Police Department Officer Daniel Faulkner, following a street altercation involving his brother. He is widely believed to be innocent and his imprisonment a "frame-up"; widespread police manipulation of witnesses, dismissal of testimonies, failure to corroborate evidence at the crime scene, and reported racism and corruption with the police force and courts surround his case. The struggle to free Mumia continues. www.mumia.org
95 *Rebel Grrrl* #2, Chicago, IL, 2002, pp.2
96 Blase, Cazz. personal correspondence with author, 20 May 2007
97 See Kearney, Mary Celeste, "Reconfiguring Feminist History through New Role Models", *Girls Make Media*, London: Routledge, 2006, pp.174–180
98 Huggy Bear mention their influences in Amy Raphael, Never Mind the Bollocks: Women Rewrite Rock, London: Virago, 1995, pp. 146–172. Kathleen Hanna talks about "writing the body" in Daniel Sinker (ed.), Punk Planet: The Collected Interviews, New York: Akashic Books, 2001, pp. 58–75. Judy Isaksen discusses écriture féminine and Riot Grrrl   105 texts in "Identity and Agency: Riot Grrrl's Jouissance", Enculturation, 2:2, Spring 1999, http://enculturation.gmu.edu/2_2/isaksen/
99 Hamer, Caroline. personal correspondence, 23 May 2007
100 Kaye, Rachel. personal correspondence, 16 May 2007
101 White, Emily. "Revolution Girl-Style Now!: Notes From the Teenage Feminist Rock 'n' Roll Underground", *The Chicago Reader*, 25 September 1992
102 Scarlet, Sophie. personal correspondence with author, 16 May 2007
103 Hamer, Caroline. personal correspondence with author, 23 May 2007
104 *Call to Arms* #1, Toronto, 2001
105 Jesella, Kara and Marisa Meltzer, *How Sassy Changed My Life: A Love Letter to the Greatest Teen Magazine of All Time*, New York: Faber and Faber, 2007
106 Greer, Germaine. "Girlpower", *The Whole Woman*, London: Doubleday, 1999, pp.315
107 Stoller, Debbie. *Bust Guide to the New Girl Order*, London: Penguin, 1999, pp.36
108 Kelly, Christina in Susan Corrigan, "Who Are the Riot Grrrls", *i-D The Sound Issue*, 115, April 1993, pp.23
109 Vail, Tobi. *Jigsaw* #5, Olympia, WA, 1992
110 Jesella, Kara and Marisa Meltzer, *How Sassy Changed My Life: A Love Letter to the Greatest Teen Magazine of All Time*, New York: Faber and Faber, 2007, pp.79
111 Dani in V.Vale (ed.), *Zines!* Vol. I, San Francisco: V/Search, 1996, pp.62
112 Star, Bec and Vicki, in *Twinkle Eye Fizzy* #2, Hornchurch, 2001
113 *Kablooie* #1, Marion Station, PA, cited in Joan Livingston-Webber, "How Sassy Are Grrrl Zines?", Paper presented at the Annual Meeting of the Conference on College Composition and Communication, 17 March 1994.
114 Hamer, Caroline. personal correspondence with author, 23 May 2007
115 CrimethInc, www.crimethinc.com
116 Chidgey, Red. Girl Track Record, Clacton, 2004
117 For a survey of zines counter-cultural position see Roger Sabin and Teal Triggs, *Below Critical Radar: Fanzines and Alternative Comics from 1976 to now*, Hove: Slab-O-Concrete, 2000. For an assessment of Riot Grrrl's co-option by academics, and the way in which most studies downplay the homo-erotics and feminist separatists aspects of early Riot Grrrl cultures (which link to "womyn only" elements of the WLM), see the oeuvre of Mary Celeste Kearney. Commentary on the Riot Grrrl appropriation by the commercial press, as well as some original Ameri can articles, is archived on-line by Lea Thompson, http://cerebro.cs.xu.edu/~tankgirl/twelvelittlegirls/papers/mediagrrrl.html.
118 Huggy Bear, *D-Generate*, London, 1993
119 Webb, Susy. "After the Riot", *Discorder*, 2003, www.ams.ubc.ca/citr/discorder/archive/2003-03/riot.html
120 Chan, Kristy. Riot Grrrl Review, www.geocities.com/westhollywood/9352/
121 Triggs, Teal. "'Generation Terrorists': *The Politics and Graphic Language of Punk and Riot Grrrl Fanzines in Britain* 1976-2000", Reading: University of Reading, Unpublished PHD Thesis, 2004, pp.202
122 Bleyer, Jennifer. "Cut-and-Paste Revolution: Notes from the Girl Zine Explosion", in Vivien Labaton and Dawn Lundy Martin (eds.), The Fire This Time, New York: Random House, 2004, pp.47
123 Hilde in *Female Perversions* #1, Finland, 2002
124 Nijsten, Nina. personal correspondence with author, 19 May 2007
125 Greta, personal correspondence, 26 May 2007
126 Nijsten, Nina. personal correspondence with the author, 19 May 2007
127 Hanna, Kathleen. *Bikini Kill* #2, Washington DC, 1991
128 Heywood, Leslie and Jennifer Drake (eds), "Third Wave Activism and Youth Music Culture", *Third Wave Agenda: Being Feminist, Doing Feminism*, London: University of Minnesota Press, 1997, pp.204
129 Marinucci, Mimi. "Zines", in Leslie L.Heywood (ed.), The Women's Movement Today: An Encyclopedia of Third-Wave Feminism, Vol.1, Greenwood Press: London, 2006, pp.374
130 Nijsten, Nina. personal correspondence with author, 19 May 2007
131 Kaye, Rachel. personal correspondence with author, 16 May 2007
133 Hamer, Caroline. personal correspondence with author, 23 May 2007
134 Fraser, ML. *"Zine and Heard*: Fringe Feminism and the Zines of the Third Wave", Feminist Collections, 23:4, Summer 2002, pp.6
135 Randie, *Media Whore* #5, Malden MA,.2004.
136 Bookmobile, www.mobilivre.org; Grrrl Zines A-Go-Go, www.grrrlzines.net/agogo.htm
137 Heywood, Leslie L. (ed.), *The Women's Movement Today: An Encyclopedia of Third-Wave Feminism*, Vol1, Greenwood Press: London, 2006, pp.284.
138 The ZineBook website has comprehensive listings of Zine Libraries and Archives, www.zinebook.com
139 Smith, Erica. personal correspondence with author, 28 May 2007

BAD LANGUAGE BAD CONFESSIONS BAD

ART, POLITICS AND HOW ONE GRRRL JOINED THE FEMINIST RIOT

SUZY CORRIGAN

Hot topic is the way that we
rhyme
Hot topic is the way that we rhyme
One step behind the drum style
One step behind the drum style
Carol Rama and Elanor Antin
Yoko Ono and Carolee Schneeman
You're getting old, that's what they'll say, but
Don't give a damn I'm listening anyway
Stop, don't you stop
I can't live if you stop
Don't you stop
Gretchen Phillips and Cibo Matto
Leslie Feinburg and Faith Ringgold
Mr. Lady, Laura Cottingham
Mab Segrest and The Butchies, man
Don't stop

Don't you stop
We won't stop
Don't you stop
So many roads and so much opinion
So much shit to give in, give in to
So many rules and so much opinion
So much bullshit but we won't give in
Stop, we won't stop
Don't you stop
I can't live if you stop
Tammy Rae Carland and Sleater-Kinney
Vivienne Dick and Lorraine O'Grady
Gayatri Spivak and Angela Davis
Laurie Weeks and Dorothy Allison

Stop, don't you stop
Please don't stop
We won't stop
Gertrude Stein, Marlon Riggs, Billie Jean King, Ut,
DJ Cuttin Candy,
David Wojnarowicz, Melissa York, Nina Simone, Ann
Peebles, Tammy Hart,
The Slits, Hanin Elias, Hazel Dickens, Cathy Sissler, Shirley
Muldowney,
Urvashi Vaid, Valie Export, Cathy Opie, James Baldwin,
Diane Dimassa, Aretha Franklin, Joan Jett, Mia X, Krystal
Wakem,
Kara Walker, Justin Bond, Bridget Irish, Juliana Lueking,
Cecelia Dougherty, Ariel Skrag, The Need, Vaginal Creme Davis,
Alice Gerard, Billy Tipton, Julie Doucet, Yayoi Kusama, Eileen Myles
Oh no no no don't stop stop

—LeTigre, 'Hot Topic'

Portraying both the attitude and portions of the syllabus behind the riot grrrl movement, the Le Tigre song "Hot Topic" is in many ways a blueprint of aesthetic influence on punk rock feminism. The band's lead singer, Kathleen Hanna, is seen as a figurehead for riot grrrl because of her earlier recordings with Bikini Kill; but here, almost a decade after the formation of the earlier group, she reinforces the feminist and queer politics agenda in the art that most inspired a generation of third-wave feminists. In many ways it enjoys a more mainstream acceptance than it did nearly two decades ago, when groups like Guerrilla Girls used eye-catching and media-friendly campaigns to draw attention to the lack of parity or opportunity for female artists in what was a booming art market.

20 years ago, before being leveraged away from young people by a government eager to characterise complainants as threats to American national security, a culture of demonstrated protest still existed, meeting perceived challenges to human and political rights with suitable derision and with responses cribbed from 'art terrorism' and other forms of non-violent response. These protests were staged to support everything from AIDS awareness, anti-war causes, racial equality of opportunity and reproductive rights.

To continue in the same metaphor, 20 years ago, young Americans knew there was a culture war going on in terms of gender, sexuality and freedom of expression in much the same way they've realised another equally serious one is being fought now. Today, a re-appraisal of radical art by women from the 1960s and 70s, the second wave of feminism, suggests that a public hungry for a way to register its non-compliance with the new 'responsibilities' of the post-9/11 age has found a foothold in a mainstream increasingly alienated by social policy. One which rewards the rich at the expense of all others, especially women and minorities, who can only succeed in prescribed roles consistent with the value systems represented by only one per cent of the world's population. Today, when spurious wars against the concept of terror are orchestrated with a particular and coercive concept of 'freedom' in mind, the art from women of my mother's generation—and queer artists from my own—dissected notions of community, egalitarianism, freedom, gender and individuality. There are now new reasons to channel the political through the personal; retrospection in the form of an alternative creative canon only reinforces this.

The Le Tigre lyric lists inspiring figures from art, film, literature and music whose femininity or queer stance foregrounds their practice and who have also offered connectivity

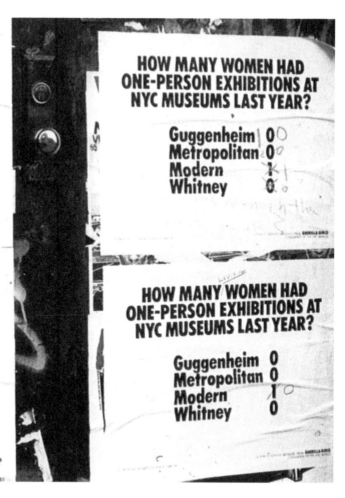

to younger generations of creative women; the queer stance is underscored by the addition of gay artists and activists. All those listed in the lyrics are also body-oriented; many of these came to the attention of Hanna and students like her at art colleges in the late 1980s when AIDS and abortion rights struggles in America made 'fellow travelers' out of undergraduate feminists and the first LGBTQ groups. Very simply, we felt our right of control over our own bodies was under attack, our freedom of expression was being challenged as 'obscenity' while pornography flourished unchecked, and the people who were doing it to us were judged hypocrites at one end of the scale and as murderers at the most extreme. Artistic expression and protest were a corrective response to these conditions. Mainstream culture's paternalistic nature sought to ignore, punish or silence the non-compliant; those who came together under that category saw this as a challenge to be met with private stonewalling, public protest and rebellion. For young women of the time, raised to believe in meritocracy and the power of education, coming up against obvious male representations of the status quo unrepentantly reinforced that authority. Even in 'safe' areas such as the arts, this was a rude and politicising awakening.

"Hot Topic" also inverts the idiom of 'songs about girls'. Itself a kind of tribute to Judy Chicago's *The Dinner Party*, where places are set for 39 honoured guests from the world of female struggle, the women (and men) named in the song are inspiring, but not through any passivity or victimhood. Scanning the roll call of 'independent' artists, filmmakers, writers and musicians Hanna lists, many 'suffered for their art' in very real terms, whether it was the character assassination of Fluxus artist Yoko Ono in popular culture, the censorship suffered by Julie Doucet in comics publishing, or Aretha Franklin, whose lack of conformity to a physical type impeded her early singing career. Linked to younger artists whose

Left: Le Tigre group shot depicting JD Samson, Joanna Fateman and Kathleen Hanna. Image courtesy of Tom Sarig.
Right: The Dinner Party: Installation view. © Judy Chicago, 1979. Gift of the Elizabeth A Sackler Foundation Collection: The Brooklyn Museum of Art, Brooklyn, NY. Photo © Donald Woodman.
Opposite: Examples of Agit-Prop approach taken by the Guerrilla Girls in the 1980s and 90s. © Guerrilla Girls. Courtesy www.guerrillagirls.com

struggle to succeed has been made that little bit easier by the work of their antecedents, the lyric itself is a history lesson given by an erudite female author. In most forms of popular music, songs about girls are written by men. The 'girls' described are usually objects or subjects, muse figures, vexing and unattainable—it is difficult to work out the root of the obsession; sometimes the love described parses just like hate. In any event, women are brought to life in the eye of male beholders, exalted for qualities men seek out in women and berated for qualities they don't. Creativity and incisiveness are seldom amongst the qualities that attract the average songwriting male to compose a lyric about a woman. In pre-twentieth century art, outside of a few notable or noble exceptions, women participated in the process as object and subject, but rarely as creator or patron.

Like many girls of her generation, Kathleen Hanna was a beneficiary of second-wave feminism; she has claimed her first awakenings to 'girl-positivity' came along because her homemaker mother volunteered helping victims of domestic violence, had a subscription to *Ms* Magazine and in fact brought the nine-year-old Kathleen to a rally in Washington DC where the magazine's founding editor, Gloria Steinem, addressed the crowds. The experience of massed solidarity with other women and the positive energy this generated stayed with Hanna, who moved to Olympia, Washington to study photography at Evergreen State College. Evergreen, by the mid-to-late 1980s, was one of America's most radical art schools, attracting undergraduates from all across America who were drawn to both the programme of studies and Olympia's politically-aware (some said, even then, 'politically correct') art and music scene, which centred around the K Records label run by Calvin Johnson of the group Beat Happening.

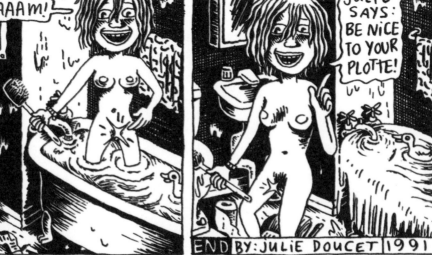

A significant distance from Seattle and the groups who would later be called 'grunge', K Records artistes and their Olympian peers were more likely to be inspired by the post-punk groups on British indie labels; some of the lovingly-crafted releases on K Records evoked an imaginary, idealised childhood while others revisited the most laughable 'teen-sploitation' films of the 1950s and 60s. In a way, the K Records scene's leading lights were the first 'kidults', exhibiting a collective nostalgia for youthful activities and pastimes they'd missed or skipped the first time around; perhaps as one-time misfits or loners, they'd even been excluded. Appearances were deceiving: dressed brightly in infantilising clothes straight out of a *Dick and Jane* reader, K-kids had angst-filled interior lives. In Britain, their equivalent was the Cutie, anaemic meta-teens obsessed with the minutiae of retro youth culture, seemingly reliant on a diet of penny sweets and Monster Munch. Cuties also wished for a kinder, gentler world, formed groups and entered into correspondence with K Records artists. Musical proficiency was not an issue: most of the bands were experimental in nature or happy to learn as they went. Songs, while not an afterthought, were part of a whole conceptual package of presentation: accompanying fanzines, manifestoes, slideshows of self-created and sampled images, slogans in childlike scrawls or in interesting fonts, retro clothing styles and a belief in autonomy in artistic production so as not to suffer compromise by mainstream culture. It was DIY with a design degree and an ironic take on apple-pie representations of the American baby boomer generation, as subverted by the boomers' children, whose future was filled with unexpected new ambiguities and conflicts.

Hanna made spoken-word performances around the subject of domestic violence throughout her time at Evergreen and worked at strip clubs to support herself. This was not an uncommon strategy for art students in the late 1980s; one of my summer roommates from college subsidised her unpaid work

Former porn star and feminist performance artists Annie Sprinkle on stage.
Image courtesy of Annie Sprinkle.
Opposite: Julie Doucet, "Clean Up Time", from *Dirty Plotte 4*, 1991. © Julie Doucet, used with permission from *Drawn & Quartered*.

experience assisting a prominent female artist by taking work at a phone-sex call centre, faking heterosexuality for four-hour shifts a few days every week. Mostly, it was about the money—if you dyed your hair, pierced your nose or were otherwise judged superficially to be a non-compliant female, sex-industry employers would hire you whereas mainstream bosses baulked.

Photography and art students who'd read Cixous, Irigaray or Kristeva and pondered the direction of society's overall gaze chanced transforming the study of theory into the practice of being gazed upon themselves. As feminists, the front-row view of the chauvinism industry was just a bonus. These young women who pioneered stripping for cash emerged in a climate where performance artists such as Karen Finlay and Annie Sprinkle devised routines around the nexus of sexuality, role-playing and visceral transgressions, reclaiming or defiling the vice aesthetic as a form of opposition to a conservative parent culture. Although it paid the bills, stripping for cash was not one more way to comply with the aspirations of a capitalist or paternalistic society, nor was it about lap-dancing the way to equality. Fetish culture, once embraced by punk heroines such as Siouxsie Sioux, became a nod to the need to cover oneself in latex now AIDS had arrived, and the burlesques of rubberised bondage some women created were a not-so-oblique reference to the repression that caused (in both men and women) a desire to escape which sometimes manifested itself sexually.

Hanna herself did not become properly radicalised until the college's administration cancelled one of her on-campus photography exhibitions. A joint project with classmate Aaron Bausch-Greene, the pair's explorations of AIDS and sexism were removed by Evergreen and prompted Hanna, who felt censored, to form Neko Case, a feminist gallery space run in conjunction with friends Heidi Arbogast and Tammy Rae Carland, where exhibitions and punk shows alike were staged. By this time, it was more difficult to be a young artist in America; many who made challenging, political work in response to social conservatism worried about the impact of withdrawal of important National Endowment for the Arts grants from artists whose works offended complaining church leaders and religious pressure groups. Gay artists were especially vulnerable to financial censure as conservative groups lobbied the NEA to cut their grants or propagated images of controversial work without the permission of the artist, as was done to the late David Wojnarowicz. Men like Robert Mapplethorpe were pursued for their transgressions while wasting away from full-blown AIDS, while those challenging religious symbols like Andres Serrano with *Piss Christ*, also had their grants withdrawn.

Riot grrrl itself began in 1991 with a multimedia approach and inclusion of the visual; originally Hanna wanted to take a leaf out of Steinem's book and launch a magazine harnessing the talents of female contributors but when the first riot grrrl meetings were called in Washington, DC, the brainstorming sessions that took place indicated most women who attended wanted to promote shows and women-only activities and learn to play music so they could form groups of their own. Tired, also, of encountering situations where their participation was limited by male contemporaries jostling for attention and undermining female expression by casting women in the role of follower and followed, the ideal of female collaboration and a stated desire to function as a community of women united against male oppression in all areas attracted hundreds of girls on the punk scene who no longer tolerated this shortchange. So that's what happened, mixed in with a healthy mistrust for mainstream media, after all an extension of a consumer-led, chauvinistic world. Firstly, riot grrrls were capable of making their own media and communication networks and wanted to keep these underground, perhaps because many of the initial actors in riot

"Untitled" (*We have received orders not to move*),
Barbara Kruger, 1982. © The artist.
Courtesy Mary Boone Gallery, New York.

Bad Girls

BAD ATTITUDES · BAD LANGUAGE · BAD CONFESSIONS · BAD FEELINGS £4.50

Penny Arcade + Nicole Eisenman + Nan Goldin
Deborah Levy + Peggy Phelan + Riot Grrrl

grrrl had watched close friends in grunge bands like Nirvana become co-opted by global (corporate, mainstream, male) media and saw the way that fashion and the sudden obligations of superstardom impacted on 'real people' for the first time—something anyone in a 'scene' learns when one group or individual is elevated above contemporaneous peers. Second, it was more important for these women and adolescent girls to celebrate themselves in autonomous and 'safe' surroundings at a time when many were being awakened to continuing gender inequality and keen to respond in dynamic, witty ways making the most of their beliefs and education. After all, what is the point of cultural theory without accompanying cultural practice?

On 3 December 1993, the Institute of Contemporary Art in London hosted GRRRLSTYLE REVOLUTION NOW!, an event inspired by riot grrrl and held in conjunction with its *Bad Girls* exhibition and season of feminism-related events. Although the young female participants revelled in a series of collective art projects, discussions, films and performance pieces, a sizeable amount of cultural and media critics broadly wondered: 'where the hell is the bloody music?'. They'd expected to see the baring of souls (or at least a few magic-markered midriffs) set to a jagged soundtrack of girl-positive lyrics. Instead the organisers (myself included) decided it would be a far better idea to interpret our influences in art, film and literature in such a way that we could fill the non-exhibition areas of the gallery with the DIY efforts of 30 young women from around Britain who had become involved with riot grrrl, only a handful of whom played in the groups who were subject to heated and very threatened music press debate. We were, to a woman, fed up with the pigeonholing of our passion into one art form—punk rock music—and by aligning ourselves with a generation of oppositional female visual artists a decade older than most of us, we hoped to show both more varied interests and that, as a generation, we were capable of challenging the canonical for something better and rejecting social models we hoped would fall out of date. We wanted to know art that spoke to us about the lives we aspired to lead just as much it spoke to us about those lives we had learned from. If that meant nominating a canon of our own, so be it. We revelled in telling the world what exactly was happening without its permission.

Discussing things amongst ourselves, we discovered heroines from Frida Kahlo to Cindy Sherman as root cause for our inspiration, as important to our journey toward that moment as a love of independently produced records. These artists, filmmakers, performers and writers (for these practitioners crossed disciplines and traditional boundaries both to classify and create their narrative) represented both struggle and triumph to the young women of the mid-1980s and early 1990s who had been led to believe by their working mothers and by notions of meritocracy that theirs would be the generation that moved beyond fighting with boys or each other for the prizes of capitalism or companionship. At the time there was

Front Cover of the exhibition catalogue
for *Bad Girls* at the ICA, 1993.
Image courtesy of Susan Corrigan.

very little mainstream appreciation for contemporary feminist art, which, along with the punk aesthetic of photocopied fanzines and common ground shared with queer politics, underpinned this underground's aesthetic-in-common.

Artists who now fit the queer canon were deeply important to riot grrrl; despite being male (and in many cases reliant on the usual masculine tropes of the auteur and the muse) their attitudes and stance conveyed in their practice remained inspirational. Despite his death in early 1987, Andy Warhol remained pop's ultimate picker; the lives of every single social misfit with ideas above their suburban station were, if anything, post-Warhol. The art we gravitated to, or in some cases made, was as instant as advertising and made to be reproduced quickly and cheaply, whether in pixel or super-8 films, fanzines, performance, photographs, posters, or records or video art—you could do all of this, and have your moment in the spotlight. Maybe even 15 of them. You could make an image into an icon through repetition (the British punk stance of 'fake it 'til you make it' also owes a debt to this stardust thinking). In Britain, the late Derek Jarman's films and writings challenged the censor while their activist creator grappled with HIV and used his more opulent productions to place a queer spin on history, which he'd studied to degree level before his father agreed to send him to art college. In 1987 he made a series of videos for The Smiths which served as a taster for the artier end of that group's audience, but particularly films like *The Devils*, which made the hypocrisy of religious leadership manifest in his set design, or Caravaggio, his biopic of the Renaissance thief and painter where the juxtaposition of classic and modern objects in the *mise* was just as fascinating as the gay sex many of us had never seen, much less experienced. Looking back, John Waters may well be the first director of queer cinema: *Female Troubles* introduced his childhood best friend and transvestite Divine as a turd-eating housewife, while elegantly but wryly explaining to detractors and fans alike that he made films about everything he'd get in trouble for doing in real life—which was something art was for. My own realisation that art could be as effective a form of protest or non-compliance as any man with a guitar came with exposure to the work of Barbara Kruger and Jenny Holzer. Their stark phraseology and dissection of human social interaction appealed to the writer in me and spurred me to articulate my own reservations about those areas with more acuity and sarcasm than before.

Cindy Sherman, who to this day eschews definition as a feminist, used her dress-up and cosmetic boxes in a career of role-playing portraits in character—I was down with that; identity politics may not have had a name in my brain at that point but I could see how she was messing with perception and selfhood. It was good to have people out there who seemed to agree with me on that level; I'd only just managed to find people like them in real life a few years earlier when a band of articulate punk girls in my school noticed I was being bullied by 'posers' and announced one day to the ringleader: "if you have a problem with her, then we've got a problem with you". We weren't merely rebelling, we were 'deconstructing the rules'. We viewed all rites of passage as somewhat absurd (a friend pursuing a boy was asked, 'have you tried the usual social rituals?') and worth lampooning. Experiencing shows and hanging out downtown—itself an obvious rite of passage—was a life-or-death subject. Many of us were running away from family settings where there was inequity, nobody home—or the wrong sort of person waiting there. Like many people who became involved with riot grrrl, it was only on hindsight that I realised how many of us had been able to make what I call 'privileged observations' because we either had no idea we were so close to history or a 'scene', or we ignored established cliques or hierarchies as if we were Courtney Love refusing to wear a backstage pass in the name of egalitarianism.

People in Britain, media included, were also largely ignorant of the climate in America that motivated the original riot grrrls. Yes, we could pinpoint an exchange of letters between a group of undergraduate-age women reacting to race riots in Washington, DC, in the summer of 1991, and the wider female anger arising from allegations of sexual misconduct by an about-to-be-ratified Supreme Court justice, but to leave it there would

GUERRILLA GIRLS DEMAND A RETURN TO TRADITIONAL VALUES ON ABORTION.

Before the mid-19th century, abortion in the first few months of pregnancy was legal. Even the Catholic Church did not forbid it until 1869.*

*Carl. N. Flanders, Abortion, Library in a Book, 1991

A PUBLIC SERVICE MESSAGE FROM **GUERRILLA GIRLS** 532 LA GUARDIA PL #237, NY 10012

be glib. Although the push for an equal rights amendment had fizzled a decade before, equal opportunities legislation and affirmative action programmes enabled girls' aspirations even if equality of result was not itself forthcoming. Comprised of a generation coming of age at the dawn of the AIDS crisis, we had conflicted attitudes to sex and sexuality; also we inhabited the vulnerability which came with our 'status' as possible victims of the first conservative challenges to reproductive rights enshrined in 1972's Roe v Wade case decriminalising abortion.

It's easy to remember the exact moment I became politicised on behalf of other women, in a school hallway by the lunchroom in the winter of early 1983. A classmate in the year above me became pregnant and decided to have an abortion. Because of her age and the laws in my state, her parents would have to be notified and permission granted. There was a loophole my classmate thought she could jump through: you could go to Family Court without the knowledge of your parents to be declared a 'mature minor' and therefore fit to decide about termination oneself. She did, got her ruling and chose abortion. Next term, a middle-aged man began leafleting girls as they boarded school buses, safe in the knowledge that he was allowed to distribute them on the public property that was the sidewalk between school limits and the bus. These graphic full-colour flyers showed us what 'our babies' would look like and contrasted that with aborted foetuses of a similar vintage. Only a few voices rose to ask him what he was doing creeping around us, not at his job, at his age. The rest discovered what good spitballs the brochures could make, and pelted the guy through McDonalds straws. It seemed clear-cut at the time: judgemental men telling women what to do with themselves once more, punishing the 'fallen' and never the

Guerilla Girls Demand a Return to Traditional Values on Abortion, Guerilla Girls, 1992.

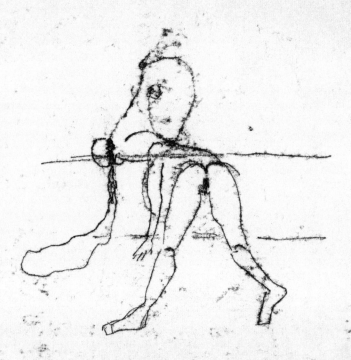

father. We were reading *The Scarlet Letter* and something of it remained two hundred years later. They didn't like it when we claimed control of our own wombs in law and retaliated by claiming it was all we ever discussed: misogynist analysis of women's aesthetic production—"it's all about their abortion/boyfriend/lesbianism/periods/rape" whatever the discipline seemed deployed as a tactic to prevent women from speaking, or to interrupt when they did. This tendency to reduce continues to this day when critics discuss Sophie Calle or Tracey Emin; and it usually parses like a howl of jealousy.

If you were becoming an adult in the 1980s, it was tempting to ask both yourself and those in charge if your own body was ever going to belong to you, if your only true value to society, once impregnated, was as a milch-cow. If you really wanted to put the frighteners on after Leaflet Man, you could follow that with a ride home on the municipal school bus that passed the Planned Parenthood clinic and its pathetic 50-something lone male (back in the 1980s it was always that one guy) 'pro-life' picket to a home where, punctuated by PSAs for HIV on the TV, you could settle in for the evening with Margaret Atwood's *The Handmaid's Tale*, a terrifying vision of the future where a nebulous fundamentalist regime had co-opted reproduction following an unspecified biological disaster. It was male authority writ large; to a teenaged girl with an active imagination, it was also probably already happening to someone elsewhere in the world. In addition to all the usual teenaged anxieties regarding sex and sexuality and the greater likelihood that we were being raised in less traditional family arrangements, my generation of adolescent girls had to cope with a massive conservative backlash which was at pains to suggest that non-compliant females were no better than dead sluts.

Don't just leave me here, Tracey Emin,
1997, monoprint. © The artist. Photo : Stephen White.
Courtesy of Jay Jopling/White Cube (London).

This male authority was obviously fallible and fractured but it sat there like a particularly obnoxious relative at a family gathering, winding up any individual that did not share his point of view. It could hire or fire you, place you in a competition with other women and name itself as winner of that contest, determine whether men and women alike approved of your appearance and conduct—not to mention, even still, race or sexuality—and decide which forms of intelligence were going to be rewarded, which victors would determine the writing of history. If he was admonished for his lack of respect to those who dared disagree, this 'authority' only bayed louder to assert conservative values and the power to choose them, if only to spite others, because this was a perk of being one of life's winners, which he'd become by holding those same values. Anyone who offered a challenge to this was either a 'liberal', a loser, 'queer', or was judged to have some deep psychological flaw or STD that did not enable them to see how the world was supposed to work. It was a privilege of dominance to believe such things; the rest would have to accept submission while being constantly and wistfully told how free they were compared to others around the world ('look at how they treat *their* women'). A young woman might well have detected a seething hatred she couldn't explain, but felt was directed at her, begun to connect that sense of male entitlement with the way women on the margins of this society were treated, seen examples of abuse, bullying or preferential treatment in the home, noticed that displays of female flesh were socially okay when it was a male idea, but subject to brouhaha otherwise. Depressingly, they might have also borne witness to the activities of young male peers who considered themselves 'liberal' but whose transgressive behaviour towards women they knew showed exactly which forms of disrespect were still enabled and encouraged by the larger society.

Rebellion flourishes like fungus in a mushroom cave at such times; the desire to escape the constraints of petit-bourgeois conservatism and the brickbats of its unquestioning adherents causes young people in its firing line to seek information and stimulation outside of that model. In 'college towns' and smaller American cities, the DIY punk scene attracted a cross-section of young people: bookish, exhibitionist, gay, musical, political, united in their common disaffection for a hostile parent culture that didn't understand. There was little incentive to do so; most of America was preoccupied with conspicuous consumption and confidently awaited the spoils promised by Reagan-era trickle-down economics. Rusted-out city centres pointed to industrial recession; artists and punks looking for cheap 'space' trickled in, just as poor as the less educated disadvantaged groups so recently vacated. Pockets of counterculture were small and disorganised; in these pre-internet days culture expanded slowly and speculative letters to others working on A5 fanzines or running performance spaces took days and weeks to arrive. There was only a limited industry dedicated to art and music inside such towns, but creative expression happened despite this, as exhibitions and gigs took place side by side in warehouses and house-party basements. This was an intelligent cohort prepared to question and pick apart any and all received ideas whether it finished at college or not, happy to work a few crap jobs to finance art of their own making.

In relativism (the idea that no one person's system of values is intrinsically superior to any other) there was a bulwark, a defence of our difference that made sense and ratified our equality to anyone and our rights to express ourselves. Americans, whatever their background, want to believe that all are created equal, all are entitled to freedom of expression and the right to be heard and incorporated into a narrative of democratic decision-making. After all, reasoned the young men and women on these burgeoning scenes, this was not a *lifestyle*, this was just life. The exhibitionism or violence of the moshpit, the disrespect for the establishment inherent in punk-rock values (which included rejecting conservatism for a democratic form of socialism and cruelty-free consumption) paled in comparison to the disrespect the establishment still showed to minorities, including women, in thought and deed, not to mention images made in the name of aesthetics and stimulation which served only to denigrate the women who weren't on the page or the canvas or the screen.

In my second year of high school, in autumn 1983, my hometown of Minneapolis, Minnesota became the first American city to attempt to seek damages for human rights violations caused by pornography. This development was, in part, the result of the legal work of Catharine MacKinnon and the late Andrea Dworkin, who argued that pornography was a violation of women's civil rights. Dworkin and MacKinnon's planned civil rights ordinance characterised pornography as a form of sex discrimination and defined 'pornography' as *the graphic sexually explicit subordination of women through pictures and/or words*, when combined with one of several other conditions.

In the model ordinance drafted by the women, Dworkin and MacKinnon gave the following legal definition:

1. ''Pornography' means the graphic sexually explicit subordination of women through pictures and/or words that also includes one or more of the following:

    a. Women are presented dehumanised as sexual objects, things or commoditiesor

    b. Women are presented as sexual objects who enjoy humiliation or pain; or

    c. Women are presented as sexual objects experiencing sexual pleasure in rape, incest, or other sexual assault; or

    d. Women are presented as sexual objects tied up or cut up or mutilated or bruised or physically hurt; or

    e. Women are presented in postures or positions of sexual submission, servility, or display; or

    f. Women's body parts-including but not limited to vaginas, breasts, or buttocks- are exhibited such that women are reduced to those parts; or

    g. Women are presented being penetrated by objects or animals; or

    h. Women are presented in scenarios of degradation, humiliation, injury, torture, shown as filthy or inferior, bleeding, bruised or hurt in a context that makes these conditions sexual.

2. The use of men, children, or transsexuals in the place of women in (a)-(h) of this definition is also pornography for purposes of this law.

3. "Person" shall include child or transsexual.

Uproar: these robust intellectuals were every conservative's nightmare, in appearance and deed. I didn't know much about these giants of second-wave feminism at the time, but as the luck of privileged observation would have it, I was close to my uncle, a lieutenant detective on the city's vice squad. In charge of rehabilitating runaway sex workers, he clearly saw the connection between the human trafficking in teenaged girls he encountered every day, the top-shelf magazines that acted as a gateway drug to the sex industry and how this was a license for misogyny that had been left unchecked until now. It was not unusual for a nosy child to encounter the graphic truth of the case files left on the desk in his study. A 20 year veteran of a division known as 'Morals' when he joined it, my uncle would be one of the bill's frontline enforcers. After winning a place in the statute books, the ordinance was cited as un-constitutional by the Mayor and therefore vetoed on the day of its passage, 30 December 1983.

My uncle explained that as much as he personally would have loved to uphold that law, which the City Council had asked the women to investigate as the result of an expansion in 'adult' shops, a judgement of pornographic obscenity was diabolical to reach because images of nude women appeared in many beautiful, acceptable forms, could be seen as 'speech' and therefore were protected by the First Amendment of the American Constitution. Like any cop, he also saw it as a matter of (what else?) paperwork. On a practical level it was far easier to pursue a 'vice lord' for property crimes of money-laundering and tax evasion than to invest any time and money in pursuing him for the content of the pornography he produced, however graphic—and if the pictures were depictions of violent assaults on women, there were already laws on the books for that.

This episode highlighted the priorities of the society I was going to have to navigate as an adult female (rape, and the idea that most men who committed the act didn't get convictions, was an idea which had already reached me. As did my own idea that it was irrational to expect me to amend my day-to-day behaviour to appease this hypothetical rapist) while also teaching me that freedom of expression was possible on the wilder shores of permissiveness because no court in the land dared tango with the almighty First Amendment.

Also, let's face it—a vast pornography juggernaut rumbled across American culture, filtering into all forms of media that used sex to sell products or impose unattainables on female consumers, who men were encouraged to fetishise, buy and discard like any other commodity. *Deep Throat* became a mainstream hit and sex shops opened in suburban strip malls (no pun intended), selling an idea that consenting adults were free to do as they pleased, and proceeded to sell enhancements for the games people believed other, happier, couples were enjoying in the bedroom. Prostitution chic ruled: the 'slut' meme was rife and ripe; in the days before Madonna there was... whore. Sandy from Grease wasn't anything to Danny without her cigarettes, hairspray, spandex and stilettos. Jodie Foster went from *Freaky Friday* to *Taxi Driver* in just over three years. Back when airbrushing was still something stoned guys in my town did to their party vans, porn managed to reassert itself as an aesthetic in art and advertising alike: pert, peach-like behinds encased in designer jeans, full lips plump in a mimicry of labia, dragging on Virginia Slims. This backlash against second-wave feminism took hold in the mid-1970s following the failure of the ratification of the Equal Rights Amendment; in many ways this was a further cultural rebuke of all women, put in their place—fantasy kitchens and fantasy bedrooms, where scanties and glossy compliance reigned. Of course it was an escapist, glamourised version of the vice industry that could be brushed off by its creators as 'just a fashion statement' as in the art of Allan Jones and the photography of Guy Bourdin, both typifying a fetishistic, almost edible gloss, providing a palpable contrast with the contemporaneous work of Carolee Schneeman and evidencing the gulf opening between the sexes. The sexual revolution and the 'zipless fucks' both men and women felt entitled to participate in soon showed that equality of opportunity was not the same as equality of result when they did. Both artistic and commercial realms were just like all those other worlds—finance, language, property, religion, science and the workplace—where expectation of just and respectful treatment was determined by gender or race.

By the time Dworkin and Mackinnon drafted their ordinance, the 'freedoms' that marked the age of sexual revolution were on the cusp of being lost. The mainstreaming of pornography in art and advertising had roughly the same effect that the lingering use of Page Three Models has in Britain still does, rendering it quotidian. Discos—once the home of polysexual disinhibition at the dawn of the gay rights movement—became yet another venue for heterosexual courtship rituals as America learned to do the Hustle. Additionally, there was the usual problem any government has when they attempt to define obscenity— plenty of citizens of every imaginable libertarian bent happy to pillory this effort as a form of rebellion, including feminists and other women. Considering the conservatism of the American government at the time, and their repressive stance towards artists who also grappled with the meaning of obscenity in some very exhibitionist work, the law as statute proved to be impossible to put into practice without deprivation of important expression.

The 'consensus' that dictates what images have the most power, as icons or idols or sexual objects—is not just a shallow bit of fun, as those who laughed off women's objections to traditional depictions tried to argue, treating the argument itself as a joke. It was a perfect expression of heterosexual male privilege. Girls in punk scenes already ran a gauntlet of paternalism to get to the seedy neighbourhoods where their record shops and preferred gig venues were; their interest in fashion was oppositional to mainstream peers in the sense that the girls dressed both provocatively and defensively enough to rile classmates, parents and teachers. They might have started out as weekend Euro-punks

Left: *Interior Scroll*, Carolee Schneemann, 1975, performance photograph. Image courtesy of Carolee Schneemann. Photograph: Anthony McCall. Right: *Illinois Central*, Carolee Schneemann, 1968–1969, photo collage. Image courtesy of Carolee Schneemann. Photograph: Landscape —Art Sinsabaugh, Action—Fred McDarrah. Opposite: *Do women have to be naked to get into the Met. Museum?*, Guerrilla Girls, 1989. © Guerrilla Girls, courtesy www.guerrillagirls.com.

making pilgrimages to independent record stores to buy the Duran Duran interviews in *Melody Maker*, but exposure to new ideas widened their perspectives considerably and gave them better art, film and music to discover. Punks at the time were seen as loiterers without intent to consume anything. Because of image, the treatment we received from authority figures was the same as if we had already physically or verbally challenged them. Anti-establishment sympathies bloom when young people are seen in this light; joined to other political sensitivities with abortion, censorship in the arts, civil rights, homophobia, nuclear disarmament and racism, a lack of faith in authority figures to treat all comers fairly, provokes cynicism over the motive for so doing. In the punk community, those at the business end of every ism and phobia going were able to draw collective strength, whether organising benefits for uninsured musicians, supporting co-operative or independent businesses or organising chaperones to navigate the Planned Parenthood picket. A rebellious girl participating in these activities courts more opprobrium than her male counterpart; constantly told that her attitude and presentation will determine her (sexual) desirability and therefore her ultimate worth, it is always clear that her bad behaviour will, literally, cost her. She doesn't need to be told men set the market rate.

The young women who would form the backbone of riot grrrl were active in towns and cities like this, their consciousness raised by having the entitlement to equality they'd been educated to embrace dashed just as quickly as it came time to enter higher education and the world of work. At university, the work of feminist artists and thinkers was, for many, on the syllabus for the first time, as was work by practitioners 'of colour'. That syllabus was rich with the efforts of second-wave feminist artists like Judy Chicago and Carolee Schneeman as well as writers whose attitude to physicality ran the gamut from guarded to exhibitionistic; sexuality and its signifiers acquired intellectual baggage. The terms to adequately express dissatisfaction with outdated social models, such as colonialism, the court system and imperialism, were suddenly available for debate. In discovering their own feminism, some opined that men might not even be necessary, or even better, decided that man's abject slavery to his genitalia might as well be exploited to pay tuition fees. Feminism's third wave had begun.

Back in American centres of cultural capital such as New York and Los Angeles, where commercial pressures were just as important as political pressures, a handful of art practitioners, curators and gallerists organised anonymously to form Guerrilla Girls in 1985 in an effort to challenge male supremacy in the visual arts. Their tactics and presentation were directly inspirational to riot grrrl, as they agitated for greater representation by female arts practitioners who felt marginalised in a booming art market. A self-described 'terrorist, subversive organisation', Guerrilla Girls used both illegal flyposting and modern advertising techniques to get their messages across, all the while disguised in gorilla masks, fishnet tights and miniskirts. Slick and professional, their use of the newly invented desktop publishing tools enabled the creation of an arresting 'corporate identity' attacking complacency around inequality with a sarcastic, wry vigour.

"We tend to shock people with the information that we give them. In no other profession in Western culture—medicine, Wall Street, whatever—are women as badly discriminated against as they are in the visual arts. Painting has traditionally been a heroic male activity, for example. There is potentially more money in art than in any other field, and the boys want to keep that for themselves. There's not enough of a historical precedent to allow women to participate", one Guerrilla Girl told me in 1991.

1980s New York, where the Guerrilla Girls first came together, was at the time the capital of the art world and therefore the place where auction houses, museums and high society came together to celebrate their own dizzying successes; downtown art stars were feted as new Warhols by uptown dealers and top collectors appeared to lap the whole circus up. It was therefore strange to see Guerrilla Girls criticised for complaining from what 'the disadvantaged' would doubtless consider an elite, privileged position where they should consider themselves lucky to make any money from art at all, criticised by 'liberal' contemporaries and gatekeepers for biting the hand that feeds. It is a familiar attitude to feminist protest, held even by those on the left side of politics, and one each new generation of feminists hopes to surmount yet inevitably meets. Never mind that many of Guerrilla Girls' anonymous contributors worked at institutions, sat on grant and tenure committees and saw up-close the rationale behind decision makers' choices and the way those decisions left women and minorities at a further disadvantage. They were supposed to just suck it up in exchange for being allowed to compete at all.

By the late 1980s, Guerrilla Girls really hit their rhythm, with campaign advertisements appearing on the sides of New York City buses. In 1989 a painted, reclining nude was captioned "do women have to be naked to get into the Met?" along with statistics that reported less than five per cent of twentieth century art displayed at the Metropolitan Museum of Art was *by* women artists, but 85 per cent of the nudes were of women. Using soundbite-sized bits of scholarship and deconstructed four-colour printing, their messages did not just address the art world but pointed to wider abuse and discrimination of women by the same status quo that relied on a specific Western canon to determine the benchmarks of aesthetics and value. Of course art, commerce and ideas of worth are interwoven.

Speaking truth to power was not the exclusive preserve of female artists in the 1980s. Having seemingly only just won the right to equality of treatment in the workplace and the

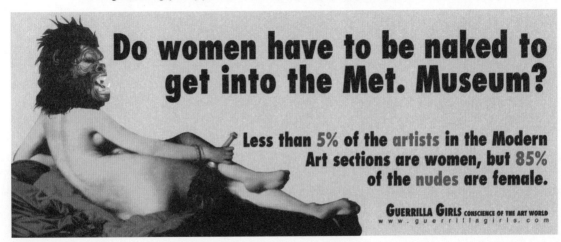

community, gay men joined the women on the art picket as, from 1984, AIDS contributed to a climate of fear and prejudice against them. While anyone can get HIV, the disease's early appearance in downtown bathhouses imperiled New York's gay community. Many fought back as part of the campaign group ACT-UP, which formed in the mid-1980s to publicise the plight of AIDS patients left marooned by politicians and the American healthcare industry and to educate the public about the parameters and responsibilities of safe sex. HIV cut across class and racial lines, ACT-UP argued, so a public perception of 'good AIDS' patients (haemophiliacs, babies) versus 'bad AIDS' patients (flamboyant gays, intravenous drug users) was not merely disingenuous (especially when members of New York's establishment known for homophobic beliefs and sharp practices were diagnosed HIV positive) but this hypocritical state of affairs also compounded the suffering of patients.

In 1987, artist members of ACT-UP were asked by New York's New Museum of Contemporary Art to create an installation, *Let The Record Show*, exhorting passers-by to involve themselves with the fight against AIDS and offering relevant statistics in the manner so effectively employed by Guerrilla Girls. Already well known for the graphic shorthand of SILENCE = DEATH, the ACT-UP group dubbed themselves Gran Fury in tribute to their righteous anger and the most common marque of American police car. Like Guerrilla Girls, Gran Fury had access to advertising hoardings and the PSA budgets underwritten by that industry: their messages soon appeared on the sides of buses and between the adverts on subway train cars; in a mock newspaper, *The New York Crimes*, a one-off sleeved around commuters' copies of *The Times* highlighting AIDS stories seldom covered in the newspaper of record. With Gran Fury joined by the more confrontational stance of Outpost, a pressure group formed to "out" culturally powerful individuals who remained in the closet, usually when it was felt that their lack of identification with the gay community was financially or socially motivated.

When the money afforded by the boom years of the 1980s ran out, and the ending of the Cold War removed the 45 year threat of mutually assured destruction, these identity politics and desire to question the social model remained as intellectual fodder to underpin the growth of a conflicted yet confident new generation. Young gays and lesbians were part of a larger counterculture made up of the 'dissatisfied customers' of North American society, influenced by artists and musicians, where individual sexuality was both central to that individual and also part of a wider spectrum of 'outsider' desire. Young Punks who Questioned Heterosexuality—an interrogation panel that took in gays, lesbians, students of art and language theory, feminists of every gender—delighted in teasing the mainstream with a scatology borrowed liberally from the 'bent' filmmaking of John Waters and a desire to subvert cultural and social norms. Existing in tandem with this exhibitionism were

Guerrilla Girls on the prowl. © Guerrilla Girls.
Courtesy of www.guerillagirls.com

expressions of introspection and self-exploration, committed to films, records and zines. This was queercore, a strain of punk that used sexuality as a point of departure and identification; queercore's adherents came from across the LGBTQ spectrum and challenged capitalist gay culture in the same way straight punks attacked hypocritical heterosexuals, and their numbers could be counted from college towns to North American capitals. You didn't have to be gay to see the attraction of queercore, either—anyone who questioned bog-standard sexuality and the clichés of coupledom within capitalism found collaboration and friendship possible there.

Within a movement called New Queer Cinema, evolving when queercore artists and zine editors applied their theories to their own film work, the most arresting images were provided by a Milwaukee 15 year old—Sadie Benning—whose father made a birthday gift of a Fisher-Price Pixelvision camera to her, enabling her to start making lo-fi films. Fisher-Price toys have an iconic place in American childhood; durable and made of bright plastic, most children (including me) owned barnyard and household play sets with Little People figurines depicting a nuclear family; lo-tech cameras, cassette and record players were just as important in introducing technology to young children as the other toys were used to inculcate traditional social values. Long discontinued even in 1990, the Pixelvision camera used cassette tapes as film, and the high-contrast, lo-resolution images it produced perfectly mirrored the girl's experience as a young lesbian commenting on her place in the world from the relative safety of her bedroom. Although totally toy-town, Pixelvision in the right hands offered lo-fi clarity of intent.

By the age of 19, Sadie Benning's videos had appeared in the Whitney Biennale and been retrospectively featured at New York's Museum of Modern Art. Most of her early videos were no longer than a pop single and their sharp contrast and collaged or handwritten transitions evoke the fanzine aesthetic as the films tell the evolving story of one girl's coming out and its outcome. In *It Wasn't Love*, Benning shoots a 'road movie' without leaving her room; hers is a journey of imagination and self-discovery nevertheless. The room proves difficult to leave, although staying there can only ever be temporary, because of the horror and violence outside where Benning is pilloried for her sexuality and set upon by bullies, realising she too is implicated in a sprawling cycle of violence when she eventually vanquishes one tormentor. *A Place Called Lovely*, acknowledges her abuser's victimisation by his own abusive parents and shows childhood as a battleground where her inability to play 'the good white girl', compliant and heterosexual, has come about because she has noticed that accepting this role disempowers women as a whole.

In *Girlpower* 1992 Benning elucidates many of the feelings riot grrrls, by now active across North America and Britain, were busy negotiating and replicating in their own films, records and zines: "I built my own world inside my head. I had imaginary

Grrrls, Grrrls, Grrrls, Riot Grrrl Fly Grrrl Posters. ICA, 4 December, 1993. Image courtesy of Susan Corrigan.
Opposite: Still from Sadie Benning's *It Wasn't Love* video. © Sadie Benning. Image courtesy of The Video Data Bank.

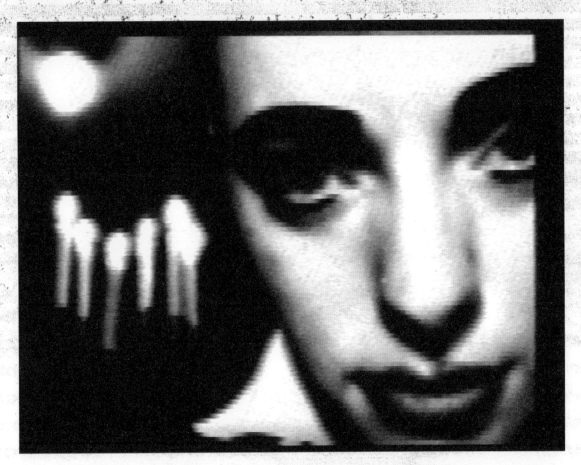

friends, make believe love. I traveled to far away places and did as I pleased. I fought the law and, of course, made my own rules." *Girlpower* envisages an autonomous teen girl culture, active in its pursuit of desire rather than willing to be the passive recipients of whatever crumbs of attention men saw fit to bestow upon them, or their 'market'. It dreams out loud in the hope that somewhere else, the reality of 'girl love forever' will coalesce. Four years later, of course, a clutch of music industry executives who'd probably never appreciated 'girl power' in its original context co-opted the term for a manufactured pop group comprised of female archetypes recruited from stage schools.

The mid-1990s anti-feminist backlash that followed the peak of riot grrrl's brief journey overground is difficult and uncomfortable to pick out, with the 'post-feminist' era declared in a number of books by idiosyncratic authors such as Susan Faludi, Camille Paglia, Naomi Wolf and Elizabeth Wurtzel. All 'cool', all more easily absorbed into a culture where women's arguments are encouraged by male bystanders and then dismissed as shrill— none of whom were able to get past that old canard about the shaving (or not) of armpits determining what kind of woman you were under your skin. The new girl power was bound up in the harnessing of new commercial markets selling carefree debauchery to women who worked just as hard as 'the boys' and therefore were entitled to play just as hard. The physical displays made by riot grrrls on their own terms were echoed by the traditional star system of the manufactured end of the music industry; riot grrrls did this for reasons of art and catharsis (principles, not money, were at stake) whilst exhibitionism or a desire for fame fuelled what was, after all, just showbiz.

Aided by the internet, riot grrrl soon went back underground, appealing to the next generation of girls, who were under more pressure to conform sexually and visually than their predecessors had been, and more vulnerable to the influence of fashion and peer pressure; young women were encouraged to appreciate the aesthetic of pornography and imitate it; the post-feminist would say that a woman had the freedom to choose to do so and those who didn't probably had something worth hiding from men. That font of all pornography, the internet, was now just as important to young women as guitars and handwritten letters had been to girls less than a decade before. Girls could now meet each other on message boards and link to each others' blogs, where affecting prose equal to anything in the first riot grrrl zines was a mere mouse-click away; MP3s traveled across continents, swapped by excited girls who'd never find a copy of the first Huggy Bear 7", not even on eBay. Cheap technology made the means of musical production even easier to access than to film with Pixelvision. Fittingly, in 1998, Sadie Benning, then 25, took a temporary hiatus from filmmaking when joining Kathleen Hanna and Joanna Fateman in the original lineup of Le Tigre; because of her age and practice, she'd long been networked into both queercore and riot grrrl. A circle of consistent and radical action completed itself in this group, and is one of many collaborations made possible by the alliances formed by politically aware young people who refused to be put asunder by differences which had scuppered the prospects of earlier, more easily divided, protestor cultures.

Although riot grrrls wanted revolution girl-style NOW—and for a while in 1992 and 1993 it looked like we might get exactly that—enormous changes in the larger political climate and global issues have conspired to delay that gratification somewhat. Homophobic crimes are still front-page news in the small American towns that gay teenagers run screaming from at the first opportunity; violence against women is still perpetrated in the name of half a dozen different gods, only one of which is money; reproductive rights are variable between American states and most western countries and women still tell themselves that men are feeble creatures because they've learned a bit of pole-dancing, are comfortable commodifying their own body, and competition between women for men or other prizes is just playing to win.

We may have to go back to the intellectual drawing board of art and academia to fight this latest, remixed version of the perpetual culture war waged by the holders of heterosexual male privilege against all others. What kind of girl riot could happen right now? This time, those who inhabit that bastion have even larger amounts of money and status at stake, and more to lose; the rich recycle out of virtue, not necessity. This pay-and-display culture is redolent of late 1980s New York, the art world booms again and those with new money and the attendant influence speculate upon its products and try to second-guess their future value. Male artists who demonstrate the 'heroic' are having a pretty good time of it, but 20 years after Guerrilla Girls attempted to raise the consciousness of Manhattan's pedestrians, the teenagers and university students attracted to queercore and riot grrrl have grown up without giving up, becoming artists, curators and gallerists themselves, determined to participate on equal footing. Representation by female artists, while still not equal to men, took off in the 1990s with the advent of the Young British Artists and their American and Japanese counterparts. As clampdowns on the public's freedom of expression and right to gather in protest become more stringent, radical art is bridging the gap of participation in a phase of inspiration; whether the content is anti-war, anti-discrimination, anti-racist or anti-religious, it stands there for those of us who cannot speak or have not found our own true voices. Yet.

Shelly Mars in Annie Sprinkle's, *Sluts and Goddesses*,
at the ICA *Bad Girls* exhibition, 1993.

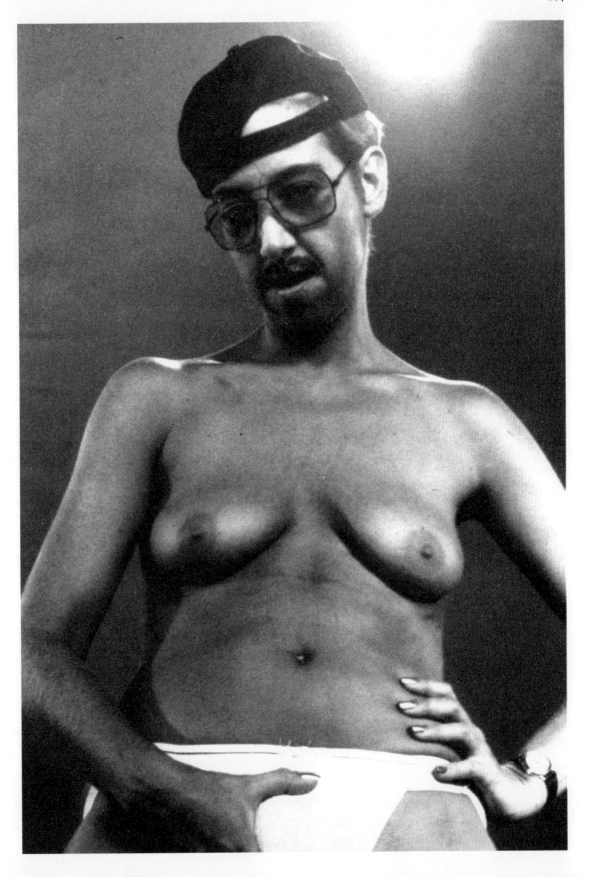

AN AMERICAN RIOT GRRRL TIMELINE

Julia Downes

1982

K Records is set up by Calvin Johnson.

1986

Go Team form (Line up: Tobi Vail, Calvin Johnson, Billy Karren).

Candice Peterson starts as an intern at K Records, eventually becomes joint owner.

1987

Erin Smith becomes a Beat Happening fan and starts her fanzine *Teenage Gang Debs*.

K Records starts the International Pop Underground 7-inch single series.

1988

Donna Dresch starts *Chainsaw* fanzine.

Tobi Vail starts *Jigsaw* fanzine.

Kathleen Hanna sets up the art gallery Reko Muse with her friends including Tammy Rae Carland and starts volunteering at Safespace.

Maximum Rock 'n' Roll does a "Women's Issue" (June).

Cynthia Connelly, Leslie Clague and Sharon Cheslow put out *Banned in DC*: Photos and Anecdotes from the DC Underground on Sun Dog Propaganda (1 November).

1989

Go Team tour America and meet Fugazi and NOU in DC.

Sharon Cheslow's *Interrobang* zine focusses on punk and sexism.

Kathleen Hanna reads *Jigsaw* and starts interviewing bands whilst on tour with Viva Knievel.

SPRING

Erin Smith visits Olympia, meets Calvin Johnson who introduces her to Lois Maffeo.

FALL

Lois Maffeo moves to DC and Erin Smith plays guitar at shows with her.

Molly Neuman and Allison Wolfe are next-door neighbours in dorms at University of Oregon in Eugene, Oregon. They start singing songs a capella at parties

1990

SPRING

Molly Neuman visits Allison Wolfe in Olympia and sees many shows including Beat Happening, Nirvana and Melvins at Grange Hall. They read Tobi Vail's *Jigsaw* fanzine.

SUMMER

Molly Neuman and Allison Wolfe have the idea of starting a radio show and fanzine to promote girls. Calvin Johnson asks Molly and Allison to play a gig on Valentines day 1991.

Corin Tucker starts telling people she's in a band called Heavens to Betsy.

FALL

Corin Tucker moves to Olympia to attend Evergreen College.

Bikini Kill form (line up: Kathleen Hanna, Tobi Vail, Kathi Wilcox, Billy Karren).

WINTER

Molly Neuman returns to DC for Christmas and makes the first *Girl Germs* on a xerox machine at her Dad's office. She is also introduced to Erin Smith via Calvin Johnson, they become pen-pals.

1991

Kathleen Hanna puts out *Bikini Kill #1* fanzine "a color and activity book".

First Bratmobile show—14 February at The Surf Club (line up: Allison Wolfe and Molly Neuman) in Olympia with Bikini Kill and Some Velvet pavement. This might have been the first official Bikini Kill show as well.

Tobi Vail puts out *Jigsaw* #3 subtitled "angry grrrl zine".

Bikini Kill demo tape "Revolution Girl Style Now" starts off self-released then gets distributed by K Records.

SPRING

Allison Wolfe and Molly Neuman visit DC in Spring break and practice as "Bratmobile DC" at the Embassy with Christina Billotte, Erin Smith and Jen Smith.

Allison Wolfe and Molly Neuman see and subsequently meet NOU.

Sharon Cheslow receives letters from Ian MacKaye and Tim Green about Bikini Kill and angry grrrl zine.

Mount Pleasant riots, Roe v Wade legislation under threat.

Allison Wolfe receives the "we need a girl riot" letter from Jen Smith.

SUMMER

Bikini Kill tour with NOU (May/June).

Kathleen Hanna, Molly Neuman, Allison Wolfe, Tobi Vail stay in DC for summer.

Kathleen Hanna forms The Wonder Twins with Tim Green and Suture with Sharon Cheslow (guitar) and Dub Birdzell (drums).

Erin Smith interns at *Sassy* magazine in New York (June).

Allison Wolfe and Molly Neuman create the first *Riot Grrrl* fanzine in Molly's dad's office.

Riot Grrrl fanzines handed out for free at shows around DC.

Need for meetings expressed to discuss issues of sexism, share information/means of production and encourage/support each other. Mailing and phone number lists of interested girls and women gathered at shows.

First Riot Grrrl meeting is held at Jenny Toomey's house, they continue at various locations including Positive Force House. Many creators of the *Riot Grrrl* fanzine don't attend the meetings. Kathleen Hanna and Erika Reinstein attributed as main organisers of meetings.

Corin Tucker starts Heaven's to Betsy with her best friend Tracy Sawyer. They are asked to play the International Pop Underground by Michelle Noel.

Bratmobile play shows in New York and DC (line up: Allison Wolfe, Molly Neuman and Erin Smith)

Slim Moon sets up Kill Rock Stars and releases the LP/CD compilation *Kill Rock Stars* with help from Calvin Johnson.

20–25 August International Pop Underground Convention at Capitol Theatre in Olympia Opening night is Girls Nite "Love Rock Revolution Girl Style".

Riot Grrrl Olympia begins to hold meetings at various locations including Martin / Ray apartments, Evergreen, dorm rooms, etc.

Molly Neuman and Allison Wolfe move to Olympia and attend Evergreen.

FALL

Slim Moon releases wordcore vol 1 KRS 101 Kathleen Hanna "rock star" / Slim Moon "mean" split 7".

Bikini Kill #2 "Girl Power".

Sassy magazine covers riot grrrl for the first time.

1992

Heavens to Betsy are recorded by Molly Neuman in Olympia and Bratmobile are recorded by Tim Green at the Embassy. Split 7 inch *My Secret/ Cool Schmool* released by K Records.

Mark Wobensmith's fanzine Outpunk evolves into a record label to release queercore bands. *There's A Faggot In The Pit* and *There's A Dyke In The Pit* (includes Tribe 8, Bikini Kill, 7 Year Bitch and Lucy Stoners) 7" are released.

Riot Grrrl New York began producing zines and holding meetings.

Riot Grrrl Press set up by Erika Reinstein and May Summer.

SUMMER

Heavens to Betsy and Bratmobile tour America.

Kill Rock Stars releases Bikini Kill self-titled EP (KRS 204).

LA Weekly (July 10—16) "Revolution Girl Style Now" article by Emily White.

First riot grrrl convention in Washington DC (31 July–2 August).

USA Today (7 August) "Feminist Riot Grrls don't just wanna have fun" article by Elizabeth Snead.

FALL

Newsweek (23 November) "Revolution, Girl Style" article by Farai Chideya, Melissa Rossi and Dogen Hannah.

Riot grrrl media blackout declared.

1993

The Washington Post (3 January) "Grrrls Only; From the Youngest, Toughest Daughters of Feminism—Self Respect You Can Rock To" article by Lauren Spencer.

Team Dresch form (line up: Donna Dresch, Kaia Wilson, Jody Bleyle, Marci Martinez).

SPRING

New York Times (14 February) "No Longer Rocks Playthings" article by Ann Powers.

Kill Rock Stars and Catcall Records release Bikini Kill *Yeah Yeah Yeah Yeah* / Huggy Bear *Our Troubled Youth* split LP (KRS 206/ Catcall 001).

Kill Rock Stars releases Heavens to Betsy *These Monsters are Real* 7".

SUMMER

Kill Rock Stars releases Bratmobile *Pottymouth* LP/CD.

Bratmobile tour America with Heavenly and Huggy Bear.

Rolling Stone (8–22 June) "Grrrls at War" article by Kim France.

Billboard (7 August) "Women Rockers Create Their Own Alternatives" article by Evelyn McDonnell.

Kill Rock Stars release Bikini Kill *New Radio* 7" (KRS 212).

Kill Rock Stars release Bikini Kill *Pussy Whipped* LP/CD/CS (KRS 218).

1994

Kill Rock Stars release Bratmobile *The Real Janelle* 12" EP/ CD-EP (KRS 219).

(March) Kill Rock Stars release Heavens to Betsy *Calculated* LP/CD (KRS 222).

Bratmobile break up on stage at a show in New York.

Kill Rock Stars release Team Dresch Hand
Grenade 7".

Riot Grrrl Convention in Omaha.

Riot Grrrl Convention in Tacoma.

Tamra Spivey sets up Riot Grrrl American Online
(AOL) message board.

Donna Dresch's Chainsaw fanzine develops
into a record label and beings releasing records
by The Fakes, The Need, Team Dresch, The
Frumpies, Sleater Kinney and *Free to Fight*
compilation. The online message board provides
a crucial space for discussion and community.

Jody Bleyle sets up Candy Ass records based in
Portland, Oregon.

1995

Kill Rock Stars release Bikini Kill *The Anti-
Pleasure Dissertation* 7" (KRS 250).

Kill Rock Stars release Pussycat trash *Amore* 7"
(KRS 249).

Kill Rock Stars release Bikini Kill *I like Fucking / I
Hate Danger* 7" (KRS 253).

Riot Grrrl Los Angeles formed. Riot Grrrl
convention in Los Angeles.

Chainsaw and Candy Ass records co-release
Team Dresch *Personal Best* LP/CD.

Candy Ass releases *Free to Fight* double LP and
Team Dresch tour with self-defence trainer Alice
Stagg, Sue Fox.

Chainsaw and Candy Ass records co-release
Team Dresch *Captain My Captain* LP/CD.

1996

Kill Rock Stars release Bikini Kill *Reject
All American* CD/LP/CS (KRS 260).

Kaia Wilson and Melissa York leave Team
Dresch.

Riot Grrrl DC re-formed by younger cohort
of girls.

Riot Grrrl Olympia re-formed by younger group
of girls.

Riot Grrrl Orange County formed.

SPRGRL Conspiracy Convention in Portland,
Oregon (July).

Santa Barbara 'Girl Convention' (21–23 June)

Chicago 'Grrrl Fest' takes place.

Seattle 'Girl Con' Convention (5–7 July).

Philadelphia 'East Coast Riot Grrrl Convention'.

Tammy Rae Carland and Kaia Wilson start Mr
Lady records (1996–2004).

1997

Riot Grrrl Olympia hold 'Olympia Foxfire'
Convention.

Riot Grrrl Orange County hold a riot grrrl

Convention in conjunction with Summer
Solidarity punk festival.

'Girl Conventions' in Boston, Tacoma,
Washington and San Francisco.

Academic interest in girl studies—National
Women's Studies Association hosts an academic
conference theme of 'girls'.

1998

Bikini Kill break up.

Team Dresch break up.

The Butchies form (line up: Kaia Wilson, Allison
Martlew and Melissa York) and Mr Lady records
releases *Are We Not Femme* LP/CD.

Kathleen Hanna leaves Olympia for Durham,
North Carolina and makes Julie Ruin solo album
which is released by Kill Rock Stars (KRS 297).

Kill Rock Stars release Bikini Kill *The Singles* CD
(KRS 298).

Temple University has the first officially
recognised and funded Riot Grrrl chapter.

Puget Sound Girls Convention.

1999

Riot Grrrl Boston Convention at YMCA in
Cambridge, MA (20–21 August).

Riot Grrrl Eastside (Seattle/Bellevue).

San Francisco 'It's a Girl Thang: Third annual
Young Feminist Conference" (April).

Riot Grrrl New York and Riot Grrrl DC host
convention at New York University Womyn's
centre.

2000

First Ladyfest is organised and held (Olympia,
Washington) 1–6 August.

Rock 'n' Roll Camp for Girls founded in Portland,
Oregon as a summer day camp.

2001

Ladyfest Midwest (Chicago, IL) 16–19 August.

Ladyfest East Hampton (Easthampton, MA)
24–25 August.

Ladyfest East (New York).

Ladyfest Indiana (Bloomington, IN) 5–8 April.

2002

Ladyfest Lansing (Lansing, MI) 11–14 April.

Ladyfest Bay Area (SF/Bay Area, CA) 24–28 July.

Ladyfest DC (Washington, DC) 7–11 August.

Ladyfest Orlando (Orlando, FL) 29 September.

Ladyfest East #2 (Brooklyn, NY) 19–22 September.

Ladyfest South (Atlanta, GA) 10–13 October.

Ladyfest Los Angeles (Los Angeles, CA)
8–11November.

2003

Ladyfest Florida 6–9 March.

Ladyfest Philly (Philadelphia, PA) 20–23 March.

Ladyfest Seattle (Seattle, WA) 26–30 March.

Ladyfest Lansing (Lansing, MI) 10–13 April.

Ladyfest Texas (Austin, TX) 23–25 May.

Ladyfest Out West (Denver, CO) 18–22 June.

Ladyfest Orange County (Orange County, CA)

Rock 'n' Roll Camp for Girls opens institute in North East Portland.

Ladyfest Bay Area (San Francisco, CA) July 30– August 1.

Ladyfest Biblebelt (Denton, TX) September 30-October 3.

Ladyfest East (New York) October 29-November 1.

Ladyfest South #2 (Atlanta, GA) 4–7 November.

Willie Mae Rock Camp founded in New York City.

2004

Ladyfest Lansing (Lansing, MI) 15–18 April.

Ladyfest Texas (Austin, TX) 27–30 May.

Ladyfest Ohio (Columbus, OH) 28–31 May.

Ladyfest Richmond (Richmond, VA) 30 April–2 May.

Ladyfest Seattle (Seattle, WA) 24–27 June.

Ladyfest Bay Area (San Francisco, CA) 30 July–1 August.

Ladyfest Biblebelt (Denton, TX) 30 September–3 October.

Ladyfest East (New York) 29 October–1 November.

Ladyfest South #2 (Atlanta, GA) 4–7 November.

Willie Mae Rock Camp founded in New York City.

2005

Ladyfest Hawaii (Honolulu, HI) 3–6 March.

Ladyfest Lansing (Lansing, MI) 14–17 April.

Ladyfest Arcata (Humbolt County, CA).

Ladyfest San Diego (San Diego, CA) 14–17 July.

14–17Ladyfest Olympia (Olympia, WA)–July 28–31

Ladyfest Buffalo (Buffalo, NY) Summer

Ladyfest Out West (Denver, CO)–August 5–7

Ladyfest Ohio (Columbus, OH) October 7–9

Ladyfest East (New York, NY) October 14–16

Ladyfest North Carolina (Durham, NC) - October 21-23

Ladyfest Out West (Denver, CO) 5–7 August.

Ladyfest Ohio (Columbus, OH) 7–9 October.

Ladyfest East (New York, NY) 14–16 October.

Ladyfest North Carolina (Durham, NC) 21–23 October.

2006

Ladyfest Hawaii (Honolulu, HI) 3–5 March.

Ladyfest Bay Area (San Francisco, CA) 30 June–7 July.

Ladyfest South (Atlanta, GA).

Ladyfest Las Vegas (Las Vegas, Nevada).

Ladyfest SATX (San Antonio, Texas) 19–21 October.

2007

Ladyfest South #3 (Atlanta, GA) 25–29 January.

Ladyfest Las Vegas (Las Vegas, Nevada).

Ladyfest Chicago 28–21October.

A BRITISH RIOT GRRRL TIMELINE

Julia Downes

1986

Talulah Gosh formed.

1987

Karren Ablaze! starts *Ablaze!* magazine.

1989

Paul Cox starts club-night The Sausage Machine @ The White Horse.

Andy Roberts, Jen Denitto and Tammy Denitto start playing together (Linus).

Heavenly formed.

1990

Erica Smith starts *GirlFrenzy* with money diverted from paying the Poll Tax.

1991

20 September—first Huggy Bear gig with Heavenly.

K Records *Riot Grrrl* newsletter released.

December—second Huggy Bear gig: Heavenly's Christmas Party.

Mambo Taxi formed.

1992

March/April–Huggy Bear 1st 'new sound' gig @ Bull and Gate.

Huggy Bear play Rough Trade shop, Covent Garden.

April—Karren Ablaze writes a *Riot Grrrl* manifesto, inspired by her conversation with Tim Green of NOU.

Avocado Baby formed.

Slampt Underground Organisation set up by Rachel Holborow and Pete Dale.

Pussycat Trash formed.

June/July Huggy Bear interviewed by SMJ & ET.

Sally Margaret Joy "Revolution Grrrl Style Now!" 10 October *Melody Maker*.

Voodoo Queens formed.

1993

Riot Grrrl #1 fanzine released.

Riot Grrrl London released.

Riot Grrrl Leeds-Bradford zine released.

Huggy Bear on The Word 12 February.

Huggy Bear on *Melody Maker* front cover 27 February

March/April: Huggy Bear and Bikini Kill British tour.

Valentines day gig Huggy Bear, Blood Sausage & Linus at Richmond, Brighton.

March 3rd Bikini Kill, Huggy Bear and others @ the Conway Hall, London.

International Women's day 8 March.

Huggy Bear *Our Troubled Youth* / Bikini Kill *Yeah Yeah Yeah Yeah* LP released on Catcall.

20th March "All-girl" gig Bikini Kill, Huggy Bear and Linus @ the White Horse.

April "Woman-only" gig Hole and Huggy Bear at Subterrania.

Girlygig at The Monarch.

Bratmobile British tour with Huggy Bear/ Heavenly.

Huggy Bear tour America and Japan.

October Heavenly/ Lois British tour.

Grrrlstyle Revolution at the ICA, 4 December.

1994

26 February Piao! festival at The Emerald Centre, Hammersmith, London. 35 bands including Heavenly, Gorky's Zygotic Mynci, Prolapse, Frantic Spiders, Pussycat Trash, Avocado Baby, Witchknot, Beatnik Film Stars, Delicate Vomit, Emperor Julian, Coping Saw, Mambo Taxi, Sister George, Hood, I'm Being Good, Lollyshop,

Th'Faith Healers, Schwartzeneggar, Linus.

Piao! distro and club night at Laurel Tree.

June/July: Heavens to Betsy & Pussycat Trash British tour.

December: Huggy Bear play last gig at the Laurel Tree with Skinned Teen.

1995

Voodoo Queens, Pussycat Trash and Mambo Taxi break up.

April: Club Vaseline begins upstairs at The Garage.

Slamptumentary is released.

1996

Mathew Fletcher coins the riot grrrl term for Oxford English Dictionary.

Mathew Fletcher commits suicide.

1997

Melting Vinyl set up in Brighton.

1998

Valerie formed Queeruption at 121 centre in Brixton.

Lo Fi Fest at Star and Garter, Manchester with Red Monkey, Red Kross.

2000

Last Club V on 2 September.

Le Tigre British tour.

2001

Slampt's farewell festival.

Ladyfest Glasgow—First British Ladyfest, 12–14 August.

2002

X-Offender club night starts at Retro Bar, Manchester.

Ladyfest London, 2–4 August.

Pussy Whipped club night starts at Bar Phono, Leeds.

2003

Ladyfest Exeter 24–27 April.

Ladyfest Bristol 11–14 August.

Local Kid (Bristol).

Irrk Records set up.

Unskinny Bop club night (London).

Here shop opened in Bristol.

Homocrime (London) 30 August : *Homocrime #1* The Gossip and The Battys at Needles.

Ladyfest Manchester, September.

Mass Teens on the Run club night starts in Manchester.

Club Motherfucker starts up (London).

2004

Ladyfest Birmingham, 9–11 July.

Bring Yourself Fest—Local Kid.

Kaffequeeria starts up (Manchester).

Shake-o-rama (Manchester).

Ladyfest Dublin.

Ladyfest Exeter, 16–18 April.

Peppermint Patti starts up (Cardiff).

2005

Andy Roberts is killed in a tragic hit and run accident.

Ladyfest Brighton 20–23 October.

2006

Ladyfest Bournemouth.

Ladyfest Cardiff.

Ladyfest Newcastle, 22–24 September.

Nomocrime (final Homocrime) 3 June at Mayville Community Centre/ Bardens Boudoir.

FAG. Club starts up (Cardiff).

Female Trouble starts up (Manchester).

Cafe Kino opened in Bristol.

2007

Ladyfest Leicester.

Ladyfest Cambridge, 26 March–1 April.

Ladyfest Leeds, 10–15 April.

Ladyfest Nottingham.

2008

Ladyfest London.

Ladyfest Cork.

RIOT GRRRL DIRECTORY

Anna Feigenbaum

This directory features folks and spaces connected to riot grrrl. Some of the listings are directly affiliated with riot grrrl culture and politics, while others share a similar ethos. All the groups, spaces and websites listed here express a commitment to grrrls, feminism, queer politics, DIY culture, and unapologetic creativity! This list is just a starting point for finding riot grrrl and riot grrrl-inspired stuff going on in the Britain and North America. There is way more riot grrrl to be found around the world, much of which you can track down through the web links listed below.

BANDS & PERFORMERS

On these bands and performers' websites or myspace pages you can hear music, download songs, check tour dates, join their networks or buy a copy of their CDs.

The Bobbed Hair Bandits (no label)
www.myspace.com/thebobbedhairedbandits
This Manchester-based DIY band is named after a famous female gangster. They site riot grrrl acts Julia Ruin, Bratmobile and Heavens to Betsy amongst their influences.

Drunk Granny (FAG club)
www.myspace.com/drunkgranny
Formed in 2005, Drunk Granny is an indie rock band from Cardiff put out by fag club's record label. Drunk Granny claims to sound "like a hole cover band". They play at benefit gigs and DIY shows throughout Britain.

Gina Young (Exotic Fever Records)
www.ginayoung.com/
www.myspace.com/ginayoung
Influenced by the riot grrrl movement while growing up in Washington DC, singer/songwriter Gina Young produces music that is influenced by, and inspires, queer feminist communities.

Jean Genet (Manifesta Distro)
www.myspace.com/jeangenet
Live act performance duo, Jean Genet, have been playing together since 2004. Their queer songs and queerer stage antics have made them a favourite at gigs and festivals.

Lesbians on Ecstasy (Alien8 Recordings)
www.lezziesonx.com/
www.myspace.com/lesbiansonecstasy
Montreal-based Lesbians on Ecstasy, or LOE as they are called by devotees, have put out two albums that remix iconic lesbian music with dancefloor beats. LOE tours North America and Europe, bringing a third wave feminist bent to their stage performances.

Party Weirdo (Stitchy Press Records)
www.myspace.com/partyweirdomusic

Party Weirdo formed in 2006 in Dublin, Ireland. Their music features flute, cello and toy instruments along with bass, drums and guitar. Songs like "Chart Your Menstrual Cycle" creatively express their feminist politics.

Vile Vile Creatures (no label)
www.myspace.com/vilevilecreatures
Vile Vile Creatures is a Manchester-based band inspired by early riot grrrl acts, feminism and queer politics. They combine these influences in their own work, producing sharp critiques over heavy 'punk-disco' guitar and drums.

Wet Dog (no label)
www.myspace.com/wetdogthebest
Wet Dog is a DIY all girl, London-based three piece band—drums, bass and guitar—who play gigs and festivals around Europe.

FESTIVALS & EVENTS

The festivals and events listed here encourage folks to participate. You can join in already planned gatherings or start your own local group of organisers.

Girls Rock Camps
www.myspace.com/girlsrockcamp
www.girlsrockcamp.org
www.myspace.com/rocknrollcampforgirlsuk
www.girlsrockuk.org
Directly inspired and created by women in the riot grrrl movement, the first girls rock camp took place in 2001 in Portland, Oregon offering young women a space for empowerment and self-expression through the creation and performance of music. Portland's Rock 'n' Roll Camp for Girls now offers multiple summer sessions and is featured in the film Girls Rock! The Movie and the forthcoming book Can Rock. There are now girls rock camps in many locations, joined together through the Girls Rock Camp Alliance. The first Girls Rock UK! will be held in Summer 2008. Girls rock camps are volunteer-run and community supported.

Ladyfest
www.myspace.com/ladyfesteurope (current information)
www.ladyfest.org (archive of past festivals)
The first Ladyfest took place in Olympia, Washington, in 2000. Since then Ladyfest has continued and proliferated in cities throughout the world from Monterrey, Mexico, Malmo, Brighton, to Ottawa, Canada. Ladyfests feature women performers, as well as workshops for participants, on topics ranging from knitting to self-defence. The Ladyfest Europe website offers discussion boards that contain news and information on international Ladyfests, as well as a 'start your own' ladyfest guide. While most Ladyfests carry out riot grrrl's punk feminist tradition of DIY production and grassroots organisation, some festivals have taken a more commercial route, such as Ladyfest South Africa. Also, because festivals have different organisers and take place in different countries, ideas about gender and feminism can be as different as the music they showcase.

Queeruption
www.queeruption.org
London was home to the first Queeruption in 1998. Every year

since, a queeruption gathering has taken place that brings together Queer artists, performers, anarchists and other activists from many different countries. Queeruption is organised by and for queers and folks of all genders and gender identifications. The Queeruption gathering is a multilingual event that features shows and workshops, as well as skill-shares, communal cooking and spontaneous DIY creations. A number of cities and regions host groups linked to Queeruption that do local actions and benefits.

ZINE DISTROS & RECORD LABELS

Kill Rock Stars
www.killrockstars.com
One of the only remaining female-led record labels in the America, since 1991, Kill Rock Stars (KRS) has worked from a DIY ethics supporting queer-positive, feminist bands. KRS put out music by many early riot grrrl acts including Bikini Kill, Bratmobile and Heavens to Betsy. Women outfitted punk bands Mika Miko and Erase Errata are currently signed to KRS.

Manifesta Distro
www.manifesta.co.uk/zines
This not-for-profit distro run by Leeds-based collective Manifesta (see below) distributes zines, crafts and stationary. Re-assess Your Weapons and the Rag are some of Manifesta's riot grrrl related zines. They also distribute recordings of Jean Genet (see above).

ORGANISATIONS & GROUPS

These groups are always looking for new performers and community-based support. If you are interested in working with one of the collectives, get in touch! Contact information is listed here, or on their websites or myspace pages.

FAG club (Cardiff, Wales)
www.fagclub.net
Fag Club is a collective that works from a DIY feminist ethic, releasing records and putting on events. They create spaces for quags (queers of all genders and sexualities) to cultivate and share their creativity, politics and desire to play. FAG Club is open to performers and people interested in creating events that express the group's mission.

Female Trouble (Manchester, England)
www.myspace.com/femaletroublemanchester
Female Trouble is a recently formed group of Manchester-based 'feisty females'. Inspired by grrrl zine distros and discos, they plan to organise gigs and club nights as well as start a new zine called desperate living.

Girl Zines-A-Go-Go (California, USA)
www.gzagg.org/
Based in Southern California, Girl Zines-A-Go-Go is an all-woman collective that designs and runs regional, community-based workshops to empower young women through zine-making. They also works with other DIY media groups and they helped San Diego State University start up the West Coast Zine Library. Expressing their DIY ethic, the collective assists other folks to start up zine workshops in their own communities.

Kaffequeeria (Manchester, England)
www.kaffequeeria.org.uk

Kaffequeeria is a collective working out of Manchester that brings together vegan food and DIY queer culture. In response to the commercialisation of 'gay pride', they organise their own not-for-profit cafe night (or kaffe night), clubnights and workshops.

Local Kid (Bristol, England)
www.localkid.co.uk
Bristol-based Local Kid is a DIY punk feminist collective that put out a record label as well as organising and promoting gigs. They are pro-queer, pro-girl and pro-participatory.

Lola and the Carwheels (Sheffield, England)
www.myspace.com/lolaandthecartwheelssheff
Based in Sheffield, Lola and the Cartwheels is a collective for grrrls and bois aiming to create riot grrrl/queer-friendly events. They also have plans to start up a zine distro and are currently working with other collectives to put on gigs and clubnights.

Manifesta (Leeds, England)
www.manifesta.co.uk/
www.myspace.com/manifestaleeds
The Manifesta collective, based in Leeds, aims to cultivate free self-expression, organising inclusive music, art and cultural events for folks of all genders and sexualities. Manifesta hosts the monthly club night, Suck My Left One (named after a Bikini Kill song), and has future plans for creating hands-on music workshops, as well as a record label. Also see Manifesta Distro listed above.

Miss G_Project (Ontario, Canada)
www.themissgproject.org/
The Miss G_Project is a young feminist grassroots organisation working to initiate curriculum on Women's and Gender Studies in secondary schools in Ontario. High school and university students across the province work locally in their communities to raise support for the proposal.

Peppermint Patti (Cardiff, Wales)
www.peppermintpatti.co.uk/
Peppermint Patti is a not-for-profit, volunteer run promotion group that puts on shows headlining women fronted acts at Chapter in Cardiff, Wales.

Power Camp National/Filles D'action (Montreal, Canada)
www.powercampnational.ca/
Power Camp National (PCN) is a grassroots feminist organisation that works with girls and women. They run popular education, skill-based and artistic workshops to encourage girls to reflect on their experiences in empowering ways. PCN also publishes a guide on how to start similar such organisations in your own community.

Radical Cheerleaders (various locations)
www.nycradicalcheerleaders.org/
www.myspace.com/radicalcheerleadingbook
Radical Cheerleader groups are collectively run cheerleading squads that foster a body-postive, queer-positive environment. Working from a DIY ethos, squads make costumes, pom-poms and political cheers for performances at benefits, rallies and protests. There are active radical cheerleader groups in various cities around the North America and Europe—and where there isn't an active

squad, existing collectives will help out people that want to start one. Some radical cheerleaders are currently working on a zine anthology to document the last ten years of radical cheerleading.

Wotever (London, England)
www.woteverworld.com
The Wotever team cultivates spaces for queer people of all sexualities and genders to come together. Bar Wotever hosts a weekly open mic and film screening night. Club Wotever, Club Fukk and Wotever Gig showcase genderbending DJs and performers. Wotever also hosts a number of workshops and talks serving the queer community.

LIBRARIES, INFOSHOPS & OTHER SPACES

Bibliograph/e (Montreal, Canada)
Le Cagibi, 5490 St-Laurent
Montreal, Quebec Canada
www.bibliograph.ca
www.myspace.com/bibliograph
Bibliograph/e is Montreal's zine library. Its 5,000-plus collection features work by feminist, queer and independent-minded people. Bibliograph/e also runs workshops, artist talks and film screenings.

Cafe Kino (Bristol, England)
3 Ninetree Hill, Bristol, UK
www.cafe-kino.com
Located in Bristol, Café Kino is a non-profit, workers' co-op that serves inexpensive, ecologically-friendly food. The café also hosts a range of musical and other performances. Café ino is also used for curated exhibitions of independent artists and as a meeting space for the local Stitch n' Bitch.

Sallie Bingham Center Zine Collections (North Carolina, US)
www.library.duke.edu/specialcollections/bingham/zines/
Women's Library (London, England)
Anchor Zine Library (Halifax, Canada)

LISTSERVES, WEBSITES & INTERNET NETWORKS
The resources below will connect you with much more information on Riot Grrrl past and present.

Grrrl Zine Network
www.grrrlzines.net
The grrrl zine Network is a web based network founded by Austrian feminist and zine writer, Elke Zobl, in 2001. The Grrrl Zine Network is a global forum that fosters transcultural dialogues between contemporary grrrls, ladies, queers and trannies engaged in DIY media projects. The network serves as an active meeting place, as well as an archive housing writing and interviews from zine-makers and distributors around the world.

Nextgenderation
www.nextgenderation.net
Nextgenderation is a transnational European network linking activists, researchers and students interested in feminist politics and ways gender intersects with other forms of oppression.

The Nextgenderation website archives writing on these issues. Nextgenderation also hosts a popular listserve that offers regular information on feminist actions and events across Europe.

Riot Grrrl Online
www.hot-topic.org/riotgrrrl/
Riot Grrrl Online is a riot grrrl resource and information site. It serves as an archive of riot grrrl materials including articles on women's issues, band profiles, grrrl quotes and a live forum for chatting about all things riot grrrl related.

Pink Noises
www.pinknoises.com/
Pink Noises is a riot grrrl-inspired online archive of interviews, music-making resources and suggested readings on women and music. The website serves to recognise the work of women DJs, electronic musicians and sound artists, while also making technological information available to women and girls interested in electronic music production. Next year, webmistress and sound artist, Analog-Tara, will update the site to include new interviews.

Queer Zine Archive Project
www.qzap.org
Started in 2003, the Queer Zine Archive Project (QZAP) is a 'living history' archive of new and old zines by queer authors. This online archive was established to preserve the work of queer zinesters and make zines available to more people interested in queer communities' DIY publishing and creative production.

Worse Than Queer
www.worsethanqueer.com/
Involved in the American riot grrrl movement throughout the 1990s, Nguyen was one of the most prolific writers on riot grrrl. Mimi Nguyen's website, worse than queer—taken from the lyrics of Bikini Kill's song 'suck my left one'—archives her journal entries from the time and her articles for *Punk Planet*. She edited two volumes of the challenging and influential zine *Evolution of a Race Riot*.

Front cover of *Jigsaw* #5 1/2.

Produced by Tobi Vail of Bikini Kill.

tHE Jigs@w

number 5 1/2

RIOT GRRRL ZINES DIRECTORY

Red Chidgey

These notes provide a history of international riot grrrl zines from 1991 to the present day. They include influential Olympian/Washington zines, which were produced while riot grrrl was emerging, and those published by riot grrrl "chapters" or groups after the network spread. This is not a definitive directory and there are glaring omissions from active North American chapters (such as Olympia WA; Washington DC; New York; and Los Angeles). As zines are ephemeral publications that quickly fall out of circulation, these summaries provide an indication of riot grrrl discourse over the past two decades. Beyond this list there are also hundreds of individual girl zines which do not mention riot grrrl explicitly, but are very much influenced and shaped by the network.

Listings and reviews of grrrl-associated zines and comics are featured in the now-defunct *Factsheet Five*, *Action Girl Newsletter* and *Riot Grrrl Review* meta-zines (available in select zine libraries and archived on-line). Zine histories can also be found at Riot Grrrl Online, Experience Music Project Riot Grrrl Retrospective, Grrrl Zines, and Zine Wiki. Excerpts from grrrl-associated zines are published in *Girl Power*, *A Girl's Guide to Taking over the World* and *Zines!* (volumes one and two).

Riot grrrl zines are internationally archived in academic libraries and info-shops. A comprehensive directory of global zine libraries and archives, and a history of zine publishing in general, can be accessed at www.zinebook.com.

Jigsaw Tobi Vail
Olympia, Washington 1988–present

Not strictly a riot grrrl publication, this zine inspired Kathleen Hanna and Kathi Wilcox to befriend Vail, which then led to the formation of the band Bikini Kill. The term 'grrrl' first appeared in this zine as a parody of the Women's Liberation Movement's use of 'womymn' (reclaiming the word 'woman' from 'man'). Vail's linguistic trick later inspired the use of 'grrrl' in the riot grrrl zine, a name then appropriated by the mainstream media to describe the rise of punk rock feminism and its 'soundtrack bands'. Issue four features Hanna's article "Jigsaw Youth", which is reprinted in the liner notes to Bikini Kill: The CD of the first two records. In Jigsaw, issue five, Vail records her alienation from the term 'riot grrrl' through its proliferation and media distortion. *Jigsaw* contains detailed stream of consciousness articles, scene reports, fanzine reviews and interviews with bands and film-makers. Issue eight, 2003, includes writing by Layla Gibbons (Skinned Teen) about "Musical Youth" and resistance. Issues are put out periodically at www.bumpidee.com

Girl Germs Molly Neuman and Allison Wolfe
Washington DC; Olympia, WA, 1990–1992

With the motto "Spread as many girl germs as you can", this "pro-girl, pro-punk rock, pro-underground" zine was created by Bratmobile members Molly Neuman and Allison Wolfe. The second issue charted the rise of an angry grrrl brigade in Olympia: "There's something going on…. There's this total revolution dancing scheming daydreaming sidewalk-stalkin' bigdealhappening." The fifth issue discusses the media attention: "OK everyone—here's proof we don't have to rely on external Powers That Be for shallow dualistic capitalist 'let's watch those girlies kill each other off and rob 'em blind while they're not looking' fucked up 'analysis'

of our work. We can critique each other's work and create channels for real dialogue and criticisms amongst each other and groups/people who have real, challenging criticism of our works, and not have to wallow in the Media Monsters' (and its many supporters) dumfuck bullshit."

Girl Germs, issue three, 1992

Features: "Square and Circle Club" pro-dork editorial; letters received from readers of *Girl Germs*; domestic violence story; article on Chinese cultural identity; incest story; uncovering masturbation myths; "Girls Rule" and girl solidarity; short stories; interview with band Love Child; band recommendations; "When you meet a lesbian: Hints to the heterosexual woman"; Sadie Benning profile; fanzine reviews; communication and power rant; history of Molly and Allison's friendship; fanzine writing tips.

Girl Germs, issue four, 1992

Features: Collages, Review of IPU Girl's night; lesbians sleeping with guys; "So what's punk", "Memory" illustration of abuse; poems; personal rants and recommendations; demo and fanzine reviews; letters; interview with 7 Year Bitch.

Channel Seven Corin Tucker and Erika Reinstein
Olympia, WA, 1994

Corin Tucker was in the band Heavens to Betsy, who played their first show at the IPC Girl's Night. Erika Reinstein was an organiser for Washington DC Riot Grrrl chapter, author of Fantastic Fanzine and co-founder of the Riot Grrrl Press. Features: Critique of TV-like consumption of music and underground culture; "Rethinking Riot Grrrl" and race and class critiques; a history of the Riot Grrrl Press distribution project; recommended bands, fanzines and record labels, "dear upper middle class white girl" and a personal experience of class prejudice within the riot grrrl movement; Heavens to Betsy lyrics and tour dates; the racism of expecting non-white women to do anti-racist work for white people; a transcript of a conversation between Erika and May Summer about class backgrounds and middle class assumptions.

A Call to Arms, issue one Toronto, August 2001

Features: The feminist backlash and underground feminism; member profiles; "What Riotgrrrl/Feminism means to me"; "Anarcha-Feminism", poems and art; "A Reflection on Girl Only Space" essay; "Who is the real slim shady" critique of rapper Eminem; "Riot Grrrl (to me) Is" article on body image.

A Call to Arms issue two, Toronto, Canada, October 2001

Features: definitions of activism and activist, "Riot Grrrl Toronto" manifesto; Grrrl Love Sticker designs; What radical means; McManifesto and activism against multinational fast-food chain McDonalds; "Identifying" and being an activist not a label; "Revolution of One" and personal style of activism; photos from the anti-FTAA protests in Quebec City; Interview with Kathleen Hanna; flyer for mobilisation against WTO on 9 November 2001; Mobilise for Global Justice schedule of events;

Mobilise for Global Justice schedule of events; "Dear Kathleen" letter about Le Tigre playing at Michigan Women's festival (which has an anti-trans policy); "the activist and the schoolgirl", a reflection on grassroots activism; homemade stickers designs; list of online activist resources.

A Call to Arms, issue three Toronto, February 2003

The Body Issue. Features: "It's time to create our own media" editorial; self-defence tips; "Enslavement Blues" and transgender body issues; a look at "Barbie" advertising; "Beauty Hurts" illustration; "Heart Hating Body" poem; "Not Making my Mood Light" and addressing fatphobia by a think girl; "Humyn Hidden Agenda" poem; thoughts on Carme Wilson's anorexia; sexism in gay guys; "Could I get a booth, please" and body self-consciousness; "Radical Cheers" for radical cheerleading; "Alternative Menstrual Products" information; "Self Breast Exam" instruction; online resources.

In Spite of the Night Riot Grrrl KW
(Kitchener-Waterloo, 2002)

Features: "Intro to Riot Grrrl"; 'the tragic quest' of unattainable beauty myth standards; "Ways to Accept Your Body and Change Society"; "Two Shots" story of abuse victim Stacey Lannert killing her father and sentenced to life imprisonment; "Cuntology: a few facts about grrrl parts"; "No Clit in the Pit" and women's experience in hardcore punk communities; "Real Girl Power" manifesto.

Riot Grrrl Riot Grrrl London, 1992

Features: "A call to make fanzines" and "go forth and Riot Grrrl!!", comic strips; street harassment and talking back tactics; creating alternative music and communication cultures; "three chords now form a band"; "the Sex Pistols stole their equipment", girls don't have the same luxury; poetry; "daddy fucking dearest" family rant; "Fuck Men What about the Boys?" street harassment for prepubescent; "We're not Men Haters" but we're going to fight; girls up front and angry at gigs; a letter to Sally Margaret Joy from a male reader of her riot grrrl *Melody Maker* article; spoof profile on band Buffalo Tom; beauty myth rants; book review of Camille Paglia's Sexual Personae; "Bimbocide" death to bimbos; extract from Margaret Atwood's Good Bones; "Hey Lame Girlfriend" and mockers of riot grrrl; Nancy Spungen and Courtney Love (Spot the difference); book review of Deborah Spungen's And I Don't Want to Live This Life; attack on Johnny Pigozzi; menstruation rants; "Get a Bike! Get a Life!" and the feminist merits of cycling.

Leeds and Bradford Riot Grrrl!
Leeds, 1993

Compilation of the chapter's three "fastzines". Features: Contributor profiles; Herstory of the Leeds and Bradford chapter; "Girl Power Explosion" and riot grrrl media; rants on women in rock, street safety, demystifying rock'n'roll; local resources; condemnation about speaking out as a feminist; tips on starting a fanzine; flyer for American Riot Grrrl Press; "How to make records and tapes and cds" info; newspaper article on abortion rights in Poland; "The 'G' Word" about the girl in Riot Grrrl;

... Garbo was not accidental 1931

She was a waitress. I thought I was in love with her. Nights I drank
root beer floats and watched her. like a flamingo take orders and
deliver food. She would ask him what the fuck did he think he was
doing smoking cigars in the non-smoking section. Each night he asked
for a table in the non-smoking section because it was her section
and he smoked-cloves, cigars, banana peels-he smoked and blew smoke
rings at her butt when she turned her back after asking him what the
fuck did he think he was doing. He ate pie. He ate steak and eggs and
wiped drool from his mouth. She became a frustrated waitress and no
longer looked at me when she took my order.
    Then he threw a pipe at her pretty face and babbled, ranted about
his right to smoke in the non-smoking section as long as there were
people in the smoking section who weren't smoking. He babbled and brown
drool formed on his lips. He tore the fake plants from the fake dirt
from the planters that seperated the two sections.
    A truck driver pulled him up by the shirt, asked him who the fuck did
he think he was hurting a woman ain't no real man that'll hurt a woman.
    The frustrated waitress cried, rushing to the restroom. The tired
elderly manager along with the truck driver threw the ranting man out
and he shook his fists for he, too, was frustrated and he too was in
love with the waitress. I paid for my root beer float and left into
the night. I picked up the pipe from the floor before I stepped out,
stuffed it down in my purse. It smelled of vanilla and warmth.
    I walked home to my room of similar fragrances, passing bus stops litter

girl in riot grrrl; "Action is simple" and strategies for everyday activism;
collages; "What the NME did not print" article; rants; newspaper article on
women's art event at the ICA; ads for girl culture projects.

Vaginal Teeth Leeds, 1998

Features: Intro to the first Leeds Riot Grrrl meeting in five years; "soul
sparks fly and the words mean nothing" personal account of riot grrrl
history; collages and Jacky Fleming comic; "Agony Uncle Vic…" spoof
problem page; "Wank Image of the Fortnight"; "What we do at Riot Grrrl
Meetings"; "Riot Grrrl for everyone"; "no heavy shit" and mental health
issues; "Scarlet red and lost" short story; "looking the part" and riot
grrrl stagnation; "Hey Riot Grrrl…"; "Why Grrrl Love is the Best" ode to
a best friend; "Stuff about Grrrl Love" and "support first, then action";
"unlearning myths about grrrl friends".

Riot Girl London, issue one, London; 2000

Features: "Why Be a Riot Grrrl?" manifesto; "What Riot Grrrl Means to
Me", "My Feminism & Sexism in Rock"; "One Step Behind the Drum
Style" and a celebration of female drummers; "Marker Pen" and the need
to move beyond "Old American Riot Girl", "Respect" and girl's invisibility
in music culture; "Clair's Body Image" and a personal look at the effects
of "body fascism"; Babes in Toyland interview; "Brainless Tart" and
"The Sexual Double-Standard; poems and collage"; "Riot Grrrl London
manifesto".

Riot Girl London, issue two London, 2001

Features: A personal article on street abuse and resistance strategies;
"Evolution Girl Style Now" and riot grrrl moving away from a punk rock
focus; a pro-sex manifesto; "My Feminism" article on feminist pride;
a piece on whether Riot Grrrl should go over-ground; "Don't treat us
like children" article on women's art; "Sexual Apartheid in Iran" leaflet;
"Gender Blind?" article on abortion and equality issues in feminism;
"Why I'm a Feminist" piece; "What every grrrl needs to know" about
menstruation activism; "So wot the heck is riot grrrl", an explanation of
the scene; "Grateful?", acknowledging the gains that past women have
made for young women today; an interview with British feminist Natasha
Walter; "Punk Rock is Not Just for Your Boyfriend"; "the agit-prop activism
of the Guerrilla Girls; Women's Street History Projects" and fly-posting
tips; "Riot Girl London" manifesto.

Riot Girl London, issue three, London, 2002

Features: Busting stereotypes in "The New Riot Grrrl"; a personal reflection
on pornography; male feminist pride; Anti-ageing and Anti-Beauty Myth
collages; women's magazines and the link to eating disorders; a discussion
of Kathleen Hanna and exclusion; a critique of Yoko Ono and John Lennon's
the "Feminine Revolution"; "The Brotherhood" on patriarchal "men-only"
spaces; "Redefining Beauty" from advertisers and pornographers; riot grrrl
quotations; "Preaching to the Converted" and a defence of Ladyfest; Riot
Girl London manifesto.

thebrendanmay21@yahoo.com

photocard number
29212

name
E K NICHOLS

signature
E Kate Nichols

Education
Transport
Service

photocard number
31003

name
ADAM CRICK

signature
Adam Crick

Education
Transport
Service

photocard number
31003

name
Tasha

signature
B Lynch

Education
Transport
Service

photocard number
31003

name
PIERCE (the fierce
panda

signature

RiOT GRrRi eSSEX ziNe

The Riot Grrrl Midlands Zine

The Nerve Riot Grrrl Central England
place unknown, 2001

Features: "Riotgrrl Suck Because" manifesto; "Working Grrrls" and corporate equality issues; "Verbal harassment: how to get your own back"; "Love is familiarity, Romance is fairyland" critique of relationships; "Social Mannequin" poem; "Love Is…" article on queer parenting; "How Many Times Have You Heard Guys Exaggerate the Size of Their Dicks?" and reclaiming women's sexual organs; anti-fashion and anti-TV art; "On Being a Girl Who is Straightedge" personal reflection, "Ignorance = Fear = Hatred" article on homophobia; "Miss Bell's guide to first date dos and don'ts" satirical etiquette; "Breaking the Mould" and anti-conformity arguments; "Recommended Reading; Interview with Tamra from Lucid Nation"; Ladyfest Scotland flyer; "You've got the Power" grrrl-positivity; "Heroines schmeroines" and real-life lady role-models; "Sense{less} Minorities" poem.

Riot Grrrl Essex Clacton, 2002

Features: "Riot Grrrl Essex" Manifesto; Riot Grrrl Wales; "An Insidious Tool of the Patriarchal Hegemony Writes A Critique of Feminism and Riotgrrl" essay on the danger of identity politics; "Ain't I a Woman?" deconstructive quotations from academia; "On Not Playing Dead" a re-printed essay by Kathleen Hanna on capitalism, objectification and performance styles; flyer for the Fawcett Society; "Fighting Back" self-defence comic; Interview with SuMay from Gingerbeer (Lesbian London listings project); "Alone in bed with a magazine", a feminist guy's perspective on lad mags; Crimethinc's "Eight things you can do to get active"; zine flyers; "Race and Riot Grrrl" article on discrimination in punk feminism; "So how does a boy get into riot grrrl" reflective piece; "Rebranding Feminism" article on the Fawcett Society's feminist conference at the ICA; Ladyfest London flyer, "Ladyfest 2001, Glasgow and what Riot Grrrl means to me" article, news clipping on gender war in the Congo; "A Postmodern Critique of Feminism" and Judith Butler; photos from the Fair Trade March in London; "Oppression + Lies + Isolation = Alienation" manifesto on communal living and activism.

All Hands on the Bad One Riot Grrrl Midlands
place unknown, 2004

Features: "Sleater Kinney—A Biography and Review"; "About Riot Grrrl Midlands"; "Green Anarchy"; "Are There Really Two Types of People" article on free-thinking and the media; Riot Boi interviews, "Borderline Business" and mental health disorders; book reviews; "I'm afraid of Britney Spears" and how the pop singer is a bad role-model for young girls; "Mini Rants!" on Royal Mail, Boy-obsessed girls, Patronising Customers and Sexist T-Shirts.

Riot Grrrl Europe
Rotterdam, The Netherlands; 2001

Features: Riot Grrrl Europe Manifesto; news from the scene in Austria and Scotland; report from riot grrrl Holland's first meet; "Emancypunx" riot grrrl in Poland; a report from the Riot Grrrl London picnic; Le Tigre interview; Directory of European grrrl zines and distros; "Hear Us Roar!" survey responses on the meaning of riot grrrl; "Not Here to Please You" anti-porn article.

Eye Scream **Riot Grrrl Netherlands ·**
Leiden, 2001
Features: introduction to RGNL; "Who's Who" contributors profiles;
Interview with band Lady!Die; music and activist project Bunnies on
Strike; "The day to open your eyes" on realising gender stereotyping;
"Punkrock in the Netherlands"; interview with band Lulabelles; interview
with band The Riplets; recipes; "Witchnight-Woman take back the streets";
comic on self defence for women; interview with band Barbitch; article on
band Blue Moon Dying; interview with band Bambix; interview with band
Missfed; interview with band Facehugger; poster activism; review of One
Trick Pony band.

Flapper Gathering **Riot Grrrl Belgium/Nina Nijsten**
Flapper Gathering **, issue one (Masmechelen, 2002)**
Cover Illustration: Allison Wolfe. Features: Belgium scene report;
Bratmobile gig review; "Battle Dress" poem; "White Paper" and personal
reflections; O G Panty Complex Interview; "Making Feminism Cool
Again", Le Tigre band review; "Boombox recording" tips; "Afraid of
Radical Change" and reflections on what revolution means; "Fight Street
Harassment" tips; "Living in a Bell Jar" and the glorification of dead
artists; book, zine and music reviews, slogans for patches and flyers.

Flapper Gathering **, issue two (Masmechelen, 2002)**
Cover Illustration: Chicks on Speed Features: European Grrrl News; Riot
Grrrl Q&A; Ladyfest Leuven; "Where Have I Been" short story on rape;
The Haggard review; "My Body Doesn't Fit Me Although It Suits Me
Perfectly" story; Ocean DIY label releases; Chicks on Speed review; Riot
Grrrl Archive Project; Vrouwentongen Caravan Art Project; "Die Bitch"
interview with Veruska Outlaw; Riot Grrrl Benelux Picnic; "Living in Bell
Jar" and social expectations; Profile on Corin Tucker; Guitar Chords Demo;
"Feminism is Not…"; Lappersfort Anti-Road Demo; Reviews and Links.

Flapper Gathering, issue three (Masmechelen, 2003)
Cover Illustration: Tanja from Bunnies on Strike Features: European
Grrrl News; Riot Grrrl Weekend; Beauty Standards; Bunnies on Strike
Interview; Anti-Fur Demonstration; "My Disillusionment in Hardcore";
Anti-War Activism; Interview with Riikka from Ladybomb distro; "Blood
Red" menstruation article; Women's Day Ladyfest Amsterdam benefit;
Alternative Bookfairs; Boycott List; "My Gender Theory" article about
trans-gender; reviews.

Flapper Gathering, **issue four (Hasselt, 2004)**
Cover Illustration: Manuela from Bunnies on Strike/Ladyfest Amsterdam/
RGNL. Features: European Grrrl News; Article on body hair; Ladyfest
Amsterdam; Interview with spoken word artist Jeanne Spicuzza; "Soul
Sister" and finding community; Ladyfest Liege; "Rape and other Torture in
Iraq": Statement from the Global Women's Strike; Art and Activism Reports;
"My Gender Theory" article on gender-blending; Reviews and Links.

Riot Grrrl World Newsletter

"Newsletter for and by Riot Grrrls and Queer Punx from all over the World", downloadable online. The idea was suggested by Jenni (Emancypunx) and Hilde (Lady!Die, Riot Grrrl Europe) and the newsletter's goals include networking between RG chapters, spreading information, creating a flyer, and inspiring people to participate. Each issue is edited by a different grrrl in a different part of the world.

Riot Grrrl World Newsletter, issue one, edited by Flapper's Gathering Nina Nijsten from Belgium, November 2003

Features: News (RTL, all-girl HC band from Brazil split up); Definition of riot grrrl; Grrrl Zine Network link; Women on Waves in Poland information about abortion access; "Riot Girl London" manifesto; Riot Grrrl events (Ladyfest, Expo in the Villa, Babwa fest, Concerts); review of "The Expo-Crass Art and Other Pre Post-Modernist Monsters"; riot grrrl Chapters (Argentina, Brazil, Europe, Poland, Belgium, Chicago, Los Angeles); Rebel Girl Distro.

Riot Grrrl World Newsletter, issue two, edited by Clit Rocket's Veruska Outlaw from Italy, May 2004

Features: "Riot Grrrl World Herstory"; "Take Back the News"; "Collectif Féministe Activiste et Non-Mixte à Istanbul, Turquie"; "The Erotic poem"; "Womanifesta" manifesto; "Women's Spaces: An endangered Species" article.

Riot Grrrl World Newsletter, issue three, edited by British riot grrrl Heather Williams from, 2005

Features: M+H postcard project in Barcelona by Las Peludas/The Shaggy Girls (hiding pro-woman postcards in clothes shops); "Women, Art & Activism" networking event in Barcelona; Information on rg chapters (Fredericksburg VA, USA; Belgium; UK) and Ladyfest (Brighton; Poland).

ACKNOWLEDGEMENTS

We owe a serious debt to all the grrrls who shared their experiences and stories with the authors and allowed us to use their photos, zines and flyers in the book. This volume wouldn't have been possible without your support and enthusiasm.

Also, we would like to thank Anjali Bhatia, Blackwell Publishing, Cornershop, Amelia Fletcher, The F-Word, Galactic Fanzine, Matt Haynes, Hazel Grove Library, John Rylands, University Library of Manchester, Kirby Fanzine, Angela McRobbie, Lucy O'Brien, Bill Savage, Keith and Lindsey Blase, Amy Brachi, Debi Withers, Cath O'Connor, Melanie Maddison, Rachel Kaye, Jacob McMurray, Allison Wolfe, Tobi Vail, Ziggy Hanaor, Marguerite Deslauriers and Pat Graham.

A big thank you goes out to Raven Smith for his discerning eye and to Charlotte Frost, Carali McCall, Nikos Kotsopoulos and Renee O'Drobinak, who were instrumental in pulling this book together.

© 2007 Black Dog Publishing Limited and the authors. All rights reserved.

Black Dog Publishing Limited
Unit 4.4 Tea Building
56 Shoreditch High Street
London
E1 6JJ

Tel: +44 (0)20 7613 1922
Fax: +44 (0)20 7613 1944
Email: info@blackdogonline.com

www.blackdogonline.com

Editor: Nadine Käthe Monem
Assistant Editor: Blanche Craig
Designer: Julia Trudeau R.

All opinions expressed within this publication are those of the
authors and not necessarily of the publisher.

British Library Cataloguing-in-Publication Data.

A CIP record for this book is available from the British Library.

ISBN: 978 1 906155 018

Black Dog Publishing is an environmentally responsible company. *Riot Grrrl: Revolution Girl Style Now!*
is printed on Munken Print White, a FSC certified paper.

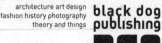

architecture art design
fashion history photography
theory and things

www.blackdogonline.com